Memories and Reflections

Memories and Reflections

ROBERT LLEWELYN

DARTON · LONGMAN + TODD

First published in 1998 by
Darton, Longman and Todd Ltd
1 Spencer Court
140–142 Wandsworth High Street
London SW18 4JJ

ISBN 0–232–52280–4

A catalogue record for this book is available from the British Library

Designed by Sandie Boccacci
Phototypeset in 10/13.5pt New Baskerville
by Intype London Ltd
Printed and bound in Great Britain
by Page Bros, Norwich

Dedicated to fellow pilgrims
in the joyful hope
that we may be an encouragement to one another
in the fellowship of love and prayer.

Contents

Contents

Prologue

A NUMBER OF PEOPLE have told me I ought to write a book of memories and reflections but I have always firmly refused. Then one day in 1996 there came a letter from a lady known to me in America who has the gift of prophecy. I have written of her in chapter 25. The message given was that I should write just such a book. I have learnt that prophetic messages should be treated cautiously and read with discernment and I needed to spread this one before the Lord for several weeks before being able to accept it. I had to take into consideration that most of me knew what was in the message before I read it and that it confirmed what others had urged upon me. Hence the decision to write it was taken. It is in fact a book written under obedience.

I am not at liberty to quote the full message which is tender in the extreme. But about a tenth of it runs as follows:

> The book should be one to encourage the Church and its people in these times, to build them up and to increase their faith. I [Jesus] ask you to tell stories of the people in your life and of their witness. Write about the people you know and have known. Write about yourself and your story as well. You have met and known people from all over the world, and many remain close to you now. Think of those who inspire *you* and encourage you with their faith and faithfulness. And write.

I am surprised if my life should be of interest beyond that of family and friends and a few who have enjoyed my earlier books. But the second half is less about me and more on prayer and spirituality which may be helpful to share. I have not asked any publisher to commission this book. In the last resort it is the publisher who is the author's safeguard. If he considers the manuscript of insufficient interest that is it. I shall at least have done the writing.

I have referred to my publisher as 'he' but it may equally be 'she'. When it comes to inclusive language I like to use it, but it is an art in itself and I am not skilful in combining meaning with elegance. In chapter 26 (page 212), for example, it has been pointed out that I might have used 'she' throughout in place of 'he'. But that would have laid me open to the charge that I thought only women could be rogues, whereas the use of 'he' opens the possibility to both sexes. For, like it or not, the dictionary still makes 'he' (and all that goes with it) an inclusive word and confines 'she' to one sex only. Thus, as I have written elsewhere, a man-eating tiger would eat women as well as men, whereas a woman-eating tiger would, by definition, eat women only. Consistently with this I always refer to the devil as 'he' and so far no one has complained.

However, wherever it can be done without being inelegant I prefer not to use the masculine to include the feminine. I don't like praying for all men according to their needs, and I hope that one day I shall not be asked to affirm that Christ came down for us men. In each case 'men' could be dropped with advantage to both sexes.

I have been able to refer to notes in only five chapters: the two on Medjugorje, Lourdes, the Zen retreat, and my visit to the L'Arche community recorded at the end of chapter 17. In the others, memory, with a few date promptings from my sister's diary, has been the only source. I may sometimes be at fault in recording the sequence of events.

My friend Sheila Waller has been good enough to read the manuscript and offer suggestions and corrections. But I am particularly grateful for her help on a wider scene. As I wrote the manuscript I was doubtful in some cases as to what should appear in the final draft. On reviewing it I have sometimes wondered lest I have been wearying or intrusive about myself or the family and it has been particularly valuable to have the opinions or convictions of a detached observer. Needless to say the final responsibility must be mine.

ROBERT LLEWELYN

1

Early Days

I WAS BORN ON 6 July 1909. I was the second child in what was to grow up to be a family of five. My brother Griff had arrived almost exactly a year before. The house being now too small, my parents moved to Rosendal, a spacious house nearby situated on the north-east corner of Sarlsdown Road, about halfway between Exmouth and the village of Littleham. There was a good family-sized garden, about three-quarters of an acre in all. My father wanted to buy the house, but could not raise the necessary £1,000. That doesn't seem a lot of money, but it was equivalent to almost £58,000 today.

Exmouth was a growing seaside resort, and Littleham an old-world thatched picture-postcard village. It, too, was growing and, on a post office being opened, a villager told me it was becoming more and more like London every day. Its beautiful parish church lay almost a mile across the fields from our house. Sunday by Sunday we would walk together to attend matins at eleven. It was something of a fashion parade, though then, as now, church was what you made of it. Matins was for the gentry, evensong for the village, though sometimes there was a mingling of the two. Holy Communion followed matins once a month, a blessed day for us children for then there was no sermon. When we were older we used to stay on, and I used to wonder why the little old lady in front of us dropped down on one knee during the creed. It was a villager who made it all plain. 'E came down for we, so we goes down for 'e.' The textbooks have never given me a clearer theology.

I have three early memories, but I cannot remember their order. One is of being sprayed with sea water on a rough crossing to the Isle of Wight. Another is of my father's (1910?) Daimler being towed away by two horses. The third, though chronologically probably the first, for I was but twenty months and six days, is the death of my little brother George.

I was off to St Lawrence on the south coast of the Isle of Wight in the summer following the death (11 November 1910) of my great-grandmother, Mrs Pelham, whose home it had been for many years. My mother and her sister – a favourite aunt always known simply as Addie – were brought up at St Lawrence (Lisle Combe[1] today) from early childhood, and their widowed grandmother – Dardar as we called her – was as a beloved mother to them both. I am told she had many admirers and she was spoken of in almost reverential tones. A story recorded for posterity tells how in her young and vivacious days (though I think her vivacity lasted to the end) Queen Victoria and Prince Albert, when in residence at Osborne House near Cowes, would sometimes drive over for afternoon tea. According to family lore, no notice was given other than a postilion being sent ahead to say the royal couple were on their way. Prince Albert, it was said, greatly enjoyed these visits and one suspects he instigated them. Doubtless the Queen, as always, shared his happiness. But she never came alone after his death, the memory (it was assumed) being too poignant for her. Though one would imagine that the horse-drawn journey of about fourteen miles would of itself have been a sufficient disincentive.

No food was allowed to be wasted from Dardar's household. Leftovers were neatly packaged and my mother and her sister Addie would, as children, take them to the cottages of the poor. The conditions of many were pitiable and my mother used to say how greatly these gifts were appreciated. Doubtless it sounds patronising to many in these very different days. I prefer to side with St Vincent de Paul who would tell the rich that the poor would forgive them their charity for the love which they bore them. And Dardar's genuine care could be in no doubt for she would personally crochet shawls over many months to give to the poor at Christmas. Incidentally her MP husband,[2] who died when he was thirty-eight, had been largely responsible for the labourers' wages being substantially raised through the country. It may well be that he and his wife encouraged one another on this issue.

My mother and Addie were educated at St Lawrence by governesses. One was Rose Wyatt who later became my godmother. She was by then a CMS missionary in Mombasa. I remember her largely for her remarkable gift with animals. She retired to Whitwell, close to St Lawrence, and of an afternoon would go out amply armed with bones, to ease the frustration of the chained dogs in the neighbourhood. She had a story of a country stationmaster in Africa being driven to near seizure when she attempted to shake hands with a lion awaiting transportation. My mother's other governess was Miss Church, who also became a missionary, this time with the Zenana mission.

Hardly surprisingly my mother became a firmly biblically-based Christian. I don't think it occurred to her in her early days to question her faith, and she looked to my father to help when our own questions were beyond her. From her governesses she received the education suited to her times. She played the piano and had a pleasant drawing-room singing voice. Thus aided, after reading Bible stories on a Sunday afternoon, she would engage us in hymn singing in the evening. My favourite hymn, scorned by the church hymnals, had to be found in *Golden Bells*, 'Pull for the shore sailor, pull for the shore'. Its theology escaped me, but its imagery held me and perhaps it ushered in a desire for a career in the Navy. I shudder to think how many battleships might lie stranded on foreign shores if that had been fulfilled.

My mother, born in 1879, was second in a family of eight girls and one boy. Her father, Gilbert Spencer-Smith, and his wife Edith, who was Dardar's daughter, lived at Maidenstone Heath, Bursledon, about seven miles from Southampton. They had a beautiful old house, the garden running down to the lane which ran alongside the River Hamble. My grandfather had been in the Army, but retired in his early thirties to become what was known in those distant days as a gentleman farmer. Cynics were known to say that such a one raised nothing except his hat, but it wasn't quite that way with my grandfather, though admittedly the control belonged to my grandmother who had a flair for such a venture. I seem to remember pigs and chickens and a few cows; but have no recollection of crops. I was never much interested in such matters though the stables drew my attention and William, the coachman, is a well-remembered, colourful figure. Speaking of stables I should perhaps add that I am not able to ride, though I have clambered onto the backs of various steeds but not with notable success. My limited experience in the saddle ended in India in my mid-fifties with a John Gilpin style approach to a Government House party. Pedestrians stood back in helpless wonder as I flashed by. I can hardly say I kept my seat, and certainly not my dignity, but at least on arrival I was still aloft. I have some sympathy with the opinion that horses are dangerous at both ends and uncomfortable in the middle.

My grandfather's main interests were shooting and attending sales. He had a high reputation as a shot and a keen interest in antique furniture;

moreover, he loved a bargain. He was generous to us, his grandchildren. Every term when Griff and I were at boarding school he would send us each a pound, untold riches for a small boy in those days. But he had pet economies, the most irritating of which was the absence of an inside lavatory for the male members of the household. Instead there was an outside contraption consisting of a hole in a board set over a bottomless pit, though not so bottomless that evidence of earlier users did not arise. There was, too, the possibility of various flying creatures zooming around and finding irresistible the new resting place offered from above. Grandpapa used to say it was all very healthy, but not everyone shared his hygienic views. My brother Griff would sometimes run up to the railway station, penny in hand. I think I was generally braver, or perhaps merely penniless, and sat it out.

Dardar's lady's maid, Katie, became an important influence in our family life. Dardar had appointed her on trial at the early age of fifteen in place of her aunt who had left to get married, and later she became her secretary and general manager of her affairs. After Dardar's death she settled down in Dawlish which is close to Exmouth, and she would spend long times with the family and was a tremendous support to my mother. She was capable and unflappable, and seemed equal to every situation. In later life I learnt that she always wished she could have been a doctor. She would surely have done well, but in those days there were no facilities for teaching those who could not afford to pay their way. Katie died in her hundredth year keenly anticipating a joyful reunion with her beloved 'Mrs Pelham' whom she had served so faithfully for many years.

My second memory is that of my father's Daimler being hauled away. He had had the car when he was General (and travelling) Secretary of the Primrose League for the South West. It must have been provided free with the job for he could never have afforded to run it. Our gardener, Gregory, was taught to drive, for my father was unpractical with machinery. I don't think one had many lessons in those days – I had only two, and that was some fifteen years later – and Gregory was not skilled. My father told us Gregory once ran over a policeman's foot; one hopes the car had pneumatic tyres. It certainly had no self-starter or windscreen wiper, and paraffin lighting added to the hazards of night driving. But my father, who in later life never aspired higher than a baby Austin, used to speak affectionately of it and especially extolled its climbing capacity on the Devonshire hills. The speed limit of twenty miles an hour was often ignored but at a certain amount of risk as there were quite a few police traps around.

The Primrose League, I should explain, was a Conservative association founded in 1833 in honour of Benjamin Disraeli, Earl of Beaconsfield. My father was an eager politician and being a good public speaker was presumably well suited to the post. The Member of Parliament for his constituency hoped he would stand in his place when he retired. But that would have been beyond his means and in any case Dad valued family life too deeply to embark on a political career. Indeed he shortly found he could no longer be a Conservative and switched to Liberal which meant, of course, relinquishing his Primrose League work. Later he became an ardent speaker in the Liberal cause.

My father, who was eleven years older than my mother, came from Warwickshire, where his father had retired after a career of tea planting in Burma. I never met his parents, though his mother's gentle and serene face used to shine down upon us from the dining-room wall at Rosendal. He was at Oxford in the early nineties, but he never took an honours degree as he devoted most of his time then and in later years to playing games. He was a gifted all-rounder, but not at the top, except at badminton where he was partner to Sir George Thomas, who was the British singles champion on several occasions. Thomas was also British chess champion and used to be working away at his pocket board as they travelled together to tournaments. One of the treasured letters of my youth is from George Thomas who, in his microscopic hand, wrote to me at my father's request to give me a few chess 'wrinkles'. Athletics was my father's forte and on one occasion he just beat the fifty second mark for the quarter mile, a distinction which I think was held by only one other (at least in England) at the time. Of course the time is much faster today but in those days you ran on grass tracks and in gym shoes, and had no professional training as we now know it. He never passed his talents on to me.

My father was devoted to us children, and we to him. He was ambitious for us and wanted us to excel at work and games. This was an encouragement but had its dangers, though I think he was alert to this and responded accordingly. He was a good Prayer Book churchman and, with my mother, made for us a solid Christian home. Our day started with family prayers around the breakfast table in which the servant(s), when in the early days we had them, would join. My father would read from the Bible, or sometimes we would take a verse each, and then we would kneel down and he would take the prayers. He told me later (no doubt with some exaggeration) that at the age of six I could read every word of the Bible. As I was not an especially gifted child that must say something about the education of the time. We were taught to read and write in kindergarten and at an early stage to learn our tables. I believe learning by heart, as part of the learning process, to have great value, not simply because it may store the memory with useful knowledge but because the very act of such learning disciplines and exercises the mind. I have long since been grateful that at boarding school I had to learn the Prayer Book collects by heart. They meant little to me at the time, but when I grew up the bones were there waiting to be clothed with the Spirit. But to return. Dickens was, I think, my father's favourite author. At another level, Liddon's Bampton lectures on the divinity of Christ held a fascination for him as, too, the New Testament, which he would usually read in Greek.

My last memory to relate is of the death of 'little George' on 12 March 1911. My parents always referred to him in this way. He had been born prematurely, and the skilled midwife who had brought (and was to bring) the rest of us into the world, and who had been booked for two months later, was busy on another case. Another nurse had to be hurriedly found, and her inexperience in bathing George at birth (which, I am told, should never be done to a premature baby) led to convulsions from which he suffered much and never recovered. He had lived only six weeks when my mother took me aside to the spare room and said, 'Little George has gone to be with Jesus'. I am told I at once went off to repeat the words to Manie (Mary) our cook, a warm and motherly figure who had a treasured place in the family home. My parents were heart-broken, but they had their faith and that saw them through. I never once heard them blame the nurse, who must have been devastated, and I am sure they did all they could to comfort her. Years later, when I visited George's grave, I found my parents had had inscribed on the stone the words of Jesus to Peter: 'What I do thou knowest not now, but thou shalt know hereafter.' Perhaps, as with so many other parents, the answer is now clear.

2

Wartime Memories

THE OUTBREAK OF THE First World War on 4 August 1914 stands out as my most vivid memory of early days. Griff and I were staying with our grandparents at Maidenstone, on holiday from Southlands kindergarten at Exmouth, which I had attended since the age of three. I was with our nurse, Lily, the only one of various nursemaids and governesses (so many due to war upheaval) whom I shall speak of in these pages. We watched and waved to the soldiers as their trains crossed the Hamble river on their way to Portsmouth where they embarked for France. Our return home was delayed until Lily could be escorted back: my father was nervous about her with so many troops travelling at that time. I was just five and Lily – I think – sixteen. She came from a large, desperately poor, deeply Christian family. Her widowed mother, after working all day, would sit up to the early hours knitting socks which she would sell in an attempt to meet the children's needs. For light she would allow herself only a single candle, placing it in front of a mirror to get double brightness. It was a great blessing for Lily, and the family, to be offered employment. Even so, Mrs Holmes was not going to let her daughter go into service, as it was called, without first writing to our vicar to enquire if my father was a dependable person. Lily came and she truly loved me, and I her. I lost touch with her soon after the war started and she died of tuberculosis when I was about thirteen, a beautiful death, I was told, in which heaven opened before her, and she knew herself to be with a great cloud of witnesses from the other side. I do not know whether it is possible for the departed to take on the role of guardian angels, but I have often believed Lily to be around me, even to this day.

It was Lily who wheeled Griff and me off to Southlands (girls') School kindergarten every day. I can recall little of that time. I have the dimmest memory of running into the ample aprons of the cook as I fled to the lavatory, causing her to stumble with the tray of mid-morning milk. More vividly I recall an alarming punishment, I forget what for. I was sentenced to sit at lunch between two senior girls. Looking back, I can see they were kindness itself, but I suffered agonies of shyness. This was odd because I was told I was a real little chatterbox in those days.

By now the family had grown. Dick had been born in 1912, and Joan the following year. Dick was a true countryman and, after schooling at Repton, chosen as it had been my father's school, gladly left his books behind and became a hard-working and capable farmer. He died in 1987, leaving his wife Diana, a true family friend, and two sons and a daughter. Joan, who has never married, was educated at Southlands School and then at Colwell, near Malvern, where she learnt the skills of domestic life. Riding and tennis were the enjoyments of her early days and she was gifted in both. With her varied and practical gifts and readiness to help others, she would have made an excellent Universal Aunt; she has in fact been just that, in a voluntary capacity, to many throughout her grown-up life.

My father joined up for the war, but was not to go to France until 1915. So we went to various places to be near him. For the most part he was stationed at Devonport. I remember Saltash, across the Tamar in Cornwall where we had no schooling but a beloved governess, Miss Bassett. Then there was Yelverton on Dartmoor, where I experienced my first Zeppelin raid, and where I was taken out to tea with elderly little Miss Horner, brother of little Jack Horner of nursery rhyme fame. There followed Plymouth and Plymouth College, which was just across the road from our house. It was when we were there that my father received his posting to France. I remember him gathering Griff and me under his arms and kneeling at the bedside praying for us both. He broke down with tears expecting, I feel sure, never to see us again. We loved him dearly, but were too young to realise the dangers ahead.

I think Rosendal must have been let, for we next went to Dawlish (I was still six) where we lived at Radfords, my aunt Addie's beautiful thatched house. She was away on war service nursing the troops sent home from France. As a country hotel bearing the same name, the house still keeps much of its old-fashioned charm in spite of extensive additions and alterations. Here I devoured Sexton Blakes until the summer light failed (there was no electricity), at fourpence a time. By day I attended a little school run by the kindly Miss Swann, a lone walk of nearly two miles, Griff being now away at boarding school. Although at least half the walk was through country lanes, I don't think it ever occurred to anyone to be nervous about me. Children roamed freely in those far-off days. Dawlish was also memorable on account of an explosion which shook the house. A mine had exploded two miles out at sea sinking a cargo ship; a treasure store which could ill be spared in those heavy rationing days. It was also memorable for an attack of measles and for the army of fairies which invaded my bedroom cupboard. Katie said I was imagining things, but I insisted on her looking. My temperature was 105.

My next clear memory is of 26 July 1916 when Nurse Skidmore, who had helped to bring us all into the world, announced the arrival of a new baby. I was delighted and, I may say, surprised. We were so ignorant in those days that if, perchance, I had noticed my mother's changing figure, it would have signified nothing. Reg and his hospitable wife Juliet celebrated their golden wedding in 1995. They have three daughters (two married) all engaged in active Christian work. Reg passed through Sherborne and New College, Oxford, was an accomplished games player, joined the prison service after serving in the war, and finally became governor of Wandsworth prison. I believe it is true to say (at least of earlier days) that everyone who has settled in Reg and Juliet's retirement street in Winchester has at one time or another been a guest in their house; an example of neighbourliness I admire from afar.

I was always a curious child and wanting to find out how things worked. One day when I was about nine I bought an electric torch – a rarity in those days – and figured out that if a battery gave such brilliance in a small bulb, how much more brightly would it shine if connected to the whole electric light system of the town. I removed the cap from the light switch in a bedroom, pushed in the wires (switches were crude in those days) and holding the other two ends in my right hand applied them to the torch bulb in my left. There was a blinding flash, a broken bulb, and burnt fingers. I still have to discover how it was I suffered from nothing more than minor blisters. There wasn't even an electric shock, though shock enough to my system as a whole. And the house electricity remained unaffected.

The war went relentlessly on, its casualty list climbing at an alarming rate, and these were anxious days for my mother who now had five children to care for. She managed, as I later realised, heroically, attending to the family needs and household chores, and often foregoing a part of her own rations that we might be better fed.

At long last came Armistice Day, 11 November 1918. We were still living in Exmouth and I attended St Peter's School half a mile away. The headmaster announced the news and we were all marched off to Holy Trinity Church for a packed service of thanksgiving. After that I jumped on my bike and rushed to the Beacon Hotel where our Monday dancing class was held. I said to the dancing mistress that with the arrival of peace I imagined there would be no dancing that afternoon. She said that on the contrary it was an occasion for special celebration. My nine-year-old spirits fell. I had other ideas of rejoicing. However, the big news was that my father had survived the war.

3

Boarding Schools

AT THE AGE OF TEN I was sent off to join Griff at Upcott House, a preparatory school at Okehampton on the edge of Dartmoor. It was to be my first extended time away from home. My father and mother took us by train to Exeter, gave us tea and cakes at the renowned Dellers café, and from there we went to Queen Street station to catch the Okehampton train. My father was sad, my mother tearful, but this thrice-annual separation was what middle-class parents of my childhood thought to be best for their sons. And so it might have been for many. But for those who like me had stable and happy homes I am not sure. At Okehampton we were met by a wagonette and driven the mile or so to the school. Welcoming and handshakes followed. And so to bed.

I was desperately homesick at first, but I was fortunate in that I had my brother Griff to comfort me. I was even put in his dormitory, a kindly concession, for boys of different ages were not usually put together. My father was a great believer in cold baths and had asked that while we were at school we should continue the practice we followed at home. So each morning Griff and I would make our way to the bathroom and take a dip in the water put out for us overnight. In winter this could be quite an ordeal and I remember one occasion when we had to break a thin surface of ice. But generally it was not unpleasant and the warm afterglow was a bonus missed by the other boys. Once we got into the way of things my homesickness wore off and although as term proceeded we eagerly looked forward to the holidays, we were not unhappy at school and were well looked after.

Not that the standards would bear any comparison with those of today. There were no water closets, just earth closets with buckets which handyman Pud or Chud (I believe those were their real names) would empty at intervals. For toilet paper we had to manage with yesterday's edition of the newspaper. And there was no electric light. Oil lamps lit the classrooms in the winter evenings and early mornings, not altogether a disadvantage as they also served to warm the room. There were radiators fuelled from a boiler below, but Pud, or it may have been Chud, was necessary to work it and it seems that sometimes he may have overslept.

On one occasion on almost the first morning of the term I went down with scarlet fever. It was not a disease any headmaster wanted in his school and an ambulance was quickly arranged to take me to the isolation hospital in Exeter. This involved a twenty-mile drive over roads and in a vehicle far removed from modern standards. I felt really ill and believe I was. During my six-week stay my father would visit me regularly (he was now working daily in Exeter) and would bring me apples and eggs, the latter being a great luxury at breakfast.

After about three weeks I realised I was well enough to get out of bed and kneel down at my bedside to say my prayers. Although no one else did this I have no recollection that it required any moral courage. It simply seemed the natural thing to do. But I chose the wrong moment. I was nicely under way when a nurse came in with my supper. There was about her, alas, no trace of the school of 'whisper who dares'. Instead she called out 'O my God' and dropped the tray. I must say that later she came and apologised which I thought was very nice of her.

How should it be on such occasions – to kneel or not to kneel? I recall a friend telling me that no sooner had he knelt at his bedside on his first night in wartime barracks than a boot came hurtling past his head. Next morning he returned it, saying, 'I've cleaned it, and if you give me the other one I'll clean that one too.' He had no further trouble. I admire his courage and do not question his choice as being right for him. But should it be an example to all?

I would argue that if I were to kneel down in such circumstances for the time I needed to say my prayers, I would be exercising a kind of blackmail on my companions to moderate their conversation and activity. The more decent they were the greater the pressure would be. If, perchance, they fell to silence, I would find myself too self-conscious to pray, feeling that I must get up as soon as possible to let them resume their normal behaviour. I would also feel I was silently rebuking them and that would help no one. The way for me would be to follow my ordinary practice of attending to my prayers earlier or to say them in bed. In school the dilemma was resolved for us by a compulsory two-minute silence.

But some would say an opportunity for witness would have been missed. That nurse who dropped the tray may have been influenced for life by seeing me kneeling at my bedside. But it wasn't done as an act of witness, though it may have been so incidentally. It was done because I thought it to be the proper and natural thing to do. If it had been done simply to witness to others in the ward, there would have been something phoney about it, and it would have deserved to work the other way.

Not everyone would agree with me. A widely read pastoral theologian of my youth tells the story of himself travelling on an overnight journey by train. He was alone in the carriage and planned to kneel down and say his prayers. Alas, he was joined by two 'prizefighters' at the next stop and he considered a new strategy was needed. He was in one of those old-type carriages in which a lavatory opened off each compartment. Here indeed he could enter into his closet and attend to his devotions as he pleased. In he went, emerging ten minutes later to find both prizefighters on their knees.

The answer must be that you can make no rules. The one who kneels does well if conscience would afflict him if he did otherwise. And he who prays earlier or between the sheets does well if he knows that to kneel would simply be an act of self-conscious witness making real prayer impossible.

I was always one for catching colds or infectious diseases and I recall the end of one summer term when I had to be kept back at school for a few days as I was still infectious with German measles. This left me to travel on my own, this time to Torquay where my parents had rented a house for the holidays. I was alone in the carriage when there came upon me an experience of what I must now call transcendent joy. I have often viewed it as a visitation from above. It left me dancing and jumping around the carriage in an ecstasy of delight. I think I would have been just eleven at the time.

Ringworm was to follow a little later. About a mile from Rosendal, our Exmouth home, there lived a remarkable doctor who was said to be the expert on X-rays, a fairly new discovery, in the west of England. Dr Hodgson was a fine Christian and his firm belief in the overruling providence of God spreading itself to the smallest details of our lives, influenced my father deeply. They were good friends, sometimes travelling to Exeter together, and the Christian witness of a scientist made an added impression. Dr Hodgson's life, moreover, accorded with his faith. If he ever made any money it must have all been spent on the elderly infirm ladies he cared for in his large house. On being told of my ringworm he decided that I must be given X-ray treatment to my head, and on two or more occasions I found myself in one of his several cellars which opened onto one another, filled with wires linking up his equipment which sprawled everywhere. A visit to those cellars might well have given Heath Robinson a few fertile ideas. Each time I was under the X-ray for at least twenty minutes whereas nowadays you seem to be given a burst of one or two seconds with assistants hiding behind screens. Dr Hodgson ran from one cellar to another, tripping over a wire here, adjusting a plug there, completely oblivious to any danger in his enthusiasm for the apparatus he had devised, and meanwhile I was exposed for the whole time. I must leave it to today's specialists to explain how we both survived. Perhaps it was all much weaker then than it is now. Anyway the treatment worked. All my hair came out and I was left a skinhead for the only time in my life. I had to wear a little skullcap as I was considered too unsightly for public viewing.

About two years later there followed an operation for adenoids in an endeavour to stem my frequent colds. For two guineas, Dr Hannah, the local GP, would do the job. But my father opted for a specialist, Mr Worthington from Exeter, who charged ten guineas. I recall no sign of a nurse. The kitchen table, being the firmest in the house, was moved up to my bedroom and Mr Worthington, with Hannah in attendance to administer the anaesthetic, performed the deed. I must have been nervous as I recall trying to kick one of them in my last feeble resistance to the chloroform. A very sore throat followed but there was some compensation in an exclusive diet of ice-cream for several days.

It was when I was on holiday from Upcott that Sir Alan Cobham – perhaps the most notable flying celebrity of the day – visited Exmouth to offer three-minute flights in his single-propeller aeroplane at ten shillings a time: or for a pound you could have six minutes and loop the loop. A nearby farmer made one of his fields available as an aerodrome. The luxury flight was beyond our means but we four older children managed to get together a pound and Sir Alan allowed us to squeeze into the two seats. It was a thrilling experience seeing our house and the neighbourhood from the air. We were able to loop the loop by proxy only, watching eagerly as Sir Alan took his passengers over the sea to give them the thrill they had so dearly paid for. Later my parents, with Reg on my mother's lap, shared the experience of the lesser flight. I imagine that Sir Alan, who did the round of holiday resorts, was collecting money for his future flights. Later he made history by flying from London to Australia and back.

In due course my brother Dick joined us at Upcott, and after my time Reg went there as well. My father had an arrangement with the head-master that the normal fee of £100 a year would be reduced to £70 if all four of us attended. We were taught sufficiently well for everyone (and I think there were no exceptions) to pass the Common Entrance examination into their public schools. I had set my heart on the Navy for which boys had first to go before a board of admirals. My father took me up to London by the Cornish Riviera which did the non-stop 180 miles from Exeter in three hours, slipping a coach at Reading. The interview was not a success. I was asked to tell the admirals the story of Prince Llewelyn's dog, Gelert. My father told it to me later and was surprised that I did not already know it. The prince, who had a hot temper, went hunting leaving the faithful Gelert to guard his child. Returning to find a pool of blood, he assumed the worst and plunged his sword into his beloved dog, only to find that the child was safe under the bed, Gelert having fought off a wolf in its defence. But it was not my ignorance of this story which failed me. The admirals must have quickly seen I was unsuited for their profession and they did me a good turn, though I could not realise that at the time.

There are many stories of young boys before the admirals but I suspect that most of them are made up. But one I can vouch for, since it was told me by John Christie, headmaster of Westminster School, who had been on the interviewing board the previous day. One of the admirals asked a thirteen-year-old which he would sooner be when he grew up, an admiral or a Prime Minister. 'Oh Sir, I'd sooner be an admiral.' Delighted, the admiral asked why? 'Sir, you'd need an awful lot of brains to be a Prime Minister.'

I wasn't to be put off the sea and sat and won a scholarship to the Nautical College, Pangbourne, from where I could take special entry to Dartmouth in my fourth term. Griff had already won an exhibition there the year before. Pangbourne life was tough but I was not unhappy there and I have often reflected how its training stood me in good stead in later life. We wore Merchant Navy uniform, paraded and marched to all events such as meals, chapel and class, and were frequently required to obey orders at the double. We slept in hammocks, and when the rising bell went we leapt out, took a cold shower, dressed and jumped astride our hammocks, binding them with rope and then hauling them down for stowing in the racks. Twenty-five minutes was allowed for this, but on punishment days it was reduced to twelve and then there was a real scramble, the bigger boys having to help the smaller if we were all to be down on time. Once dressed, we paraded at 7.30 and ran in ranks round a field known as the triangle. Then to a well-earned breakfast, and so on to chapel parade and classes. The college had a boathouse on the Thames, about a mile away, and there we would struggle with the oars of ships' cutters, or on holidays paddle our private and often self-made canoes. Sunday was a great day as we could fry sausages in the woods. There was no morning chapel other than the Eucharist before breakfast for those confirmed to attend if they wished. Evening chapel was compulsory. My church knowledge was sketchy in those days and when RCs were told to fall out from chapel parade that they might be segregated from C of Es, I promptly obeyed on my first day, my initials being RCL. The petty officer was flummoxed knowing that Griff was not an RC and not knowing what to make of this division in the family. Finally we got it sorted out.

Holidays were an added joy at that time for I had bought a second-hand New Hudson motorbike for £14, later to be exchanged for a new Francis-Barnet at £27. The age for a licence in those days was fourteen, or sixteen for cars. A clergyman who lived nearby had fallen off his bicycle in his eighties and decided that he must take up motorcycling instead. He was, however, too insecure to take his hands from the handlebars to put the machine into top gear. Accordingly he would lend his Royal Enfield to Griff, graciously saying it simply had to have exercise in top. And off we would go for rides together, once, I remember, to Torquay to see Bunny Austin defeat J. Brugnon of France in the British hard courts championships. How trusting our parents were! True, there was not much traffic, but there were plenty of pot-holes in the Devonshire roads, and we exercised our steeds to the full. I do not recall either of us receiving a scratch so perhaps there were guardian angels around.

I was not to remain at Pangbourne for more than four terms. My father clearly saw the sea was not for me and wrote to our cousin, Charles Russell, who was headmaster of King Edward VI School, Southampton, asking him to examine me in mathematics with a view to a university scholarship ahead. He could never have afforded Cambridge without such help. He was earning but £150 a year in office work in Exeter, and Cambridge was a full £300. I do not know how he managed as it was. Addie generously paid Griff's school fees; there must have been some private money available as well. Two or three years later, however, my father was left a substantial sum of money by the widow of a ship-owner whom he had never seen, her generosity being a thankoffering for kindness from his mother who cared for her in childhood days. There were many annuities and legacies to be paid, but he was now comfortably well off and his financial and educational burdens were lifted overnight. He loved motoring and was now able to afford a car. We had a series of baby Austins from then onwards. But this is to jump ahead. My own future was to be at King Edward's School under the tutelage of Charles Russell, where I would specialise in mathematics and work for the scholarship I was never able to win.

4

King Edward VI School, Southampton

IT WAS IN SEPTEMBER 1924 that my aunt Addie drove me from Exmouth to Southampton in her bull-nosed Morris Cowley. Long distance motoring was quite an occasion in those days and I held in my hand detailed instructions from the AA to make sure we did not lose our way. There were no large direction signs as there are today, but simply wooden signposts which could not be read until one had reached them which often meant stopping the car. Every now and then an AA man would come along on his motorbike with sidecar, and if he failed to salute we were asked to stop and ask the reason. Not that we did so, we simply inferred that a police trap was ahead and kept within 30 m.p.h. which I think was the limit at that time. It was my first long drive and I remember it well, the beautiful cliff road leading to Lyme Regis and the fast straight undulating roads in the New Forest where we must have reached at least forty.

King Edward VI School was a day school of rather over 400 boys, situated off the Marlands near the Southampton railway station. My cousin Charles Russell was headmaster and he and his wife Irene lived with their three daughters in Westwood Road about one and a half miles away. I was to live with the family and attend school daily. School fees were about £8 a term for the minority who could afford them. Most boys were recruited from the Government elementary schools with a handful from professional classes such as clergy and doctors. As I joined at a late age it was not surprising that I felt myself to be a bit of a stranger at first. But the atmosphere was friendly and I soon settled in.

Charles Russell was a priest and good scholar who would probably have risen to the top whatever discipline he had chosen. In effect he chose mathematics and became a Wrangler and Smith's prizeman at Cambridge. He had come to King Edward's from Harrow where he had been an assistant master. As a priest he was a modern churchman and represented that wing of the Church on the Archbishop's doctrinal commission. I don't quite know what modernism meant in those days, but I know Charles did not believe in the virgin birth of Jesus (it was not he, but my father who told me this) and I doubt if he believed in Christ's bodily resurrection or the Gospel nature miracles in their literal sense. But he never pressed these views on us, wanting us, no doubt, to think for ourselves and find our own way. The book of Job was his love from the Scriptures and every sixth form was well instructed in its meaning. Moreover, whenever he preached we usually knew where his text would lie.

I little realised in those years that Charles Russell was engaged on an immensely erudite history of the school from its foundation by William Capon in 1553, the last year of the reign of King Edward VI, to almost the beginning of Hitler's war. (*A History of King Edward VI School, Southampton*, by C.F. Russell, published privately.) The fortunes of the school are faithfully traced under each of its thirty-three headmasters and lives of its better known old boys recorded. Chief of these perhaps is Isaac Watts. In the year of his birth (1674) new statutes had been drawn up requiring boys in the top two forms to speak only in Latin on the school premises and requiring nine hours a day in classroom study in the summer: one hour less in winter. So perhaps it is not surprising we read of the young Isaac starting Latin at the age of four and Greek two years later. The twenty-two statutes, which had to be read out four times each year, make strange reading today. I can find no mention of when they were repealed or perhaps they merely fell into disuse. But this, though interesting in itself, is by the way. Russell describes Watts as the father of modern hymnody. I have read elsewhere that as a schoolboy Isaac complained to his father of the mediocre nature of contemporary hymns and was advised to try his own hand. In all Isaac Watts wrote about six hundred hymns, some of indifferent quality, but others of undying fame. Among these must surely be, 'O God our help in ages past' and 'When I survey the wondrous cross'.

One of the school houses is named after Watts, another after Edward Reynolds who became Bishop of Norwich in 1660. He is, however, best remembered as the composer of the General Thanksgiving, one of the noblest of the prayers in *The Book of Common Prayer.*

For three centuries the school mostly prospered, drawing pupils from near and far. Then with many similar schools it suffered a sharp decline in the middle of the nineteenth century having only four pupils on the roll in 1853. It closed the following year and opened again in 1860.

Numbers gradually built up to over three hundred chiefly due to the work of James Fewings who, on taking over the headmastership on St Swithin's Day in 1880, declared it to be his desire to rule for forty years. He was in fact just two years short, Charles Russell taking over in 1918. At four hundred in my day it was bursting at the seams. Within a few years a splendid new building was erected on the playing fields at Hill Lane and today it cares for nearly a thousand pupils. It probably flourishes as never before. On a recent visit I discovered it offered more than fifty clubs and societies.

Charles Russell had high ideals for the school and brought to it a wider vision. He gathered round him a talented staff and together they made King Edward's a school which did well academically and continued to serve Southampton well in many walks of life. The general tone was high: I do not, for example, remember a single case of bullying. There was a healthy balance of work and games. The spiritual side, widely interpreted, was important to Charles and we began and finished each day with prayers. Twice a week in the morning assembly a prefect would read a self-chosen piece of poetry or prose in place of the normal Bible reading. There were, too, evening prayers in Charles' home before bed.

Moving to a lighter vein I recount an incident of my day related by a more sprightly hand than my own.

> The Cellars were two classrooms, almost underground. High windows ran along one wall at ceiling height. Lionel Victor Gibson, an enterprising youth in 4A, before a Latin lesson with Exham, introduced his firework. In those days a firework with the sole quality of a large bang was a squib and cost a halfpenny. Gibson's device was no squib. It was a twopenny Thunderbolt, a veritable Rolls Royce among bangers, with the loudest bang purveyed to the general public. From his seat at the back Gibson applied a furtive match. Then, ever willing to share a stimulating experience with his friends, he thoughtfully kicked the device a few rows forward where it rested beneath the unwitting figure of Rex Shannon, idly browsing in his Latin primer. The contraption exploded with a mind-raping BAM. Memory is probably at fault when it insists that the fabric of the school leapt a couple of inches. Mere inches would be inadequate to measure the leap of Reginald Arthur Shannon, who went up like a rocketing pheasant. I don't know the school record for the sitting high jump,

but Rex must be a close contender. Sixty years on, recounting the incident, he would speak with awed wonder as of a recent event. It is my recollection that, when hearing was restored, Gibson owned up to spare the class corporate penalty and was sent to the Head for stern punishment.[1]

Corporal punishment, as was general in those days, was a part of the practice of the school. It was sparingly used and served its day well in helping to furnish a framework of discipline in which the school could function in an effective and orderly way. (I may say the engaging fore-going story was not part of the normal diet!) Though we did not always realise it at the time, it benefited miscreants along with others in contribu-ting towards a structure conducive to study and consideration of one another. So, too, at schools I had attended more recently and at those I would later serve as master or head. It must necessarily give way to other methods today with advantages and losses which others will be able to gauge better than myself. It seems to me that life has become increasingly polarised. The young people being turned out by our schools are often better, more mature, more creative, more socially and much more environmentally aware than was general in my youth. On the other hand I can never remember the open defiance of authority and widespread unruliness we are familiar with today. Lawlessness – not in all schools to be sure – soon finds its way into society, making for one of the alarming features of our time. Not the least of its unpleasant consequences is that you can hardly go outside your front door without wondering if Big Brother is watching you.

As for myself, I worked hard for the most part and played the ordinary games, though rose to honours (vice-captaincy) only in 'rugger' as it was universally called. I struggled into the cricket team and by a strange fluke won a schoolboy international in hockey, at which game I had difficulty in keeping my place in the school side. I think I must have done something uncharacteristically spectacular on a day on which a selector was watching a school match. I found myself playing outside left for the Welsh school-boys against England who defeated us by two goals.

The games which really took my heart were tennis and chess, the former because I was reasonably good at it and the latter because it fascinated me. In tennis I used (later on) to play in many tournaments and my glory was to take a set off the Japanese champion, Miki, in the year in which he won the mixed doubles at Wimbledon. But that was a lucky day and in general I never reached higher than Devon county standard. As for chess, I allowed it to take up time which ought to have been spent in pursuing a mathematics scholarship to Cambridge. I loved the game, studied its openings meticulously, and yet had no real flair for it. But I did have my big moment. I was selected to play for Southampton against P.D. Yates who was British champion of the day. Yates was playing on twenty-two boards and I think I was on board seventeen. I lasted a mere eighteen moves. But I mention the match, too, for another reason. My neighbour moved from his board to watch what was happening on board one and the steward, thinking his game was over, put the pieces back into the box. My neighbour returned to find an empty board and, of course, resigned. But Yates told him not to worry and, pulling out the pieces, put them back into place, an indication that he carried every game around in his head. Yates won on twenty-one boards and drew on one.

Southampton days were also memorable for the opportunity to watch cricket matches on the county ground just up the road from Charles' house. Here I spent many a holiday, watching perhaps all the great English cricketers of the day. In spite of the snobbishness of those days in which the amateurs were known as 'gentlemen' and the professionals as 'players' (the latter being disallowed initials on the score cards) there was both a skill and spirit on the field which is often lacking today. 'That's not cricket', derisory today, was a meaningful phrase of my youth.

Another Southampton memory is the celebrity concerts at sixpence a seat. The best performers in the country would offer their services at reduced fees so that classical music was not the preserve of the rich. Two thousand would attend and give the performers uproarious applause. All this, of course, was before most people had any opportunity of listening to radio. The singer, Peter Dawson, famous to me especially through his gramophone rendering of *The Floral Dance*, was my favourite performer. I recall, too, a visit from Clara Butt, but that was at full fees. Her rendering of 'Abide with me' remains to this day.

At the end of Westwood Road where I lived was a lecture hall where the great of the day would be invited to give a magic lantern or other lecture. One lecture stands out particularly in my mind, given by the lightning calculator, A.J. Russell, headmaster of a Bristol school. Having spent most of the afternoon multiplying 675,496 by 476,823, and doing similar sums, we would give them to Russell, who would write them on a blackboard and underneath write the answer in a matter of perhaps fifteen seconds. Unlike most calculators he shared his methods and, in case it is of interest to the reader, I may say that anyone who is moderately gifted in mental arithmetic could, with practice, write down the answer in a single line. I cannot explain the method here other than to say it is simple, but long. Long division sums were equally spectacular and although Russell explained his methods, I have forgotten them, and I am unable to reproduce them.

However, what was most spectacular of all was Russell's capacity to tell us that (say) 6 June 1171 fell on a Sunday, a calculation he would do within a second. Well, not quite, for his calculation would begin as soon as you started asking the question, which itself might take two seconds. But the answer was instantaneous and he would do the same for any date in the calendar. Here is good news for interested readers, unless they belong to the generation which can do nothing without a calculator. The calculation could be done by the average person, with daily practice for a month, within five or ten seconds. You just have to know the trick. As soon as June is said you have 4 in your head, then when sixth is said you have 6, when 1100 is said you have 7, and when 71 is said you have 4. You simply add up as the question is being asked and get 21, which being an exact multiple of 7 gives Sunday. (22 would give Monday etc.) Of course each month, each century and each year of the century has a special number and you have to know these, but less memory is involved than what we all went through in learning up to our twelve times table. Mathematical readers can easily work out the system for themselves. There are a number of variations, but for the easiest you should begin with 1 January 1900 which conveniently fell on a Monday. And you mustn't forget that in 1752 eleven days were lost in the calendar, Wednesday 2 September being immediately followed by Thursday 14 September.

In 1987 an autistic boy performed calculations as above on television. No one could conceive how he did them. But in view of what I have written it is easy to conceive how he might have done them, though it should be added that there have been child calculators who have been unable to offer a rational explanation for their extraordinary feats. The performance was reported in the *Daily Telegraph* of March (date obscured) 1987 as follows.

> Strangest puzzle of all is a third sufferer from autism ... who can give you the day of the week corresponding to any date in the calendar, past or future without pause for thought. Experts say he

has a mind like a computer, albeit an impaired one. There was
something positively New Testament in the spectacle of a
mathematical whizz from Greenwich University . . . beavering away
at the same calculations, and being beaten every time by the
unlettered innocent.

I did not see this report commented upon which seems to indicate that
A.J. Russell's art may be lost which would suggest the more reason for
recording it.

I was confirmed in my Southampton days at the age of fifteen. I can
dimly remember the occasion in Highfield Church, and Bishop Beau-
flower of Southampton who came across as a holy man in days when I
would not have been likely to have used that word. The vicar, Walter
Chitty, prepared me. Of the many things he said I remember clearly the
following two. One was that it is unlawful for a priest to wear a coloured
nightcap in bed; the other was that in my prayers I should always include
a period of silent listening to God. As to the first, I have often worn a
woolly hat (they never come my way in white) to keep my balding head
warm in wintry weather, and I pass the tip on, for we lose at least a
quarter of our bodily heat at night through the head. So far as the second
is concerned, I had little or no understanding of its meaning. I obeyed
conscientiously wondering if, like the infant Samuel, I would hear some
external voice. Needless to say, none came. Only much later I came to
understand that a listening silence makes for a heightened awareness in
which we may intuitively discern the still small voice within. But if I had
been told that at the time I would not have understood. There are some
things we can only learn for ourselves.

I left King Edward's in 1929 having been head boy my last year. Charles
Russell left at the same time. I was to go to Pembroke College, Cambridge,
he to be headmaster of Merchant Taylor's School, Crosby. There he was
to help guide the fortunes of his best known pupil, Robert Runcie,
destined to steer the Church through stormy waters in later years.

5

Cambridge Days

~᪇~

I WENT UP TO Pembroke College, Cambridge, in the October term of 1929. There were about three hundred members of the college and accommodation within its walls for only a third of that number. Hence we had to be boarded out for the first two years, enjoying college life only at the end. My own rooms were near the college playing fields, a good half-mile away. I was to read for an honours degree in mathematics. I was also hoping to get a half blue at tennis. The tennis part started off well by my reaching the final in the freshmans' hard court tournament. Mercifully, however, as I saw it later, I sprained my ankle severely at the beginning of the summer term, taking me out of the game for that term and allowing me to get a second in part 1 of the mathematical tripos, which I would never otherwise have achieved. As for tennis, the competition was too strong for me ever to have reached university honours.

I was what I would call a dutiful churchman at the time, a regular on Sundays at the Eucharist and at some other services, but hardly a committed Christian. Indeed I had a decidedly inadequate idea of what the Christian faith was about, interpreting it largely in terms of moral behaviour which prayer and worship would help one to achieve. Nowadays I would see it as a pilgrim's progress from the position of the elder brother in Jesus' best loved parable, to that of the returning prodigal. In those days there was very much in me which belonged to the elder brother, in fact as a schoolboy I used to feel considerable sympathy for him when the story was read in church. In much later life I was interested to learn that the great German mystic Jacob Boehme absolutely required his readers to be identified with the returning prodigal. A reason for this is that the prodigal must necessarily be caught up in a relationship with God whereas for the moralist this may or may not be so.

It was fairly early in my Cambridge life that I met Pat Gilliat, a fellow tennis player, who was to be my partner through many tournaments. It was not long before I discovered he was a deeply committed Christian and I accepted his invitation to his meeting place on the following Sunday. This was a small hall where about fifty like-minded young men listened to the exposition of the Bible and then knelt down and prayed in spontaneous and rather emotional terms for the conversion of people like myself. This was in fact the Cambridge inter-College Christian Union, known as the CICCU (pronounced 'kick you'). I never felt wholly at ease at these meetings, nor, I think, did Pat. We both felt the outlook was narrow – though perhaps that gave it strength – and there seemed to be a general assumption that here was the only way. However, I was greatly helped by them, the Bible became alive, and the Holy Spirit spoke through its pages. But I lacked the confident faith of my companions that Jesus had died for the forgiveness of sins and although I cried mightily to the Lord, I was left with no assurance that my prayers were heard. I felt the need to open up myself to my parents and it was perhaps this humbling of the soul which led to an experience which I now tell.

James Moore Hickson, the forerunner of the ministry of healing in the Church of England, visited our Exmouth (Holy Trinity) parish church when I was on vacation from Cambridge. I attended with my parents and remember a whole new dimension being opened out to me as Hickson spoke to us from the pulpit. He spoke of many remarkable miracles God had worked in his ministry both in England and abroad. He insisted that Jesus was the minister, and he himself but a channel of Christ's risen life. On one occasion in Africa he had laid hands on an enormous crowd from dawn till late evening, and at the end he was as fresh as at the beginning; this to impress upon us that Jesus was at his side upholding him all the time. I found myself wishing that I had some illness so that I might go up to the altar rails to receive ministry with the sick. But I need not have bothered for Hickson announced that anyone might come for a spiritual blessing. I went up with my father, who had Hodgkin's disease, and my mother, to receive the laying on of hands. No sooner had Hickson laid his hands on my head than my body, and I suppose my spirit, was bathed in a glow of inexpressible comfort and peace, and for the next two weeks I seemed to be walking on air. It was an experience I was often able to look back upon, and draw encouragement from in the days ahead. My father, I may mention, was not seemingly helped in any physical way, and when I said to him and to my mother in my naïveté, 'Wasn't it wonderful?', thinking my experience must have been shared by them, they did not know what I was referring to. However, they shared my happiness when I explained and, no doubt, gave thanks to God. I did not know in those days that it was the babes in Christ, such as myself, to whom the sweetmeats were usually given, the seasoned warriors being left to battle on in faith alone. They were perhaps the more blessed, who had not seen, but had believed. But there was still much healing to be done (indeed, does it ever end?) and before long I was once again walking through a 'dry and weary land where no water is'. But once more the 'pools were (to be) filled with water.'

I was lying awake in bed in the early morning hours and heard the clock of Cambridge's large Roman Catholic church strike three. It was, I suppose, by modern reckoning the third hour (Acts 2:15). Immediately there came upon me 'a mighty rushing wind'. I choose the words from the Authorised Version translation of the Acts of the Apostles (ch. 2) where we read that at the third hour the Holy Spirit descended upon Christ's apostles, his mother Mary, and the whole assembled company as 'a mighty rushing wind', and as 'tongues of fire' which fell upon each one of them. In my case there were no tongues, but I was conscious of a gale blowing through my thick black hair (so different now!) and through my body and through the room. The door, incidentally, was closed and, too, the only window. It seemed to me at the time that an observer would have noticed my hair blowing about, but looking back I do not suppose anything would have been noticeable to anyone but myself. It was a healing experience and I remember thinking that if there had been sick people around me I had only to lay my hands upon them and they would have been healed. I think it was all over in a matter of two or three minutes. I have no doubt, looking back, that the experience was given as a sign of hope and encouragement in the difficult days I was passing through.

Mahatma Gandhi was much in the news during my Cambridge days and I became very interested in him. His book, *My Experiments with Truth*, was widely publicised and I bought it and read it eagerly. Hearing he was to come to Cambridge I had a great desire to meet him. However, I learnt he was to make only one public appearance and that was to be to Indians only. I had several Indian friends who knew my hopes and they decided that with my jet black hair and darkish complexion I could quite easily be smuggled in. Accordingly it was arranged, and there, one night, was Gandhi before me, speaking from the stage of a theatre on the struggle for independence to the several hundred Indians from the university and neighbourhood. I have to confess I was disappointed, though that should not be taken as a criticism of Gandhi himself. He had probably been up since three in the morning, meeting people all day, and here we were at eight o'clock at night. It was not surprising that he should be mentally and emotionally exhausted. But there was a surprise to come. When Gandhi had finished answering questions, there stepped on the stage Charlie Andrews (The Revd C.F. Andrews), often described as the best loved Englishman in India. He said a few words but there was no need for them. The place had at once lit up with his radiance. I think everyone must have felt it, but perhaps not so intensely as myself. I knew at once that he was the person I had to meet and, since he was a Fellow of my own college and stayed there when in Cambridge, it seemed possible that my hopes might be realised. Later I told my experience to Mrs Hutchinson, the wife of the Master of Pembroke, when asked to tea at the Lodge. She must have got busy behind the scenes for a meeting was soon arranged.

I really forget what we talked about but that didn't seem to matter. It was the sheer goodness of the man which held me. It was only later that I learnt that his search for truth had taken him through many trials of mind and spirit. What I was aware of was the fruit of his quest, the peace and joy which flooded from him. Andrews was a great lover, able to share the sorrows and joys of the humblest and poorest Indian, and yet fearless and tireless in taking up India's case for home rule with the by-no-means always sympathetic British administrators. I was to meet him again some twelve years later in strange circumstances in Delhi. I was sleeping in his bed when he appeared unexpectedly one night. The Cambridge Brotherhood,[1] where he had a room, had laid me there after a painful attack from the sun. I opened my eyes to see Andrews looking down upon me, apparently completely happy that I should be there and not he. Once again his presence acted as a tonic. The greatest don't have to give blessings and say prayers. They are blessings, they are prayers.

Andrews was a great friend of the Indian poet Rabindranath Tagore, as I was reminded when I spent a few days at Tagore's ashram Shantiniketan, meaning 'Abode of Peace'. I had been given an appointment to see Tagore at eight o'clock one night, when the message came through that Andrews had died that morning (5 April 1940) in Calcutta, and the poet wished to be silent and alone. Tagore wrote later of Andrews' 'genuine unbounded love', and said he believed him to have been the 'highest blessing' of his life. Of death itself Tagore has written in words which have gone round the world: 'Death is not the extinguishing of the Light, but the putting out of the lamp because the dawn has come.'

The most famous person of my day at Cambridge was Sir J.J. Thomson who was then in his seventies and Master of Trinity College. He had had a brilliant young life as a Cambridge scientist discovering in 1897 the electron, a particle of one two-thousandth of the mass of the lightest atom then known. This was hailed to be the greatest revolution in physics since Sir Isaac Newton. I am not myself knowledgable on these matters but I have read that we owe it to 'J.J.' for every electronic gadget we depend upon and many that most of us don't. These include the telephone and the television, the CD player and the radio, the answering machine and the computer, the washing machine and the microwave, the central heating timer and the burglar alarm, robots and satellites, aircraft and guided missiles, credit cards and the world stock market. It may well be that indirectly he won the war for Britain for the famous Bletchley Park code-breaking computers depended on his discovery. This is just a beginning of the debt owed to this remarkable man who is said to have made the Cavendish Laboratory in Cambridge the greatest research institution in the world. I think he must have been an experimenter rather like Dr Hodgson, whose X-ray equipment I have described in an earlier chapter, as we are told that the simplicity of the apparatus was carried to 'string and sealing wax extremes'. It was said he was clumsy with equipment and relied on his aides to set the apparatus up under his instructions. Thomson was a devout Christian, accessible, generous and hospitable. Telepathy and water divining were among his ESP interests. I cannot imagine him seeking fame but it came his way and he won the Nobel peace prize in 1906 and was buried near to Sir Isaac Newton in the nave of Westminster Abbey. In my day he used to go up to the Cavendish every day reportedly intent on splitting the atom though none of us knew what that might mean for the neighbourhood if it took place. He was much too intent on his research to have any care for his clothes and the story of the time was that for years Lady Thomson had been trying to get him to buy another pair of trousers. Eventually, unknown to her, he slipped away to the shops and returned with a new pair. In the morning he went off to the laboratory leaving the old trousers laid out on his bed. Lady Thomson discovered them and, distinctly agitated, sent them post haste to the Cavendish labelled 'urgent'.

One winter when on vacation I had a truly terrifying experience. I was walking at dusk along the shore of the River Exe on a lonely stretch between Exmouth and Topsham when I found myself sinking in the mud. It was quickly obvious that any effort to extricate myself only led to me sinking deeper and I had the good sense to keep still before I was up to my knees. But the prospect wasn't bright because even if I could have maintained that level there was the tide to reckon with and within a few hours I would be submerged. My relief was immense when in the fading light I spotted two fishermen about a hundred and fifty yards away. If ever I yelled with all my might this was it! They at once came running towards me and marking time at immense speed to avoid getting sucked in themselves they heaved me out. They made light of it as though it were all in the day's work. For me it was an almost miraculous deliverance. The chance of finding two men within seeing and hailing distance at that lonely spot on a winter evening must have been pretty remote. My lasting gratitude to those two men remains though only their children would be likely to be alive today to receive it.

A staunch friend and guide through my Cambridge days was Edward Wynn, Dean of Pembroke, later to become Bishop of Ely. Himself an Anglo-Catholic and a member of the Oratory of the Good Shepherd, he was open to all comers, and my association with the CICCU did not affect the warmth of his friendship. One particular occasion stands out. He had asked me to keep an eye on Frank Briggs, an undergraduate on an adjoining staircase to mine, who was ill with pneumonia. When I went to bid him goodnight he seemed to be all right, but he died alone in the early hours. The doctor had seen him the previous evening so it was, I suppose, unreasonable that I should feel blame. But it was a shock and I needed the encouragement of an older friend. I went down to the funeral at Biddecombe in Somerset. Admiral Briggs and his wife and their family, who put me up for the night (my first experience of a naval grace, 'Thank God'), were wonderfully kind and understanding. Edward Wynn came next day and we travelled back by train together. Simply his presence was a great support. Generations of Pembroke men owe much, and some their very souls, to this deeply human and affectionate man. His holiness struck me forcibly when some years later I went for his counsel at Ely, and received his blessing.

My link with the evangelicals meant foregoing some tennis tournaments in the summer holidays to work with the CSSM (Christian Special Service Mission) on their beach mission. It was thus that I met Bryan Green (at Filey), once described by Billy Graham as 'the greatest living evangelist'. Billy could hardly have awarded that title to himself, but his high rating of Bryan greatly impressed me. When I knew him he was, I think, just thirty, emerging from fundamentalism and hence a cause of suspicion to his fellow workers. At Filey he raised evangelical eyebrows by allowing in his team two eighteen-year-old girls who not only powdered their noses but were not beyond using a dash of lipstick as well. Bryan was a whirlwind of energy: electric, dynamic, stimulating, challenging are words everyone would associate with him. He broadened considerably and was happy to conduct missions with any party which believed in the fundamentals of the Christian faith and so remained a fundamentalist in this sense only. He exercised a powerful ten years ministry at Holy Trinity, Brompton, where he was followed in 1948 by my friend Pat Gilliat of whom I have spoken. Bryan had the deep conviction that an evangelist should work from a parish base thus remaining in touch with day-to-day pastoral needs. I think his worth was never properly appreciated in England, though the church historian Bishop Stephen Neill described him as the greatest evangelist of the Anglican Church in the twentieth century. But it was America who loved him. He visited the United States about a hundred and twenty times and, in addition to ordinary evangelical rallies, spoke at more than a hundred and fifty universities and four hundred high schools. His last visit to America was at the age of ninety-two. He took on all comers including the League of Atheists at Columba University who made the fatal mistake of asking him to speak to them. Their president was converted! Tact was not one of his virtues though his directness often paid off. At one university, confronted by fifteen hundred curious and not altogether sympathetic students he began with: 'The first thing I want to say is that I am not interested in your nasty little sins. In fact most of you don't have enough adventure in you to be really big sinners. But what I am interested in is *the* sin – which is separation from God'. For the next four evenings he spoke to standing-room-only gatherings of more than two thousand students. There was fire in Bryan's belly to the end, and he could never have rested so long as a pulpit was open to him and he had the strength to mount it. After a lapse of more than sixty years I met him again in Norwich shortly before his death at the age of ninety-three. How much he had travelled (and I hope I had too) over the years from those far off restricted Filey days![2]

Largely uneventfully, Cambridge life went on. Rather to my surprise I had taken second-class honours in part one of the maths tripos. Now, in part two, I was floundering out of my depth and my hope was to achieve a third which was honoured in that tripos with the title of Junior Optime.

Senior optime was reserved for those who were awarded a second, wrangler for the privileged few who won first-class honours. Great was my delight when the news of a third (as distinct from failure) was duly announced.

I was late in deciding on a profession. Years before I had told my headmaster, Charles Russell, that there were two things I would never be: a priest or a schoolmaster. Perhaps I was unconsciously fighting against both. The first was not yet in my sights but the second followed after an interview with Dr Costley-White, headmaster of Westminster School, who offered me a post as assistant master to begin in the Michaelmas term of 1932.

6

Westminster School (1)

I JOINED THE TEACHING STAFF of Westminster School in the Play term of 1932. Westminster, in common with other public schools, has in many respects its own language and the Play term was so named to mark the performance of the annual Latin play. The only other new master was John Carleton. He had been a boy at the school and was later to become master of the Queen's scholars and finally headmaster. I was a raw recruit and somewhat overawed in my new surroundings. However, the common room was welcoming and friendly. Arnold Willett was senior master, himself a Westminster boy of Victorian days, exercising an old world courtesy becoming rapidly extinct. He was one of the last masters to be adorned in top hat (mortarboard on the premises) and tailcoat. The rest of us were deemed to be suitably clothed if we wore subfusc suits. Gowns and mortarboards were, too, the order of the day. The boys wore either tails or Eton jackets, according to stature, with top hats for out of school wear. In my early days the school was moving towards four hundred, boarders and day boys being about equally divided. Wearing a top hat and tails on bus or tube each day must have been an ordeal for the more sensitive boys, though in those class-ridden times they probably excited the envy rather than the amusement of most fellow passengers. Some boys, no doubt, gloried in the supposed sense of superiority which their clothing afforded them.

The school day began with chapel in Westminster Abbey at 9.20 and ended up-school (the word for the assembly hall) with Latin prayers in the late afternoon. It was, of course, an enormous privilege to have the Abbey as our school chapel and for boys to be able to wander round it as they wished in their free times. Those were the days before hordes of tourists were seeking admission and the steady flow could easily be dealt with without the barriers which now exist. Women were not admitted unless their heads were covered. Those who arrived without hat or scarf were required to perch a folded handkerchief on their heads before the verger (acting, no doubt, on the advice of the dean and chapter) would let them in. Such were the superstitions of those days. Yet before we feel too superior, it may be well to ask how we would react if the man in front of us were wearing a hat or cap, not out of ignorance or bravado, but for the commendable purpose of keeping his head warm in a cold church. How much are we prisoners of our traditions and culture! I recall a man in India telling me he would never again attend a Eucharist celebrated by me. On my asking why he said that it was because I was wearing shoes at the altar. He had strayed into a westernised church. In his own church it would have been a grave irreverence.

It was during my first year at Westminster that my father died. He had been ill for several years with a form of cancer and the doctors could do nothing more for him. His death took place in the Easter holidays so the whole family was together at Rosendal. The local vicar celebrated a Eucharist in Dad's bedroom with the family present, an immensely reassuring service for us all. A few days later there followed what we have always referred to as 'Dad's vision'. As we stood around his bed my father's face shone with a light not of this world, and in almost ecstatic utterance he expounded on the atoning sacrifice of Christ. I cannot remember his words and they might look plain enough if written down. It was the light and conviction of the utterance which held us. Perhaps it lasted for two minutes or a little less. I think we all knew that death could not be far away and so it proved to be. On the Tuesday of Holy Week, having suffered much, he passed to his rest. Unusually, he was buried between Good Friday and Easter, Holy Saturday as the Church calls it.

I taught twenty-seven periods a week, all but one being mathematics. The exception was Scripture which I taught to my form. Here I was bothered because we had to use a book written by Costley-White and Hardwick and I couldn't in conscience go along with all of its conclusions. Yet I did not want to be disloyal to the headmaster by disputing his writing. Finally I went along to Dr Costley-White and explained my predicament. 'Oh, that's easy,' he said airily. 'When you come across anything you disagree with, you just say that Hardwick wrote that bit'! I do not suppose there was anything in the book which would bother me today.

In his book *Dear Me* Peter Ustinov writes briefly of his days at Westminster School mentioning the eccentricities of some of the masters, mercifully sparing me. Perhaps he has forgotten me though I vividly recall him, a slim good-looking boy, tall for his years, sitting in the front row struggling with his mathematics. I must have known him quite well as one half-holiday he took me to meet his attractive Russian mother at her art shop in or off Bond Street. I remember him as a boy of high sensitivity, modest and responsive, though his talents lay elsewhere than in the subject I was assigned to teach him.

Another boy who took me, this time to his home, was Michael Wedgwood Benn. His father was postmaster general at the time and had a house (if I remember rightly) on the Embankment. His parents were out but on the staircase was a delightful child, brimming over with mischief and vitality, no less than Tony himself. Later he came to Westminster and was in one of my maths sets, sitting in the back row, no great achiever in that subject, but a great charmer, bursting with energy which had to erupt somewhere, if not always in the task before him. Michael, a splendid boy, served in the Air Force for most of the war but, alas, died of wounds in 1944. So many whom I taught in those days failed to survive those terrible years.

Almost next door to Westminster School lay St Edward's House, the London monastic home of the Cowley Fathers. Edward Wynn, Dean of Pembroke, had wanted me to meet them and was especially anxious I should come to know Father Wigram who was then in charge. I think he must have written, for I was invited to the house where I very quickly sensed that here was my spiritual home. There were four fathers in residence, Frs Wigram and Sedding, Fr Wallis who was almost blind, and Fr Bignold, the oldest, who was practically stone deaf. I had been drawn to the Christian Union at Cambridge because of the depth of their commitment, yet uneasily on account of their near-fundamentalist outlook. Here at St Edward's House there was no less commitment and a theology and way of worship with which I could readily associate. The holiness of these men made itself felt and their ascetic way of life spoke of a singleness of heart in their approach to the gospel. I knew I had found a home which had much to teach me.

It was not long before Fr Wigram introduced me to the sacrament of confession, whereby one confesses one's sins to God in the presence of a priest who gives counsel, if that is asked for, and absolution, which is the declaration of God's forgiveness in the name of the Church. In due course I made my first confession to Fr Wigram when I was about twenty-five, something I came to with a good deal of foreboding, but he was encouraging and understanding. He then wanted me to make my confession fortnightly which I did for several years, but then it seemed right to make it once a month and later on less frequently. My practice latterly has been, with the approval of my spiritual director, to go to confession when aware of the need, or it may be to mark some special occasion.

I think there are few people who would not be the better for auricular confession at certain periods in their lives. Certainly, when after a grievous fall a sense of guilt gnaws away at the soul, confession followed by priestly absolution is the healing balm God offers to restore us to peace of mind and reconciliation with himself. Confession should not be seen as a work we do to keep us right with God, for here as everywhere else we are saved by grace and not by works. It should be seen rather as a precious and merciful provision God has made available to us. Even so, this is not to deny that many saints have been and are being made without recourse to ongoing systematic confession to God in the ears of a priest, followed by formal absolution. St Paul and the apostles are surely evidence of this. There was indeed no such system available in the early centuries of the Church.

The position of the Church of England in regard to auricular confession is often abbreviated into 'all may, some should, none must'. I am not happy about all of that because it seems to me that it has to be a 'must' for everybody that they should live in peace and reconciliation with God, so the sacrament of which we are speaking becomes a 'must' where it is needed to minister to that end. I believe that in most people's lives that will be so at one time or another but not necessarily in all. The point which I think the Church of England is making is that so inexhaustible is the compassionate love of God that there is no situation, however bad, in which his forgiveness is not available without recourse to sacramental confession. That is to say there is no barrier on God's part. But there may well be a barrier on our part due to excessive guilt or want of faith, and the priestly absolution (likely to be reinforced by words of hope and encouragement) which follows auricular confession is offered that it may bring with it the assurance of forgiveness which, left to our own devices, had lain beyond our grasp. The position of the Roman Catholic Church is that the sacramental confession of venial sins (which may roughly be described as everyday faults) is strongly recommended without being strictly necessary. Catholics who have committed a mortal (serious) sin are obliged to confess it before a priest and may not receive communion until it has been absolved. The regular confession of venial sins is seen in the new Roman Catholic catechism as helping to 'form our conscience, fight against evil tendencies' and allowing us to 'be healed by Christ and progress in the life of the Spirit'.

For some, however, there are dangers in frequent confession. There are ardent, loving, sensitive and, even more so, scrupulous souls whom frequent auricular confession can hold back. Such people carry with them the burden of some peccadillo (objectively speaking it is often little or no more) until the time of their next confession arrives. Without a rule for confession they would be able to make a brief act of sorrow and acceptance of forgiveness in Christ and move on unhampered in the love of God. With a rule, in spite of their act of sorrow and acceptance of forgiveness, the burden with these people remains until it is unloaded at the next confession. Thus the experience of reconciliation and the accompanying peace of mind, which might have been theirs at once, is deferred. A wise confessor will be able to identify such people and advise them accordingly. It seems to me that the golden rule has to be that whatever practice most freely liberates for the service of Christ is the way to be followed. What may best serve one may not best serve another, and what serves one best at one stage of life may need modification at a later stage.

Unburdening to another outside the confessional, whether to priest or layperson, may meet a deep spiritual and psychological need. It is commended to us in the epistle of St James (James 5:16). The practice may be an alternative to formal confession or it may exist alongside it. Needless to say it should carry with it the same assurance of complete confidentiality as exists in the confessional itself.

In my early days at Westminster I was living in lodgings in Vincent Square about half a mile from the school. It was a quiet and pleasant spot looking straight onto the school playing fields. My furnished lodgings cost two guineas a week which included an old-style English breakfast. As the school provided lunch in return for supervision duties I was well set up for the day and a light evening meal at one of the little restaurants in the nearby Vauxhall Bridge Road was the only extra needed. I was earning the princely salary of £350 per year, about double the income of the middle-aged curate in the parish.

One night as I was returning from supper in the Vauxhall Bridge Road I came across a well-dressed man lying in the gutter. Going to his aid I found him to be dead drunk and was wondering how to proceed. At that moment a taxi came along and with the help of the driver I got him into the cab, only then realising that I didn't know where we should go. I hastily went through his pockets and finding two letters similarly addressed decided that that must be his home. We drove about ten miles out into the suburbs (fortunately only sixpence a mile in those days) by which time he had sobered up a bit though he was still unable to talk. I got him onto my shoulder and together we made our way down the little path to the front door of his terraced house. My halo was now almost visibly sprouting as I awaited the joyful reunion with his wife and her profusion of thanks. Down the stairs she came, opened the door, folded her arms and thundered at me, 'So you're the man who makes my husband drunk'. It was no moment for explanations and I fled to the gate, the taxi driver, who had heard it all, chuckling mightily. He drove me back to Vincent Square and insisted on sharing the ten shilling fare. On reflection I felt I knew who it was who contributed to my passenger's downfall. I doubt if she ever learnt the truth as her husband was too far gone to have had any idea of what was happening to him.

In the epistle which the *Book of Common Prayer* sets for the second Sunday after Easter Peter writes that there is no glory in being patient if you suffer for your faults, but that if you suffer when you do well and take it patiently, that is acceptable to God. I sometimes ask if Peter got it right. I would far sooner be in prison for fifteen years for a murder I hadn't committed than for one which I had. But public opinion seems to be on Peter's side.

I don't think the above incident ever became widely known, but the one which follows certainly did and caused a lot of amusement. It was generally put down in part to a shabby trilby hat I used to wear. The story has been distorted beyond recognition and the true version may not come amiss. I was walking home one evening when I became aware of two tough-looking men following me. Thinking they were what we would now call muggers, I quickened my pace and they quickened theirs. Catching up with me they identified themselves as police officers and wanted to know what I was doing wearing a mackintosh and carrying one as well. I didn't endear myself to them by remarking that I hadn't realised there was a law of the land against it. They took me off to a quiet spot under an archway and asked me to explain myself. Obviously the hat had not drawn out their softer side. I explained that I was a master at Westminster School about a hundred yards away and that having given a boy private tuition, it had come on to rain and I had lent him my spare mackintosh kept at the school. Having delivered the boy to his house I was now walking home with it. They probably thought that was a rather clever excuse and asked me what subject I taught. Clearly they knew no mathematics so that part of the conversation led nowhere. They said I must identify myself, so I said the headmaster would do that if they cared to accompany me to his house. This they were unwilling to do. Then I had an inspiration. The school published its own diary and the names of the masters were listed at the beginning. Pulling out my copy I said they would find my name and the same name in the mackintosh. They made the check and apologised profusely. I said they were not to worry as I would sleep all the more soundly knowing such vigilant people were around. But I found it irresistible to add that I didn't think their detective work was very thorough as obviously I'd be taking the precaution of wearing the stolen mackintosh and they hadn't bothered to check my name in that. No sooner had I said it than I remembered I had been playing in a tennis tournament and a player had run off with my mackintosh, identical to his own, leaving me to run off with his. Here was a real Wooster situation, but with no Jeeves round the corner to bail me out. I need not have worried. 'Wouldn't dream of looking, Sir. Why, Sir, we'd trust you anywhere.' Later I learned the police might be sued and fined for an incident not unlike mine, and I think they were mightily relieved to close the incident on a pleasant note.

An early event of my time at Westminster was a blackmail threat from a private detective on a charge of homosexual practice. As that particular temptation has never come my way I was able to sit loosely to the accusation. In fact so ignorant were we in those days that I had only the haziest idea of what was involved. It must be difficult for moderns to understand how in the dark we were about these things in the days of my youth. As for the young man of about my own age, who was supposed to be the other party, he was of such exemplary piety that it gave the affair much of the colour of a West End farce. Except that the farces of that day would never have ventured away from the straight and narrow. It is quite a long story and I shall have to start at the beginning.

The Oxford Group (otherwise known as the Buchmanites or more recently as Moral Rearmament) was much in evidence in those days. Groups would meet all over the country, the members pledging themselves to absolute honesty, absolute purity and absolute love, enough to tie any conscientious examiner of conscience (let alone scrupulous person) into a hundred moral knots. I have in much later life met many splendid members of Moral Rearmament (as I prefer to call it) but the movement has always struck me as being sub-Christian in that it is another version of some of the ten commandments, but this time expressed positively, described by St Paul as 'a schoolmaster to bring us to Christ'. A large part of the meetings was taken up with open confession of one's sins, something which undoubtedly proved a valuable catharsis to some, but to others forced into it by peer pressure could be damaging in the extreme. The movement had many zealous crusaders and one of them wanted me to join. I decided to go to a meeting as an observer praying that my experience might lead me to know what to do for the future.

A date was fixed and in due course we went along. Various people made their confessions, one particular person standing out. He had been in prison many times and I think we were all impressed with his frankness and honesty. After the meeting he came to me and said he was in a spot of bother with money and asked if I could lend him £5 (multiply by 40 and you get £200 pounds in today's money) which he would send back in two weeks' time when some payment due to him would arrive. One didn't carry such vast sums in those days but I said that if he would give me his address I would post the amount to him. This I duly did, I suppose by cheque or postal order. The fortnight passed and other fortnights with it and still there was no money in the post. I mentioned the matter casually to a fellow lodger who said his brother was a private detective and he was sure he would be glad to help me. In due course the detective came to see his brother and said he would come to see me shortly. Meanwhile the aforesaid young man of pristine purity looked in and I asked him if he would mind waiting in my bedroom, which opened out from my sitting room, whilst I spoke to the detective. This he was glad to do. As we were making our goodbyes the young man emerged from the said bedroom and joined in the handshakes. I thought nothing of it but the detective, interiorly speaking, must have given himself a nod and a wink.

A week or so later the detective returned and gave me the £5. I don't know how he obtained it but I am sure he had his own methods. He then presented me with a bill for his services which I (perhaps rather meanly) refused to pay pointing out I had never engaged him but that he had offered to do this for me as a friend. He replied that if I didn't pay up he would not rest till he had got me out of my job. It was obvious to him that I didn't catch on so he went on to refer to the young man emerging from my bedroom on my last visit. Obviously if at that stage I had offered him even £1 (more than a day's salary!) it would have been tantamount in his eyes to admitting guilt so I told him he could do what he liked but that I wasn't going to give him a penny.

I already had his card and as soon as he left I dashed up to his agency off Oxford Street where I met his boss, a hefty masculine-type woman who was nobody's fool and would put the fear of God into any crook. She had no problem in accepting my story and later I learnt the detective was sacked that afternoon. I fancy there must have been other complaints but that until then she hadn't had the confidence to act. Next I went off to the headmaster (Dr Costley-White) and told him what had happened, and that I had come as he might be getting anonymous letters about me. He took the matter very lightly and assured me that any such letters would go straight into his wastepaper basket. I only hope, if they ever came, he remembered to tear them up! For myself I felt I had been caught up in some rather exciting drama. But at least the Lord had given me guidance over the Oxford Group!

God looks with infinite compassion on us all. I have often wondered what happened to my blackmailer when he died. By the law of averages that must have been at least a quarter of a century ago. I cannot find it in me to look on him with less than such compassion as I have. I shall need the compassion of others when I die and it is only fair he should have mine. Though I hope it goes deeper than that and that I give it gladly and hold nothing back. Mary of Medjugorje, of whom I shall speak in a later chapter, tells the visionaries that at death most people go to purgatory, a few straight to heaven and a larger number straight to hell. But she adds (as I once heard the visionary Vicka say) that God sends nobody to hell but that if we choose hell in this life and go on choosing it that is how it will be in the next. Of course my detective may have repented and died almost a saint but I have not thought that likely. I hope he made his peace before death and at some level or another was plunged into purgatory which, as I understand it, is a one-way street in which those who join can move only upwards. But the suffering must be great especially at the lower end (though tempered by joy at the prospect of the eventual beatific vision) and so far as my prayers can help him he has them on his journey. Unless we are saints and go straight to heaven we shall all need one another's prayers at one level or another. Happy are those who can pass through their purgatory in this life (Matthew 5:4) and die ready to rest immediately in the nearer presence of God.

In 1934 my brother Griff, who had passed through Cranwell and was now well established in the Air Force, was posted to the Air Ministry in

London. We decided to share a flat and Joan generously came to be our housekeeper. The venture lasted until 1937 when Griff got married. We gave up the flat and I moved to a house in Barton Street reserved for masters at the school. Though the family tie was broken, there was for me the compensating advantage of having both the school and the Cowley Fathers virtually on my doorstep.

7
Westminster School (2)

A PERSON WHO INFLUENCED ME greatly during my time at Westminster School was Brother Douglas, the founder of the Franciscan order in the Church of England. I visited him first when I was about twenty-four and joined him digging in the garden of the Wayfarer's Rest in Bishop's Stortford. I was drawn by his warmth and simplicity and, above all, his joy and it was not long before I was visiting him in his Friary home at Hilfield, near Cerne Abbas in Dorset. It was simple in those early days and Madam the donkey would sometimes be there at the refectory window when we took our rough meals. There were just Brother Douglas and Brother Charles and Brother Kenneth. The first two were priests but liked to be known as brother since that was more generally acceptable than father in the Church of England.[1] It also helped to preserve equality between the ordained and lay brethren as the community developed. Brother Douglas was the son of a Methodist minister and once told me how greatly this background had enriched his catholicism. The Franciscans have always been able to welcome a wide spectrum of Christians into their fellowship.

At that time Brothers Douglas and Charles would spend a large part of each year sharing life with wayfarers – the word was just beginning to replace the less respectable word 'tramp' – walking from one workhouse to the next, dossing down with them for the night and doing some chore such as scrubbing the workhouse steps to pay for the hospitality. In this way they came to know many men who would later find their way to the Friary where they would share the work of the brothers for a period, and their worship if they wished to do so. In a few cases their stay might be prolonged for months or even years, engaged in a trade for which they had aptitude. The daily Offices of the little community would for the most part not appeal to casual visitors so Brother Douglas would hold informal family prayers at night, helped by a piano which had long since seen its best days. The Friars attracted a lot of interest and support and the family rapidly began to grow. Today there are more than three hundred Anglican Franciscans in communities at home and overseas.

There are many stories of Brother Douglas and perhaps some of them have grown in the telling. One of his problems was to get things right in church. He would forget the banns and then return to the church to read them to the angels only. He would offer prayers which might have been more happily worded and be unable to continue when the funny side hit him: 'Lord, we pray that our brother's heel may be healed'. Nor did it help church discipline when he asked his congregation to sing his favourite hymn adding that he had once sung it to a sick lady who had passed away during the second verse. There was, too, the occasion when, having found a Prayer Book of the reign of George III, he prayed for 'our Gracious Queen Charlotte and Princess Adelaide', and then desperately corrected himself with 'Queen Mary and all the kindly fruits of the earth.'[2] I don't think he ever quite equalled one of my predecessors at Westminster School who (I was told) once opened the creed in morning Abbey with 'I believe in Pontius Pilate' and, in his confusion, sat down.

When Brother Douglas was in London he would usually sleep with the 'down and outs' (the description of the day) in the crypt at St Martin-in-the-Fields. We would ask him in to breakfast and provide him with a good fry up as one never knew when he would get his next meal. But it was only rarely that he would accept as he normally felt he should share with his almost penniless friends.

One summer holidays I took a party of Westminster boys to camp at Hilfield and begin the digging of a swimming pool which Brother Douglas so much wanted. Just down the road from the Friary was a stream whose waters could be diverted to keep it full. Brother Douglas dug with us for a week. We made very little impression but it was a start and in due course the work was finished by the brothers and probably by the wayfarers as well. Brother Douglas had a great gift for getting others to work, teaching by example and finding idleness hard to tolerate. He would have enjoyed St Francis' description of 'Brother Fly': 'He liked neither work nor prayer but he did eat bravely'.

With the coming of war I lost touch with Brother Douglas. He became wartime chaplain at the large YMCA hostel in Parliament Square, his mission being largely to the many servicemen passing through London. When peace came he shared his life and much of his food with the crippled and near starving people of Hamburg which had been devastated by allied bombing. He was not a gifted linguist but the universal language of love overcame to a large extent his limited knowledge of German. Further missions followed until his health began to fail. Cancer was diagnosed but was unable to dim his faith and courage. The (nursing) Sisters of St Margaret cared for him in his last days and he died very peacefully at their hostel on 5 September 1957 in his eightieth year. Francis, whose ideals of poverty and simplicity had inspired him, can seldom have had a more faithful follower.

During the pre-war years I was frequently asking myself whether God was calling me to test my vocation in a religious community. If so it had to be either the Cowley Fathers or the Franciscan Friars. Each beckoned in a different way, Cowley for its hidden life of prayer, the Friary for combining prayer with a greater freedom and variety. I contended with these in my mind and I think it likely I did not offer myself for the unsatisfactory reason that I could not decide which community it should be. However, on looking back I see that neither would have been likely to confirm me after the probationary period: rightly so, for I do not think I have ever had it in me to be a good member of a community. Certainly, if I had gone that way my life would have been restricted in many respects (though no doubt developed in others) and as I look back I see it as being of God's providence that my indecision was used for his ends.

My life, however, became increasingly linked with the Cowley Fathers as the Westminster years drew on. My lodgings were now in Barton Street at the back of St Edward's House and this gave the opportunity of sharing in many of the Offices. I was sprightly in those days for I would leap out of bed as Big Ben struck six and be dressed, washed and shaved and in the Cowley chapel ready to begin prime as it struck the quarter past. Pangbourne training, no doubt! Prime would be followed by lauds and matins with the Eucharist at seven. Here I learnt the enormous value of daily Offices, taking one straight to objective realities and away from the petty concerns of everyday life. It all made the perfect start to a busy day. Compline was a further possibility at nine in the evening but the daytime Offices were rarely possible. Another important sharing with the Cowley Fathers was daily lunch for a while, taken in silence except on feast days. Here I sometimes met Brother Edward of the Village Evangelists, though never to speak to. So often have people spoken of the extraordinary aura of goodness around him and many regarded him as a saint. As C.F. Andrews radiated joy, so Brother Edward disseminated peace. Of course it is a little artificial to make these distinctions for all the fruits of the Spirit are aspects of the one love. And yet they are not fruits but fruit, for unlike the gifts of the Spirit they cannot be divided. So God's peace cannot exist without joy, nor God's joy without peace.

In 1936 I was ordained deacon in St Paul's Cathedral. For two or three years I had been asking if there was a calling to the ordained ministry: undoubtedly Cowley had helped to foster this. Dr Costley-White gave me a term's leave of absence in the summer of 1936 and I spent this time at Ely Theological College. That was all the training I had and I was woefully ill-equipped. The Bishop of London (Dr Winnington Ingram) had excused me five of the ten General Ordination examination papers; even so that left five to be worked for in about three months. I suppose that was possible as I must have come from a larger background of theological reading than that of students straight from the university. But any theology I may have I have picked up on the road and not in the schools. If you write and edit books people often think you are learned. How wrong they can be!

Ely was a good experience for me because it plugged away at my weak points. I was too individualistic and needed a greater sense of the sacramental and corporate life of the Church. My leaning was to the prophetic rather than to the priestly. Here was the reflection of the Cambridge Christian Union background as against that of the Cowley Fathers. But the catholicism of Ely, though warmly incarnational, was too 'fussy', and I could never have settled into it. Nor do I expect most of the students did once they got into the rough and tumble of parish life.

Ordination to the priesthood usually follows after a year in the diaconate, but when the time came Father Wigram did not feel able to sponsor me as he considered my views on baptism were unsound. Very likely he was right but when the Bishop of London later examined me personally he said mine were the same as his own.

> I say to my people, 'Look at that great Fulham hospital down the road. If you are taken in there you have all the apparatus of healing around you, the doctors and nurses, the operating theatres and the X-rays and the medicines, and all the rest. Of course you may reject the lot and die. But the opportunity is yours and you are given every chance if you want to take it. So, too, with, baptism. God gives you every opportunity. He plants a seed which can be watered and nourished in communion with the prayers, the

sacraments and the fellowship of the Church. The word of God is read at every service, counsel is available and instruction is given. All the apparatus of salvation is around you. You may of course reject it. You may never enter a church again. But the chance has been given you.'

That was roughly the tenor of the Bishop's words. How then did I differ from Father Wigram? I think probably it was a matter of emphasis. I needed a greater awareness of the God-breaking-through element of the sacraments. There was a good deal of Pelagianism in me in those days. The Augustinian side was yet to come. (Augustine said in effect, 'Salvation, it all depends on God.' Pelagius replied, 'No, it depends on me. If I want to be good I can, God helping me.' Augustine answered, 'But what can make me want to be good in the first place - only God. The initiative is always his.')[3]

However, the Bishop judged it suitable that I should wait a year and I was sent for instruction to the rector of a famous London church. I was told he was as dry as dust and so he was. But he did take the trouble to see me and he was patient with my youthful ardour. There were rough edges to be made smooth and I owe more to him than I realised at the time.

How well I remember my first sermon at Westminster, delivered in the Abbey at morning prayers. I was nervous beyond belief, wrote it all out and learnt it by heart. Even so, I had the script with me though had no need of it. With such over-preparation the address ought to have been a flop, but amazingly it came out spontaneously and full of life. It was on the returning prodigal, who was of course myself, a journey I am still making, I hope with my readers, and which, God helping us, we shall make to the end. For we are always returning, just as we are always being welcomed and reaffirmed in the sonship we have never lost. A number of hearts were touched that morning and especially that of a senior master for whom it was a marking point in his life. People sometimes say to me (not often!) that that was a good sermon, but one much prefers to hear that someone was helped or some heart has been moved. The well-known mission preacher of my youth, Father Andrew of the Society of the Divine Compassion, once told his Sunday evening mission congregation that he would be hearing confessions at eight o'clock on the following Tuesday night. 'Wonderful sermon, father,' said a lady as she left the church. 'Eight o'clock Tuesday' came the reply.

Shortly after my being made deacon, Dr Costley-White left Westminster to be Dean of Gloucester and was replaced as headmaster by John Christie. Christie had a brilliant mind. He had been a scholar at Winchester, took a double first at Oxford, and was then classics master at Rugby where he gained the reputation of being an outstanding teacher. He left Rugby to become headmaster of Repton and from there came to Westminster in 1937. He remained for thirteen years, taking the school through the difficult war years at Bromyard, before becoming Principal of Jesus College, Oxford.

Discipline at the school had undoubtedly grown slack and Christie's arrival gave it the spur it needed. His lithe, athletic figure, strategically placed in Little Dean's Yard, helped to scurry boys to their classrooms and, indeed, masters too. Moreover, he was almost always on time himself, an exacting discipline for a head with so many conflicting calls. His reputation had preceded him and the classical VIth and VIIth were quick to realise they had an exceptional teacher among them. Christie had a lively and stimulating mind, well stocked beyond the range of his specialist subject, and his pupils, educated rather than informed, gained far more from him than examination success.

My personal contact with Christie was largely through a group of three or four masters who used to meet weekly. Each in turn would give the others a scriptural passage for meditational reading through the week. Then on Fridays we would spend a quarter of an hour in silence in St Faith's Chapel in the Abbey and from there we would move to John Christie's study to discuss what we had read. He must have found us rather dull. Often we couldn't keep pace with his agile, penetrating mind and if we made an ill-thought-out remark he was quick to challenge us and set us right. I once said, in an unfortunate contribution, that Jesus said we must die in order that we may live. Christie replied that he was unaware that Jesus had said any such thing and asked me to show where it was written. 'No, no,' he said, 'it's not a question of dying *in order that* we may live, there is no nice little calculation involved, it's a matter of dying and *behold* we live. The note of surprise is always there. Jesus says simply that whoever dies for his sake and the gospel's will indeed live.' I have always been grateful for that rebuke and have often noted how many clergy and others have misquoted the words of Jesus as I did on that occasion.

Others in the group were W.H. (Bill) Franklin, a priest who died at the age of ninety-two in 1996, David Simpson, master of the King's

Scholars and Tom Garnett who was to become Master (headmaster) of Marlborough. I suppose it was a useful exercise and it helped us to get to know one another, but frankly it wasn't my scene. When I went to St Faith's Chapel I didn't want to have on me the burden of discussing the passage afterwards, but simply to let everything go in silence before God. St Faith's, incidentally, in those days was a favourite haunt and a wonderful refuge from the continual bustle of school life. I used to spend most of my free periods there, doing nothing as it often seemed to me, but looking back I think it was the beginning of a contemplative call. In those days the chapel was accessible through the Abbey whereas nowadays the entrance through the cloisters is normal and fewer people discover it. The chapel has an atmosphere of its own and should not be missed by visitors seeking quiet as they visit what has become a busy tourist's church, where the battle to keep prayer and worship foremost has to be continuously waged.

I once spent a memorable evening with Christie who had invited me to meet C.S. Lewis who was spending a night with him. I had, in fact, met Lewis earlier in the day when he had stopped me and asked for directions, and I had been wondering how to place him. I was the only other person present and was content to sit back and listen to the most fascinating and brilliant talk I have known. But what was said I cannot remember except that Lewis insisted that he never wrote about any sin to which he was not personally tempted. Christie challenged this – he was apt to challenge anything – saying Lewis had written on theft which temptation he felt sure was never his. Lewis replied that only the previous evening he had been tempted to down the whisky of a colleague who had been called to the phone. And so serious stuff mixed up with the banter went on.

On the religious side Christie's drawing was to the person of Jesus. Though a loyal churchman he left it by and large to others to speak of the mission of the Church. He was somewhat wary of the clergy and a priest had to prove himself to be taken into his confidence. As a preacher he was stimulating with a lively turn of phrase. A camel passing through the eye of a needle had outlasted its time to evoke merriment and delight, so it had to be instead an elephant passing through a turnstyle. In that way the words of Jesus became alive once more to today's listener. His talks in Abbey were model compositions, his own conviction and sincerity shining through.

Agapé, the general New Testament word for love, the love which seeks the wellbeing of all, running sometimes with and sometimes against the natural inclinations, was Christie's great word. Every Friday evening discussion was shot through with it and no one can have known John well without being aware that that is what he sought to live by. Whenever I hear the word now my mind shoots back to Christie and Westminster School.

In the summer holidays I would sometimes take groups of boys for excursions overseas. We had ten days touring the Black Forest in Germany, and another year a week in Oberammergau and Austria. Most interesting of all was a week's visit to a Nazi school (1937?) set up for the training of army officers. The Westminster boys used to marvel at the Nazi late-teenage youth chasing from one cover to the next, aiming with an imaginary gun and doing a 'bang bang bang' at some imagined enemy, just as they themselves might have done at half their age. In those days it seemed natural and generally acceptable to begin each day with corporate prayers and we used to leave the school for the neighbouring wood for the purpose. I think this quite impressed our hosts, more especially when they once heard a German tune emerging from the shrubbery. I used to meal sometimes at the staff table. The teachers spoke English fluently so there were no conversational barriers. In place of grace there was some sort of acknowledgement of Hitler. The boys had to respond to orders smartly, ending with a click of the heels and a Heil Hitler. Once, incidentally, we missed our bus because our arm raising to bring it to a halt was mistaken for a salute to the Fuehrer. The driver acknowledged it smartly and sped on. I was invited to attend an English class and was astonished at how well the boys could speak. The masters at the school made us most welcome and assured us, sincerely I feel sure, that war between Britain and Germany could never break out again. In a short time we – by now good friends – were at one another's throats.

It was, I think, at the end of the summer term of 1938 that I had the interesting prospect of serving on a peace mission to Germany organised by Lord Lothian. Christie had been expected to be one of a little group of about eight people, but had had to withdraw and asked if I might take his place. All was ready for us to spend a few days at a famous Berlin hotel where we would meet with some of the high-ranking German officials. I had been warned that our rooms and luggage would be searched while we were at meals and it was becoming an exciting venture, when suddenly the Foreign Office either forbade or warned against the party going. It all ended in a damp squib with a party of moderate-ranking Germans coming to meet us one afternoon in a London hotel. I don't think minds ever met and I can't think anything was achieved. For myself I was intrigued with the skill of the interpreter, said to be Hitler's own, in getting across what people wanted to say. I was a very small fish in such troubled waters and did not say a word. What useful word, indeed, could I have said?

Early in 1939 I was asked by the SPG (Society for the Propagation of the Gospel) if I would be their representative to public schools. This involved spending a weekend at one boarding school after another, preaching on the Sunday and being available for discussion or interview. I replied that I would not feel qualified to accept until I had spent at least a year with overseas missionary work. To this they agreed and I was granted a year's leave of absence from the school. Accordingly my passage was booked to India, and I was to sail on the P and O liner SS *Moloya* in a few months' time. Little did anyone know then that she would be the last passenger ship to sail through the Suez Canal for many years. But events in Europe were moving rapidly and in August the papers were announcing that war clouds were gathering. I was, in the event, to be away not one year but nearly six and my life was to be largely uprooted from England for the next thirty years.

8

The Cawnpore Brotherhood

M Y MOTHER AND JOAN saw me off at Victoria station for my overland journey to Marseilles where I was to board ship for Bombay. It was a sad parting for on that day in the middle of August war seemed inevitable. It was general knowledge that Britain was quite unprepared to meet the might of the German forces and as we said our goodbyes we must have wondered if we would meet again.

I reached Marseilles early the following morning and had most of the day before me before joining the SS *Moloya* which had left England with most of its passengers a week before. I went to a Catholic church on a hill overlooking the sea for a period of silence for I felt that that alone would revive my drooping spirits. But it was not to be as I expected. A little family of parents and children came and sat just in front of me and, quite unconscious that anyone else might be disturbed, they went through their lengthy prayers together. It was not what I would have asked for but it was just what I needed. I could not understand the prayers which were, of course, in French, but a strength reached me through the simple faith of this peasant family. Perhaps they, too, were anxious for their loved ones as the storm clouds were gathering over their country. I remember reflecting how this experience could never have happened in the staid, formal and polite atmosphere of the Church of England. It came to my mind that for Catholics church is home, a place where they may quite naturally come and be at home with God. Happily in the fifty and more years which have since passed, our Anglican churches have mellowed greatly, though to be fair many of the Anglo-Catholic churches of the day carried this happy air of informality with them. By the time I left the church my spirits had revived.

The ship sailed that evening but it was hardly a normal voyage. I suppose the thoughts of all were deeply occupied with those they had left behind. There was a tangible need for prayer and every evening a

Methodist minister or I took family prayers which were remarkably well attended. We were even given an empty cabin as a chapel for private prayer in the day.

It was not until we were in the Indian Ocean that we were told that war had been declared. I went off to find a private spot for matins and there in the Old Testament reading before me was the following story of Elisha from the sixth chapter of the second book of Kings. I quote from the Good News Bible.

> When the king was told that Elisha was in Dothan, he sent a large force there with horses and chariots. They reached the town at night and surrounded it. Early the next morning Elisha's servant got up, went out of the house, and saw the Syrian troops with their horses and chariots surrounding the town. He went back to Elisha and exclaimed, 'We are doomed, sir! What shall we do?' 'Don't be afraid,' Elisha answered. 'We have more on our side than they have on theirs.' Then he prayed, 'O Lord, open his eyes and let him see!' The Lord answered his prayer, and Elisha's servant looked up and saw the hillside covered with horses and chariots of fire all round Elisha.

The message was brought home to me that our little armies would be more than a match for Hitler's might and what the Office had given me to read that day returned often through the bleakest days of the war. It was a message of hope. I wondered how many others had noticed it and drawn comfort from it.

Black-outs were at once enforced and we were warned that there was to be no smoking at night on deck. As luck would have it I ran into a solitary smoker that first night. We were the only two who had come out for fresh air. I reminded him smoking was not allowed but was asked what the hell that had to do with me. I said I had no wish to be torpedoed and that there were hundreds of others whose lives he was putting at risk. He remained unimpressed. I was less tactful at thirty than I am now and I mused aloud that he might perhaps be a German spy. This hardly mollified his feelings and he stood his ground before me. I said I would have to report him to the captain at which he stamped out his cigarette in a torrent of abuse. I can't think I acted other than rightly though it might have been more tactfully done.

Father Whitworth, local superior of the Cowley Fathers, met me at Bombay and took me to the community house in the compound of St

Peter's School, Mazagon, a few miles from the port. I met the fathers, was introduced to the school which they ran, an Anglo-Indian boys' school, and was fitted out with a bedding roll, an essential piece of luggage for travelling in India. The following evening I was put on the train for Cawnpore.

Christopher Ackroyd of the Cawnpore Brotherhood met me at the station some twenty hours later, and took me by a horse-drawn tonga to what was to be my new home. The Brotherhood house was an L-shaped building comprising six bed-sitting rooms, a library, dining room and chapel. The building was decidedly *kutcha* (*kutcha* being the opposite of the better-known *pukka*), baked mud walls supporting a kind of thatched roof in which the birds might make their nests. My room, about ten feet square, was simply furnished with a *charpoy* (bed), a desk, an upright and a reclining chair. We shared a common purse, three missionary salaries doing for the five of us, four English, and Sirswal, a fine young Indian. Food and clothing and other necessities were met from the common purse and in addition we each had five rupees a month for personal luxuries (13 Rs equalled £1). It was thus a simple life, the hope being that our relative poverty would make us more accessible to the Indians whose lifestyle was well below that of most westerners in India. In this we were not disappointed.

We lived to a simple rule which included matins and Eucharist, a midday Office and evensong, and finally compline at night. Meals were simple, Indian style, and for the most part we thrived. We were young and idealistic, I think all of us under forty, and were inclined to discount the views of the more experienced that Europeans should not be attempting to live in this style. Though I have to say I did go down with dysentery after about nine months, and apart from a timely removal to the European style McRobert hospital I believe it would have carried me off.

I found the greatest hardship was travelling third class by train, an experience which need hardly be described as the modern reader will understand it from their television screens. But I have to say I was sometimes elevated to intermediate class, above which was second and finally the luxury of first. Air-conditioned travel had not arrived in those days.

The Brotherhood was linked to Christ Church, a Christian degree college across the road and two of its members taught there regularly. Christopher Ackroyd, the Brotherhood bursar, was an honoured professor, a splendid teacher to Indian students, and, importantly for his work, fully identified with the aspirations of wartime India for independence as soon as it might be. I was to be the other teacher, chosen to teach English for no better reason than it happened to be my native tongue. I couldn't understand my students' English and I doubt if they could make much of mine. I can't blame them if they were horribly bored as I tried to put across *The Tempest* and *Great Expectations* which were set for their coming examinations. But there was more to it than just inadequate teaching: there was a clash of personalities as well. As a newcomer from England I represented the British Raj at a time when nationalism was at its height. Once when I grasped one young man by his arm and told him, pleasantly as I thought, to behave himself, the class cried out 'violence' and disappeared to a man. Then the college came out on strike, nothing more than a political game really to get this young Englishman to apologise for his behaviour. This I did at the request of the exasperated Indian Christian principal. Honours were now even and we could start again. But to my relief I was regarded as something of a liability and my teaching work was phased out. Ackroyd, as a fervent nationalist, had no problems unless it were with the Raj itself. We used to wonder whether one of his Oxford contemporaries in the Indian Civil Service might not one day see it as his duty to put him on a charge. In effect he was shortly to be summoned to war service, was sent to the Middle East, and in a matter of months reported dead. I subscribed to his memorial fund (I had left the Brotherhood by then) only to meet him a few months later looking as well as he had ever been.

I now had much more spare time on my hands and used it in a way I shall never regret. With money I had in England I was given permission to buy a typewriter and set myself to learn a skill without which I do not know how I would ever have got through life. In my mid-eighties I have graduated to a word processor but the basic *qwerty* keys are there and the other skills are secondary. God surely did me a good turn when I grasped that young man's arm!

Michael Storrs Fox, a priest five years my senior, was head of the Brotherhood as, too, of all the SPG work in Cawnpore and its outstations. His was a steadying influence in the political climate of the time. His aim was to make the Brotherhood a place of community and prayer where people of all opinions could talk in an atmosphere of calm and understanding.

From Cawnpore I used sometimes to visit Canon Underwood who

was the SPG missionary at Moradabad about two hundred miles away. Moradabad was a railway centre and so harboured a strong Anglo-Indian colony which formed part of his scattered parish. I think Canon Underwood was something of a scholar though he wore his learning lightly and was a man of deep simplicity in heart and mind; and, too, in his outward style of life. He was a natural visitor and his people loved him. Sometimes he would hear my confession, always with wisdom and simple goodness, and I expect he was the confidant of many hearts. On our first meeting I remember he greeted me joyfully with the observation that we would be able to say compline in Latin, a subject in which, to put it mildly, I never excelled.

When I first knew him Canon Underwood (he was always so known) had a motorbicycle to help him get round his scattered district. I was his pillion passenger in days when motorbikes were more basic than they are now – and I cannot think he had the latest model – and Indian country roads were a revelation to western eyes. It must have been bad enough in front, but of course he had never experienced sitting behind. He seemed to have more sense of adventure than danger as we sped out to an Indian school, where he would take the Eucharist in an open-air chapel with monkeys dancing on the wire meshed roof. In my later years in India when he was about eighty and in another parish, he had given up his motorbike for an ordinary bicycle, something the parish had been trying to persuade him to do for many years. Once he produced a bicycle for me and taking me off somewhere one dark evening he mistook a T-junction for a crossroads and landed us both in the ditch. He was unperturbed though he must have been quite heavily shaken. But the day came when he had a nasty fall with an injury to his head and the Bishop sent me out to see him, an overnight train journey away. His only concern as he lay in bed was that he had prepared 'such a lovely sermon' for his parishioners which he would not now be able to deliver.

Once when preaching in Allahabad Cathedral Canon Underwood began by explaining that he had three points. 'My first point is . . .', which he duly explained. 'My second point is . . .', and explanation followed. 'And my third point is . . . well now, I've forgotten my third point but [leaning over the pulpit with a beatific smile] it was such a *lovely* point.' And down the steps he came. Naturally, all hearts were won. I have often used that story when I have forgotten my next point in a retreat address, and by the time I have told it we are all so relaxed that I have usually remembered what I wanted to say. I commend it to all speakers.

Following my bout of dysentery in April 1940 it was decided I should go to the hills to recuperate. There was a holiday chaplaincy at Mashobra, about six miles from Simla, sponsored by Miss Hotz who owned the Gables Hotel (also the famous Cecil Hotel in Old Delhi) hard by St Crispin's Church. Free hotel accommodation was offered in return for the taking of Sunday services. I gladly availed myself of this and had a pleasant if small congregation. I have always been a little absent-minded and to my concern discovered during my first service that I had forgotten to robe. Holy Trinity, Brompton would think nothing of that nowadays but in those times it was different and as I left the church there came across the air, 'My dear, I think he must be a Baptist'. Probably I had been distracted by the man I met in the churchyard before the service. He introduced himself to me as the cutter of the toenails of the local rajah and listed other famous toenails he had clipped. Feeling honoured to be in such company I held out my feet obediently, hoping fervently that the operation would be completed before the congregation arrived.

It seems that at the next session with his master he communicated my presence, for a card shortly arrived inviting me to luncheon at the palace. Alas, I arrived an hour late only to find the thirty or so guests taking their final course. It was not my fault as the card was wrongly marked and the troubled rajah insisted on me going through the whole meal whilst the others waited. The mango at the end, the first I had seen, completely defeated me until a guest came to my aid. It is said there is only one way to eat a mango and that is in the bath. After that experience I fervently agreed.

A few weeks into my stay at Mashobra a cable came from my mother to say my Air Force brother Griff was reported missing over France. He had been piloting a bomber which had received a direct hit. There was time to smile and nod to his observer to bail out, but Griff was having trouble with his escape hatch and by the time he managed to open it there was no chance for manoeuvre and he parachuted into a tree. He was dead when he was found and one hopes he died instantly. The details, of course, emerged much later from his observer who landed safely in spite of being shot at, and the one who found him. The latter, Mr Roberts, who was responsible for the war graves in the area, thoughtfully kept Griff's parachute cushion in case he should one day meet one of the family. Some years later, Addie, who was always devoted to Griff, visited the grave, and was very pleased to receive it. She was greatly touched by Mr Roberts' loving care in his work.

It was the reference to the smile and the nod in the observer's carefully written and considerate letter which held me. If you can smile when part of your plane is blown away and the part you're in is ablaze and you haven't yet opened your escape hatch, there must be some special grace at work. I like to think there was peace and not panic at the end.

Griff was very close to me. For the first fourteen years we had been together almost the whole time, both in schools and holidays, and in Westminster School days for three years as well. He was a much more adventurous person than I, a good athlete and games player and had many friends. I grieved greatly but my neighbours were kind and helped me through. It was, of course, a pain shared by the end of the war by almost every family in the land. Our thoughts now went out to his devoted wife Barbara with her young child Jill, and baby Ann well on the way. Barbara, who died in 1995, worked with the Admiralty helping to plot the course of convoys across the seas. I learnt later that she was in touch with my own convoy throughout the voyage from India in the last days of the war. It was a comfort to the family to know this.

I am not usually psychically aware but about two weeks after his death Griff visited me early one morning in my hotel bedroom. I did not see him but was aware of his coming through the locked bedroom door and hovering over me. Nothing was said, or perhaps it was and not picked up, but I believe that he came as an assurance that all was well.

In due course the Mashobra holiday came to an end. I returned to Cawnpore to open, under the auspices of the Brotherhood, a small day school for war evacuees until fuller provision for them could be made.

9

The Hallett War School

THE WAR SITUATION IN England was now serious and parents whose work lay in India were becoming anxious for their boys and girls at boarding schools at home. Evacuation was still possible though a lengthy business since the Suez Canal was closed. Even so, many parents took advantage of transport destined for India. The next problem was education, for the Anglo-Indian schools did not fully cater for the subjects these children would require. Hence, through the Bishop of Lucknow and the Director of Public Instruction, Mr Powell-Price, and greatly aided by Bill (later Sir William) Christie of the ICS, it was decided to open a special school in the hill resort of Naini Tal. Thus came into being The Hallett War School (named after Lady Hallett, wife of the Governor of the United Provinces), and I was asked to be its headmaster. My year with the Brotherhood was up and the Bishop of London had said I should stay in India for the duration of the war. The Bishop of Lucknow had turned down my offer for war chaplaincy thinking perhaps that this school work was my true calling. Certainly I have seen it since as the reason for my going to India and the year at the Brotherhood as a period of preparation in a strange land, without which I could never have coped with the years ahead.

The Philander Smith College, an Anglo-Indian school situated at 7,000 feet in the foothills of the Himalayas, had closed in 1940 and this was to be the site of the new school. It was unapproachable by any road and everything from sacks of potatoes to pianos had to be carried up the 700 feet above the Naini Tal lake (*tal* means lake) on the backs of coolies. They were amazingly clever as they tackled the heaviest loads, aided by ropes and long bamboos. I took over in January 1941 with instructions to open in March, but with all the alterations necessary, including the removal of a whole storey from the classroom block, though this work was under way, it seemed impossible that we should be ready in time.

Fortunately I was so inexperienced that my imagination was unable to take in all that had to be done. Otherwise my spirits might have failed.

On my first visit to Naini Tal in January 1941 I walked up to the school with Margaret Tilney-Bassett, a trained Great Ormond Street nurse who had been appointed head matron. She was a gem of a person and I could never have managed the school without her. Her husband was Army chaplain at Dinapore and I used to spend holidays there with them and their three children who were pupils at the school. We decided to ignore the pony tracks up to the school and to go straight up the hillside. About 500 feet up we were stopped by a high fence and there seemed to be no way round. We found, however, a drainpipe through which water would have cascaded in the rainy season. Margaret, having the greater girth, went first, her torch in her mouth, me following ready to pull her back in case she got stuck. As she clambered out the watchman of the premises descended on her asking for an explanation. She explained that she was to be the matron at the new school and that the headmaster was on his way behind her. We never knew what he made of it. Mad dogs and Englishmen is engraven deeply into the Indian psyche and it may be he thought all English headmasters made their debut in this way.

It was obvious when we reached the school that something drastic had to be done. Builders were everywhere, but still in short supply. The doors on the girls' lavatories had been wrongly fixed to open inwards making it necessary to stand on the seat to shut the door. There were few carpenters in the place so we sent to Lucknow for twenty who, to our surprise, all came. I had to go off to Bombay about a thousand miles away to select textbooks and equipment, for we had almost nothing except the blackboards on the classroom walls and many of them had to be replaced. Margaret remained at the school with Miss Fowle, the headmistress, to try to bring some sort of order out of chaos.

My memory is hazy but I think there were about six of us there in the month or so before the school opened. We used to meet for prayers every morning and then sketch out the day's work. Even so, time defeated us and we had to delay opening by two weeks. This, of course, meant letters to all the parents for there was no getting on the phone, pressing a few buttons, and finding you were there. How fortunate that I had learnt to type!

The first day of term arrived and we were faced with an army of parents and children making their way up the hill, some walking, others on ponies, or in dandies. A dandy was a sort of canvas sedan chair carried on the shoulders of four coolies. Hundreds of pieces of luggage followed, some strung over the strong hill ponies but most on the backs of the coolies. How those men worked, and cheerfully too!

There were bound to be mistakes for no one knew anyone else. I showed one young mother to her cubicle thinking she was a senior girl. A twelve-year-old boy asked me what sort of bloke the headmaster was. But we got it sorted out in the end. The parents departed at last and we were left in peace to face a nine-month term.

That was a problem with the hill schools. Nine months is a long time for a child to be away from home. We were victims of the climate which was manageable in the plains from December to March, but hardly so in the summer when the temperature might rise to 112 degrees or more. Also there was a serious risk of infection in the plains in the hot weather. Moreover, distances from home might be up to a thousand miles and transport was not as it is in the western world. So, instead, we had a two-week break in June and a week in October when those whose parents came up to Naini Tal could be with them.

One problem was that there was a headmaster (me) and a headmistress for the girls and the Governing Body opted for dual control. This was not always easy for either of us, though I owe a great deal to Ethel Fowle who had been headmistress of an Anglo-Indian boarding school and had had experience I lacked. She left after the first year and later became a nun in a teaching order. The Governing Body decided against dual control for the future and appointed a housemistress for the girls.

We were an interesting mix for our day, for none of our parents had chosen a coeducational school for their children in England where there was a choice. On the whole it worked out well and from later reports from home schools, to which many eventually returned, the education had not suffered. Indeed the final results in the Cambridge School Certificate – the highest we aspired to – were better than anything I had known in England. This was due to our well-qualified and dedicated staff, mostly wives of Army officers or other personnel serving in India. In these circumstances it was, perhaps, hardly surprising that we had a German spy on the staff. She was uncovered in due course. I had had no suspicion but learnt later that the girls among whom she worked, who had noticed the extent of her correspondence, had had quite a few. The circumstances of the war made it impossible for us to have many men. However, at least so far as examination results are a guide to teaching, women are, I think, generally better than men, being more conscientious in marking and preparation of lessons. They are also more wedded to the syllabus: not necessarily a good thing in the wider aspect of education.

Margaret Tilney-Bassett, of drainpipe fame, was my great helper and became a treasured friend of the family in postwar years. When her duties allowed she would be present at the early morning Eucharist and shared with me a liking for the Offices of the Church which we often said together. She was universally loved by parents, staff, children, and all. A day came when she had to leave the school and travel to her home in Dinapore for the removal of a cancerous breast. The chapel was over-crowded (we needed two sessions) on the day of her operation and there was an atmosphere there which none could miss. Perhaps there is something very special about children's prayers (our age range was 6 to 17), something the Lord finds hard to resist. At any rate she recovered in double-quick time, and the surgeon was sufficiently convinced that it was not all his doing that he charged no fees. In a very short time she was back at work.

An incident which sticks in my mind is the disappearance of a ten-year-old girl one Whitsunday after church. In that wild hilly country this was a matter for serious concern. We searched high and low but to no avail. Finally in the evening she came to light; she had been resting in a quiet spot in the scrubby hillside. Having been sent to me to explain herself, I asked if she was not lonely all that day by herself. 'Oh no,' she replied, 'I always had the Holy Spirit to talk to.' The words were said so artlessly and simply that it was impossible not to accept them and I was left musing that my Whitsun sermon had gone deeper than I had thought. Actually her reply raises an interesting theological question, though I was unaware of that at the time. In our hymns and devotions there is plenty of talking to the Holy Spirit, yet there is not one instance of it in the New Testament where the Holy Spirit is never invoked directly, but only the Father or the Son.

Odd fragments of memory return. I recall our splendid cook making me a magnificent birthday cake, but when put on display it was found to bear the words 'A happy bath day'. Then there was the young woman teacher who got the most dreadful shock one winter evening when she saw me coming out of the mist and mistook me for a bear. We did have the occasional bear around in the hills above. I never heard of one invading the school premises which is just as well as they could be very dangerous. But I never saw one in my time.

Mary Austen, who was housemistress, was an excellent English teacher and a lively and indispensable member of the staff. She had a trenchant wit which helped her not a little in her dealings with others. I recall reading on one senior girl's report, 'She believes in co-ed in the American sense with the emphasis on the co and not the ed'. We did, of course, have our boy/girl problems but they were nothing as they might be today. For the most part there was a healthy and happy camaraderie between the sexes and of course when it came to producing plays we had every advantage over the single-sex establishments. The occasional dances were also much looked forward to.

Early in 1944 the Superior of the Oxford Mission to Calcutta wrote to ask if Fr Prior of the community could spend six months with us. He had been unwell and it was judged that a long convalescence in the hills would be good for him. Fr Prior was the pastor and priest of numerous outlying Christian communities in East Bengal. It was a district with few roads but many waterways and Fr Prior's rectory was his houseboat St Mark, which he would sail from one congregation to another. I once spent a week with him on board. Wherever we went we would be sumptuously feasted. Fr Prior, after the acclimatisation of many years, had no problem here but mine was acute. I simply couldn't manage the enormous quantities of food, especially rice, one was expected to consume; yet to eat only a little seemed discourteous to one's host who had prepared what would have been a delicious meal for the Bengali palate but a distinctly demanding one for my own.

How these people loved their church! They would walk fifteen miles or more to be present at the Eucharist, which would begin when the sun was in such and such a place determined by Fr Prior. I imagine he had a watch but possibly no one else. In this outlying place a strange thing happened. A boy of about thirteen produced a booklet of Bible Reading Fellowship notes (in English) which he was reading daily. Imagine my surprise when I saw I had written them myself. I had written two simple booklets making daily comment on St John's Gospel at the request of the BRF shortly before leaving England. I never expected to see them in print, yet here they were in the middle of nowhere and in wartime too. And, in addition, a boy who could read English and understand them. Some would call it coincidence but to me it was the hand of God.

Fr Prior duly came along early in the new term and we accommodated him in a cabin about a hundred feet above the school, where he could live as a hermit or mix as he wished. He was, I think, sixty-five and with his fine flowing white beard looked for all the world like an Old Testament prophet. Naturally he made a great contribution to the spiritual dimension of our lives. He suggested holding a mission, for want of a better word, towards the end of his stay, consisting of five evening chapel addresses which were well attended. After Fr Prior had given the first four talks I had a deep conviction that I should give the last. But how to tell Fr Prior, especially as he would have already prepared what he was going to say? I need not have worried as he was confined to his bed that day and had to ask me to take his place. I don't suppose I said anything dramatic, but several came afterwards to make their first confessions and I felt clearly the Holy Spirit was at work. Some have expressed surprise that I heard the confessions of pupils (it wasn't often they wanted to come) so perhaps I should make it clear that I always offered another priest as an alternative. Naturally it was understood that what one knew as a priest one did not know in any other capacity.

I forget whether it was before or after this that a strange thing happened. I was lying awake in the early hours of the morning when, as it seemed to me, a cat jumped onto my bed landing on my stomach. The 'creature' then began pawing its way through the bedclothes and then in to me, although I did not feel any physical pain. I thought myself to have been invaded by an evil spirit. I was frightened but realised there was nothing for it but to lie back and pray. After about half an hour all seemed to be well. Two nights later there was an exact repetition and at about the same time. I then told Father Prior who, due to the cold, had moved from his cabin and was sleeping next door. He asked me to call him if it happened again so that he could come and pray at my bedside. But that was the end of it. I had known with my head that our warfare is 'not against human foes, but against cosmic powers . . . against the superhuman forces of evil in the heavenly realms' (Ephesians 6:12, NEB). Although I would not wish the experience to be repeated I am grateful to have known it at gut level. In the sixty and more years since these happenings I have never had a comparable tangible experience of evil, though I have often believed myself to be under some sort of attack before retreat or other addresses, and imagined the devil has homed in on my natural fears and tried to put some sort of spoke into the works. Not that I think Screwtape himself would think me worth bothering about but maybe Wormwood or Slubgob or some other of his minions have been on the prowl. I certainly do believe we are subject to attention from demonic forces and it seems quite a short jump from there to assume they have a leader to whom the name Satan (meaning the adversary) is traditionally given. I once read the story of a fisherman who having to be away at sea for many weeks used to preserve his catch in tanks that it might be fresh on his return. Even so, these fish never quite had the flavour of those which were freshly caught, at least not until he hit upon the idea of adding catfish to the tanks. Not all his fish can have survived, but those which did so were said to taste the better for having to be vigilant to the end against their natural foe. So, too, we are encouraged to flex our spiritual muscles, to put on the whole armour of God, when we know that an adversary intent on 'getting us' is there.

But I also find it helpful to believe, as some theologians do (St Augustine was among them), that evil is a 'no thing', an absence of good, rather as cold 'exists' as an absence of heat. If I give the reader a block of ice they may call out that it is cold. If I want to be awkward I might say that they are wrong there as it has 273 degrees of heat in it and so must really be quite warm. So I find it helpful to think that a person who is apt to be labelled as evil is, more accurately, wanting in goodness. Perhaps absolute zero in this scale of reckoning belongs to the devil alone though there are some who would say (and Origen was amongst them) that he stands, as it were, at only minus 272.99 and so is capable of conversion. If we had sufficient love and humility that we could genuinely and warmly embrace some 'hardened soul' in the Maze prison or elsewhere would he not begin to thaw, to take on some of our warmth, as a block of ice in our hands?

So which is it? Is evil a positive force, a dragon spitting fire against Michael and his angels, or is it something negative, an absence of good, a parasite feeding on a host which (parasite) could not exist apart from the presence of the host to feed on? Though the host, representing goodness, would continue to exist if the parasite were not there.[1] I am unable to reconcile these two views. It seems to me that Julian of Norwich, whom I shall come to later, believed in both, and I find I have to do the same, accepting the seeming contradiction which I cannot resolve. Perhaps some theologian reader can help me here? My reading tells me that there are two contradictory views on the manner of the propagation of light and that scientists have to hold to them both, now one and now the other, though they seem to be irreconcilable. Are we in a similar bind?

At the end of each school year some of the boys would come to me for Bible Reading Fellowship notes so as to continue their reading in the holidays. On one occasion a regular fourteen-year-old failed to appear and thinking he had overlooked the matter I sent for him to enquire. He said he had decided not to take the notes that year but instead to ask his father to supply the Bible readings for him. Knowing his father and believing him to be more fond of the bottle than the Bible I asked the boy if he thought that was a good idea. He replied: 'Well Sir, I am not expecting it to help me but I thought perhaps it might help father.' (!)

Fr Prior left us as the winter drew on. Many boys and girls had become devoted to him and corresponded with him for a long while. He had vowed never to buy a sheet of paper or an envelope so long as the war lasted so his letters came in all shapes and sizes. The Casey children, whose father was Governor of Bengal, were not above enclosing a few sheets of Government House notepaper. He was a great letter writer and it cannot always have been easy for him to keep his vow.

By the autumn of 1944 it seemed certain that the war would soon be over and the Governing Body decided to close the school at the end of that year. The boys and girls were to meet me again, most memorably, forty-five years later, by which time most were approaching their sixties, when they gave me a party in London on my eightieth birthday. I had to stay on at the school for a while but was free in March 1945 to make plans for returning to England. One had to wait one's turn in the shipping queue and it was not until May that our convoy was in the English Channel. Peace in Europe had just been declared but the submerged German submarines had no means of receiving the news as we realised when depth charges were dropped somewhere near the Isle of Wight. That night we docked at Hull from where I took the train to London to be met by my mother and Joan. As it happened I had not spent a wartime day on English soil, not altogether an advantage perhaps, but so it had worked out. Joan motored us to my brother's farm at Dummer in Hampshire and there I was to live until I took up work once more. Dick and Joan looked well, but the strains of war had taken their toll on my mother who had aged considerably. But at least we were together again.

10

Westminster and Vienna

ENGLAND WAS IN A MOOD of rejoicing when I settled down on my brother's farm, for peace was but a few days old. Food and clothes and petrol were still rationed but all threats to the safety of the country were removed; and Japan was too far off to be of general concern except to those whose families were still caught up in that horrifying area of the war. Then, within three months, came the explosions of Hiroshima and Nagasaki which not only brought devastation on a scale hitherto inconceivable, but shook the minds of men and women everywhere into realising that a new era for our world had dawned. I remember my instant reaction as I first read the news in a street in Winchester: the most momentous event since the resurrection. It was hardly a rational observation for the two are scarcely comparable: the one a beacon of hope to all who can accept it, the other a weapon of destruction threatening the existence of the planet itself.

I was still technically on the staff of Westminster School having been given a year's leave of absence which had been extended for the duration of the war. However, I was wondering whether I should now go into parish work and applied for a curacy which eventually came to nothing. I then looked towards Westminster, and John Christie offered me the post of chaplain, it being agreed that I should have the weekends free (the Abbey cared for the needs of the school on Sundays) to fulfil my obligation to the SPG, which was to visit public schools, preach the Sunday sermon, and be available in any way which might be required. I was also to be chaplain to the Francis Holland (girls') School which I was to visit once a week. It was arranged with Christie that I would not look for other work for at least three years but that if I was invited elsewhere I would be free to consider it. In the event the chaplaincy lasted only one year.

Much of that year at Westminster has been lost in the shades of memory but a few things stand out. Most of all was the daily lunch in College Hall where I sat at the head of a table next to four King's Scholars whose company and conversation were a delight. On one side was Hugh Dickinson who was to become Dean of Salisbury; next to him was Donald (A.M.) Allchin later to be a canon of Canterbury and Warden to the (Fairacres) Sisters of the Love of God. On the other was Michael Adie, to become Bishop of Guildford. Next to him was Arthur Graham-Dixon whose calling was to the Bar. I must not leave him out as he was fully with us in our lively talk whether secular or theological. Could any chaplain wish for more stimulating company? Donald has paid me the tribute of saying that I was the first person who made him see that theology was exciting. But, believe me, I am no theologian and sit very much at the feet of those who looked to me for instruction in those days.

I met Michael Adie in his retirement recently and he told me a story which has evidently done the rounds. First I had better explain that my nickname was Lulu. (I once discovered on a piece of paper a boy had not intended me to see: 'Hair as black as a negro or Zulu/This gentleman's nickname is Lulu.') The sitting-room in my flat was situated immediately below the school sanatorium. I used to sit in front of the fire saying evensong aloud not realising (as Donald Allchin told me later) that my voice was carried up the chimney into the fireplace above so that the patients had to hear evensong as well. One evening a patient called down the chimney (was it the future bishop?) a very firm 'Lulu'. I stopped evensong and said reverently, 'Yes, Lord'. Whereupon, down the chimney the voice continued, 'For heaven's sake stop saying your prayers'. I have to say the story, though founded on fact, has been richly embellished.

It makes a diversion but a school story I greatly enjoyed came from the St Paul's schooldays (and lips) of the late Brother Dennis Marsh of the Franciscans. It is too good not to go on record somewhere. As the clock struck twelve a fourteen-year-old boy emerged from his seat at the back of the maths class carrying a little mat. Setting it down in front of the class he knelt down and began prostrating himself upon it. 'Smith, what on earth are you doing?' 'Hush, Sir, I musn't be disturbed. I'm a Muslim and have to say my prayers.' The pantomime went on each day the maths lesson was held at that time. A week or two later the High Master (Headmaster) asked Mr Jones how he was getting on. He said he found it a bit difficult having a Muslim in the class and explained how Smith, being a Muslim, found it necessary to pray each day. 'A Muslim, we haven't any Muslims in the school [this was over seventy years ago]. I'll

come in just before twelve tomorrow and we shall see what happens.'
The High Master duly came in a few minutes before twelve to have a
chat with Mr Jones. The clock struck and Smith remained firmly in his
seat. Said Mr Jones, 'Smith, are you not saying your prayers today?' 'No,
Sir, I was converted to Christianity last night, Sir.' I feel sure the seeds of
a sermon lie in that story. I recall how in India I found myself hoping
my devout Indian Muslim servant would not become a Christian lest he
thought that instead of praying five times a day all that was needed now
was to pray on Sundays.

It would be tedious to go through all the schools I visited at weekends
but Winchester stands out in my memory. I had been told, with what
truth I do not know, that the boys played an A to Z game during the
sermon. You waited till the preacher had said a word beginning with A,
and that passed you on to B and so on through the alphabet. The first
one to hit Z dropped a hymn-book to show he was the winner. Obviously
X was a bit of a problem but EX was acceptable instead. The real hurdle
of course came when you reached Z which must have prolonged the
life of many hymn-books. I think this information rather unnerved me
and I got into the pulpit feeling the sermon would be a flop. Then I
caught the eye of a senior boy who looked at me with utter scorn and
contempt. The message was unmistakable: who the hell does this chap
think he is coming to talk to us; and on missions too? Immediately the
adrenalin flowed and I don't think I had ever spoken more powerfully.
Spencer Leeson, the headmaster, said afterwards how he loved a hard-
hitting sermon. I wonder what the boy made of it. Incidentally, I never
heard the hymn-book drop. I fancy I was a bit short on Zerubbabels and
Zephaniahs that night.

Roedean also stands out: partly for the bed sitting-room opening out
of the sanctuary, partly for my first girl server ever, who fainted during
the Eucharist, but most of all for the redoubtable Miss Tanner (Dame
Emmeline Tanner) who welcomed me and put a rather nervous visiting
preacher at his ease. She was a tremendous character, warm and animated
but formidable no less, and I can't imagine any of the St Trinian's stuff
so common in schools today taking place while she was at the helm.

What were the results of such sermons? I shall never know. I have no
notes or memory of what was said except that much was repeated from
one pulpit to another. They all had to be geared to the SPG and have
some missionary flavour about them. I seem to remember a true story
about an American marine being washed up on some distant island to

be fed and feted by its newly converted Christian people. When he ventured that missionaries should leave non-Christian peoples alone he was met with the observation that 'if it wasn't for missionaries *your* head would be in *that* pot'. That must surely have hit my Winchester friend with the adrenalin running so high that night. It is not, however, my favourite cannibal story which is that of the missionary dining with the cannibal chief. Says the missionary: 'Your wife makes excellent stew.' 'Yes', came the reply, 'but we do miss her.' I also relish the story of the French missionary who wrote home encouragingly that whilst after five years he had not been able to wean his flock from cannibalism he had at last persuaded them to use a knife and fork.

Sometimes on these tours I would call on my Aunt Madeline who lived in the little Dorset village of Hinton Martel. She was my mother's eldest sister and a very dear person in our lives. She was a richly contemplative soul, very high church, and although she gave virtually all her money to a Roman Catholic mission in India, she never became a Catholic herself. Hinton Martel suited her, for here at the Anglican parish church was a daily mass in Latin. She and the priest, with his beautiful dog lazing on the altar steps, were the only three who normally attended. I asked her once if the church could supply a *Book of Common Prayer* so that I might say matins. She took a knife and dug up a floorboard under which were several dusty prayer books. So much for the C of E!

Aunt Madeline was a unique character and stories around her abound. She used to take the bus periodically to Bournemouth where she would make her confession. On one occasion she mistakenly removed a suitcase belonging to a sailor travelling on to Portsmouth to join his ship. He, poor man, discovered the look-alike contained only old women's clothing. A telephone conversation followed. I never heard the end of the story but fear my aunt's vocabulary may have been considerably enlarged. Among many other memories is that of a book she gave me with one sentence so heavily scored out that not a word was legible. The writer was the holy Father Andrew, the founder of the Society of the Divine Compassion. What naughty thing could he have written which needed to be shielded from my middle-aged priestly eyes? On my next visit to the SPCK I naturally looked up the offending passage. I read: 'I have never wanted to think that the wet finger of a curate was necessary for a child's salvation'. Aunt Madeline died at the age of 93 and must have gone straight to heaven with angels and archangels clapping all the way.

In the spring of 1946 Father Wigram of Cowley, who had been my spiritual director before the war, approached me with a view to my going to Nassau in the Bahamas to open a Diocesan school. A meeting followed with Bishop Daugleish who had recently retired from Nassau, and Eric Jay, a priest on the staff of King's College, London, all of whom had been asked by Bishop Spence Burton of Nassau to propose a name. They judged me suitable and I expressed my willingness to go. Hence it came about that I was to give in my notice to Westminster to leave at the end of the school year so as to be free to travel to Nassau in October. I was sorry to leave but I don't think my work really lay as a school chaplain. I have always considered myself to be a good teacher of mathematics (examwise at least) and a poor teacher of Scripture (again, examwise at least). Before the war the masters had a little joke that I gave fifty per cent for faith and the other fifty for knowledge. I plead not guilty, but at the same time I am aware that I was more concerned in teaching the Scriptures for the purpose of living than for that of passing examinations. And I have to confess there were days when we didn't get beyond two or three verses in a whole period. But quite apart from this I did not have the knowledge to do justice to boys or girls at sixth form level. So it was just as well that I moved on. But before the Nassau episode began there was an exciting venture to come.

Vienna was amongst the cities in Europe still occupied by British, French, American and Russian troops. The serving parents in that city wanted their children to join them for the summer holidays. Christie was asked to provide a master as escort and settled on me. Accordingly the morning came in early August when on Victoria station two hundred children from about six to sixteen were handed over to me and five helpers, all of us being strangers to one another. Somehow we left Victoria on time and got everyone aboard the channel ferry. It was the roughest crossing I can remember and I was dashing here and there with paper bags for one child after another until I collapsed myself spewing uncontrollably. I imagine the other grown-ups were helping likewise but I was too far gone to notice. Recovery was quick and by the time we left Calais on a super through train to Vienna with hospital coach attached, we were all in fine form. But what a journey it was! On the last leg we decided we had lost one child along the route and were mightily relieved to find on arrival that it was our calculations which were at fault. All were safely delivered into the hands of devoted and excited parents.

I was whisked off to a posh hotel taken over by the Army and sumptuously fed. Next day the Air Force was to fly me home to London.

Somewhere about mid-flight it was found that the wheel locking mechanism had jammed, and I was told we must return to Vienna as that was judged the safer airport for a belly landing. Why so, I can't imagine. A flight sergeant told me breezily that it wasn't the fall that hurt, but the sudden pulling up at the end. Not that this was to the point as there was no chance of our dropping out of the sky. We reached Vienna to see a fleet of fire engines and ambulances to greet our arrival. The first need was to circle the airport to consume as much petrol as possible. And during that hour there was sudden rejoicing as the wheels came down after all.

Strangely there was no other plane available and I was told it would be a while before our own plane could be repaired. So I was taken back to my hotel and in the event spent ten days there. It so happened that I had been in touch with the 'Save Europe Now' association in England and for some while I had wanted to visit a European city to see conditions for myself. Here then was the opportunity handed to me as if by divine grace. I decided to visit the desperately poor and underfed people and in this I at once found help from the Red Cross, Quakers, Roman Catholic sisters and several doctors as well. It seemed obscene that I should be eating so plentifully and some of these people hidden away from the streets should be quite literally starving. CARE parcels from America containing necessities in food and toiletry were all the rage at the time and, guided by kind helpers who believed that I, as a foreigner, could do something beyond their power, I went from house to house to draw up an account of the conditions. The need was so great that I later sent my diary to the *Church Times*, listing many 'before and after' weights, which published much of it. CARE parcels quickly arrived, perhaps they were already stored away in Vienna. It was only a drop in the ocean, but it surely did bring some comfort and hope, and the courage and endurance of some of the old people I saw did a lot for me. After ten days I was taken to join my plane again and we reached London with no more mishaps. Within a few weeks I was asked to preach in Westminster Abbey and tried to bring home the plight of so many in Europe at that time for although Vienna was the most needy city in Austria there were, I had been told, many German cities in a worse way.

11

The Bahamas

Travelling to the Bahamas fifty years ago was not the simple matter it is today. I had to go by banana boat to Jamaica and then wait a week for a plane to Miami, and after an overnight stop, fly to Nassau. The banana boats took about ten passengers and chugged across the ocean at a speed of not more than fifteen knots. Eventually we arrived at Kingston and, as I had a week to wait, I travelled across the island to stay with the archdeacon of Montego Bay, who was with me on the Atlantic crossing and had invited me to visit him if I became stranded. It was a memorable train journey through the banana plantations. About midway I tried to buy half a dozen bananas but was told I couldn't have less than fifty for which I was charged a shilling. The archdeacon was well stocked that week.

At Kingston I had to leave most of my luggage behind to be taken by sea as I had no money for its air transport. Nassau was not served well by shipping and my baggage had to go all the way north to Canada and then south to the Bahamas. Not surprisingly we were separated for about three months.

On arrival in Nassau I was looked after by Canon Marshall, the dean of the cathedral. He took me to see the school I had been asked to start. Everything was ready and the buildings looked bright and gay, clothed in Nassau pink; all so different from my arrival at the previous school in India. My accommodation was small but comfortable and a servant was provided to look after me, a magnificent black Bahamian woman, Agnes by name, standing at least six foot three and with body build to match. She had a wonderful personality as well.

St John's College was not to open until January so that one could proceed at a leisurely pace. The Bishop came to see me and wanted me to join him at various functions so that I could meet and get to know people. Bishop Spence Burton – Spence as we used to call him, though to his face he liked to be called My Lord – was an unusual man, an American Cowley father who had done much to build up the community, not least on its material side. He was a millionaire in a day when money went forty times as far as it goes now. The fathers had released him to become Bishop of Nassau, and he was able to draw extensively on his personal funds to entertain the rich American visitors who flocked to the island. Whilst he entertained lavishly, he was abstemious himself, living simply in the midst of luxury, a teetotaller (at least I never saw him take a drink), and sleeping on a board bed. He had seven dogs, small wire-haired terriers, whom he would take on his lap one by one and talk to as if they were his children. Singly they were friendly enough, but if they escaped from their 'kennels' they would act as a pack and make quick work of any large dog which trespassed on their premises.

Many are the stories which surrounded Spence Burton. He insisted on clergy wearing cassocks 'at all times', and when asked at synod if they might be removed when bathing he was not amused. He also insisted on long trousers being worn under the cassock, the temptation being to wear shorts in that hot humid climate. One day on meeting a priest who had no protruding trouser legs, he rebuked him saying that he had been told not to wear shorts under his cassock. 'But, my Lord' came the reply, 'I'm not wearing any.' Like many Americans, Spence had a great gift for picturesque speech. And he was firm with his own rich countrymen. 'God doesn't count collections,' he told a gathering of the rich in the cathedral, 'he counts what is left in your pocket after the collection has been taken.' But Americans generally have the gift of colourful speech. 'I guess I'll park my hinge,' said one of them to me as he prepared to take his seat on a broiling day.

With all his unusual ways – and he used to find us English priests distinctly odd, and who can blame him? – Spence had a truly pastoral heart. He and I didn't always agree for I found it very hard to fit into Nassau's ultra high church customs. But he was patient with me and the failing was far more on my part than I realised at the time. I feel sure we shall meet merrily in heaven, that is to say if I ever reach the exalted mansion in which he probably now rests. To give one example to show what a raw recruit I was. I visited a certain church and observed from the noticeboard that so and so was boat boy on the following Sunday. This, for the uninitiated, means that he was responsible for the incense boat at the Sunday mass. 'Oh, do you do rowing?' was my innocent remark. But even after these many years I have never mastered the mysteries of liturgy and ceremonial, get hopelessly lost in processions, and in one cathedral was politely bowed out of the bishop's throne.

The school started on time and smoothly enough. We were all ages from about eleven to seventeen. There was a Government High School which catered for secondary school pupils, but Spence wanted something which offered a more marked church background and which could take on those church boys and girls who were unable to qualify for the other school. There was also an all-white school for, apart from the churches, there was a colour bar in the Bahamas at that time. We were an all-black school, not by design, but because no white parents would be likely to send their children to us. Our staff, however, were mostly white. Among them was Mrs Nelson from America who taught Latin and English and who would on occasions motor me in the summer holidays up the coast of North America to her home near Cape Cod. Then there were Father and Mrs Davies (every priest in the Bahamas was Father), he being also chaplain to the prison. And Father Roe, a dearly loved priest who lived with his mother in what should have been my house, and who died of cancer within two years. We began the day all together with a service in St Agnes Church about a quarter of a mile away. Morning and afternoon school followed, the work being geared to the Senior Cambridge School Certificate.

The modest fees we were able to charge may perhaps have paid running costs but left nothing over for the further building which was needed. For this we had either to collect money or 'earn' it through fetes on the school premises, ably helped or even run, by a dedicated band of parents. I would try my hand at collecting from the rich American colony but was never a good beggar. Once however when £50 was offered (£2,000 for today) I asked whether the donor could really afford that. 'You think I can't afford £50, I'll make it 75.' A further expostulation followed, this I confess somewhat artfully, and £100 was offered. But there was no going beyond that.

A day to remember was when I met George. I was motoring out to the hospital about three miles away when I came across a small boy in distress having lost a wheel of his scooter. Guessing that he too was on the way to the hospital I offered him a lift and found he was taking a few provisions to his mother who was expecting her seventeenth child. Not, I may add, her last. I think the final tally was over twenty. George was about eleven, a delightful child, bright and concerned for his mother, and he used to do the little bit he could to help the family by shining

shoes on Nassau's well-heeled Bay Street. I felt strongly he ought to come
to the school but the fees, small though they were, were of course beyond
him. I paid his modest fees and he did odd jobs for me and worked in
the house which after Ronald Roe's death I had taken over. By the time
I left Nassau in 1950 George was doing splendidly. I later learnt that on
leaving school he went to America with practically no money, drove a
taxi almost without rest from Friday night to Monday morning and used
his earnings to pay his way through medical school. He emerged a trained
gynaecologist, but rather than remaining in America where the money
was good he returned to serve his homeland. I met him again twenty-
one years later, the old pupils having invited me over for a 'banquet' to
celebrate the twenty-fifth year of the founding of the school. He was well
established as a leading doctor: indeed, once when George was on holiday
an expectant mother said she absolutely refused to have her baby until
he returned! It was a real joy to meet George again, and to talk with him
as he drove me around in his American car, me probably reminding
him of the broken-down scooter days.

Church life in the Bahamas was an eye-opener to me. I don't know
how it is now but in those days the clergy were an accepted and necessary
part of the community. Most people would not much miss us if we
disappeared from the scene in England, except when it comes to mar-
riages and funerals, but in Nassau our absence would have left a real
gap. The Church was the very heart of its life: even the St Agnes early
morning five o'clock mass on Wednesdays was attended by thirty or forty
people. Christmas and Easter were particularly busy times, for everyone
who received communion was expected to make their confession. I would
sit for hours in St Agnes Church with the Bahamian vicar, Father Cooper,
confessing another stream of penitents opposite me. On one occasion he
called across the church that I must hurry along and that I had only
heard seventeen confessions in the last hour. There was a paper at the
back of the church containing every imaginable sin and confessees (I am
not sure that they were always penitents) would examine themselves from
it. I recall a man who said, 'Father, I done 7, 13 and 21, for these and
all my other sins . . .' (For any nervous about the seal the numbers are
invented!) We were taught at ordination that we could never be too
careful in speaking of confession and the cautionary tale of the day was
of a priest who told a friend when lunching with him at a restaurant that
the first confession he had heard was that of a murderer. Later, another
diner arrived, and catching sight of the priest came to his table and said,

'Hallo, Father, do you remember me? Mine was the first confession you ever heard.'

But for much the most part they were true and good confessions. It is not easy to open to another the deepest recesses of the heart, and for every sin committed there are countless victories of which one never hears, kindnesses and sacrifices which are no part of the material for confession. One is generally left with an admiration for the courage and goodness of the one who has laid bear their soul, rather than with any sense of failure of which they may be only too well aware. I am not a good spiritual director, and I never expect to be, but if one can listen with an understanding and compassionate heart and say a few words of hope and encouragement and assure waverers of the reality of their absolution, that is probably in most cases what is required.

As I was writing that last sentence someone looked in unexpectedly and said the rosary with me. As we said it together it came into my mind (it has never done so before) that in spite of Nassau's extreme high church ways and in spite of its emphasis on the importance of Mary, I never once heard anything said about the rosary or saw anyone using one. Doubtless some said it privately in their homes, but I cannot recall seeing a rosary in Nassau. I knew nothing of this prayer at the time and it was only much later that I experienced the enrichment it may bring to the prayer life. We did say the Angelus at midday at the school and that meant everyone was acquainted with the Hail Mary. But whereas the Angelus is essentially an interruption, a brief moment snatched from one's work as a reminder of the things of God, the rosary, being much longer, is more of the nature of an Office, designed to bring the scattered mind back to recollection and to establish the heart once more in silence before God.

I am not given to premonitions, but in 1950 I had a settled idea that I would receive a letter on my forty-first birthday inviting me to work elsewhere. The day in July came but there was no letter so I assumed I must be wrong. But a week or two later I received a letter written on my birthday and I took serious note of it. My correspondent was Michael Storrs Fox in India who was writing on behalf of the Bishop of Lucknow to ask if I would be willing to return to Naini Tal to take over Sherwood College, the Diocesan boys' school which was suffering a decline in numbers after independence and in danger of closing. I saw it as a call and a challenge and replied positively, eventually giving notice to leave St John's at the end of the school year in June 1951. Thus I was, in

August, on the high seas again, not this time in a banana boat, but on the *Queen Elizabeth* which I managed to catch almost literally by the skin of my teeth. I forget now what the chapter of accidents was all about, but I remember clearly being nearly left on the quayside at New York watching the great ship sail away with my berth unoccupied.

1 2

Sherwood College

Y MOTHER AND MY SISTER, Joan, were now living in Charmouth in Dorset and I spent two months with them before going to India to take up my new work at Sherwood College, Naini Tal. I have a beautiful photo of my mother at the age of seventy spinning wool in her little garden. My sheep farmer brother Dick, who was then married, supplied the wool, my mother spun it and Joan, who was a talented weaver, completed the work, producing rugs or material for clothing. So they were quite a home industry.

India was more accessible than when I had first gone out more than ten years before. Then it was either a three-week voyage by ship, or a three-day flight by Imperial Airways with two night stop-overs on the way. Now the journey could be completed in little more than half a day. I flew out in October allowing for two months of term before the school broke up for its three-month winter holidays.

Sherwood College was situated on the opposite side of the lake to the Hallett War School, where I was headmaster during the war years. We were 6,800 feet above sea level and 500 feet above the Naini Tal lake. The school was one of the many schools in India which catered for the needs of the Anglo-Indian community. These were, for the most part, hardy schools placing considerable emphasis on sports and games, and Sherwood had been no exception: indeed in gymnastics and boxing it may have exceeded them all. But it had fallen on bad days and it was now in danger of having to close down. An earlier principal, who had done much to build up the school had, most unwisely, refused to fly the Indian flag when independence came to the country in 1947. This was against Government orders and was naturally seen as a grave discourtesy to the Indian State. As a result the Government grant, which was considerable, had been stopped and had not been restored when I arrived several years later. Furthermore, on the coming of independence, many of the better-off Anglo-Indian families had decided to emigrate to England or elsewhere and the numbers had fallen well below half their previous strength. The school found it hard to get by with this double loss of income. We were but 170 boys against an earlier enrolment of over 400.

It was obvious that a number of changes needed to be made. To begin with we were no longer to see ourselves as being predominantly Anglo-Indian. As we gradually built up to full strength the proportion of Indian pupils would be growing the whole time and eventually they would probably be ninety per cent of the school. Naturally, education had to be geared to their needs. Probably the changes I made were more evident to the staff who were steeped in the old tradition, than to myself, for one of them remarked to the Bishop in fairly early days that the only thing which remained of the old school was the name on the gate. I truly believe that that too would have gone if the place had been left unchanged.

The school, which was for boarders only, was situated at two levels. At the higher level was Dixon Wing for upper and middle school boys: a hundred feet below was Horsman Wing under a junior school head-mistress. Administratively it was all one, but there was little interplay between the two wings. In Dixon Wing the day began with prep at seven o'clock, followed by ten minutes' PT and breakfast at eight. At nine there was chapel, which all attended. The service was based firmly on Christian lines and parents were happy that that should be so. Although the boys were a mixture of Christians, Hindus, Sikhs and Muslims I only recall one parental request for their son to be excused chapel and that, after explanation, was withdrawn. Boys were free to take what part they wished and we had a daily minute's silence in which each would follow his own devotions. I regarded full assembly in chapel as of great importance, for it brought the whole of the middle and upper school together once a day, and any general talks or notices would be attended to in chapel. The reading of lessons was open to boys of any faith. There was never any feeling of hostility on account of race or religion and I recall that in four consecutive years the post of college captain was filled by a boy from each faith.

An interesting illustration of the above occurred following the removal of a Hindu boy to hospital for a brain operation. I had forgotten all about it until my sister Joan showed me a letter I had written at the time. The relevant portion reads:

We have just had one of our boys in hospital for a brain operation –

successful I think – due to a head injury in infancy. Two Hindus asked if we could have a special service (Holy Communion) at 6 a.m. on the day of the op. I thought it was a bit early (but prep. was at 7) so didn't announce it but suggested they should tell a few friends. To my surprise there were 150 there, mostly Hindus of course, though 30 Christians.

That would have been about our full quota of Christians at the time. Joan showed me also a number of other letters she had kept. On the principle that despatches from the front are likely to be of more interest than histories of the war I will quote from a few. The first deals with a rat which on one occasion tweaked me when in bed.

> I forget if I told you that after leaving the lower plate in a BOAC plane the dentist here made me another which has been most comfortable. But what do you think happened the other night? A rat came . . . in the morning the teeth had gone, the lower set plucked out of its cup of water. I was upset as they were such comfortable ones and I felt I should never get another like them . . . So I kept a sharp look out for any rat wearing false teeth. Then as a last desperate hope I pulled the cupboard from the wall and there just by his hole were the teeth intact. They must have stretched his mouth too much when he got to his hole.

But it was buttons which the rats went for. One of the boys woke up in the morning to find all his trouser buttons gone. I note from another letter that I lost eight buttons and caught four rats. They may not, however, have been different ones as neither my servant nor I had the heart to drown them but released them from their cage traps in the countryside. It sounds as if we were swamped with rats but it was only a few really, and that in the monsoon when their holes may well have been flooded. There were, however, larger problems. At nearly 7,000 feet we were somewhat exposed to the elements.

> We have had a hectic day. A storm hit us last night and took away about 2,500 square feet of roofing. Then a snowstorm followed. Today we are without 6 classrooms, a library, a large dormitory, a staff room, 2 staff quarters and several servants' quarters. Of course everything is soaked. However once we get the roofs on we shall be all right but it takes time up here and thick snow impedes everything at present. The boys were thrilled.

450 out of 480 have never seen snow before and snowballing has been the event of the day. The problem is to keep warm – for the boys I mean as they have no heating. They have been togged up in dressing gowns through the day. All this has coincided with a flu epidemic – not too serious but we are nursing 40. Then at the same time the new bathroom decided to leak and showered water into the tuck shop and another room. Add to this a hot tap controlling 12 showers broke, scalding a boy's back so he had to be taken off to hospital. I read Job 1 in chapel this morning! and said we had very few troubles really.

The next letter speaks of an awkward moment after breakfast.

Two days ago an imaginative and acrobatic young man locked himself into the first of 24 lavatories in a row, climbed over the five or six foot partition to the next, locked the door and so on for the whole 24. No one, of course, could get in (except into the last lavatory) so there was some disorganisation for a while. I haven't enquired who it was. It's a case of once being a joke, twice a nuisance, and thrice insufferable . . .

Then there was the occasion when I was hit on the forehead by a discus. I wasn't watching the event and was standing at an angle to the thrower about sixty feet away. I went down like a log but there was no lasting damage. My first letter has not survived but the second refers to it.

I agree they are horribly dangerous things, even in the best sporting society. Someone was killed like that when I was in England. I think the thrower was pretty relieved to see me get up on my own . . . thank you for your prayers. We can never tell how much we owe to one another's prayers. Though next time let us pray it will miss altogether!

The first of the next two letters refers to the bishop on one of his visits and the second to a problem parent.

Yesterday the poor man lost his shoes and searched everywhere as he wanted to go out. Finally they were found – on my feet! such comfortable ones too!

One of our mothers told me I was very sweet today and asked if she might have a kiss. She then tried to fling herself round me and I only just managed to escape and bundle her out of the room. We

might so easily have been caught by a boy in each other's arms.
I should have looked such a fool!

And finally.

> We have an unusual custom on the last day. Some years ago, as
> I liked to have Holy Communion most days, I said it would be at
> 5.30 a.m. on the last morning. I didn't expect to see more than
> two or three there, if that. But 10 came . . . and now at least 100
> including a whole lot of Hindus who worship from the back. We
> have a Christmas cake and tea afterwards at 6 a.m. I don't think that
> brings them, though perhaps it helps, though they only get about
> two mouthfuls each. It's cold at that hour in December, rather
> like an ordinary English Christmas morning before the sun gets
> up.

Morning and afternoon school followed daily assembly in chapel,
except that Wednesdays and Saturdays were half-holidays. Games or other
pursuits were part of the curriculum of each day. After supper there was
prep, the time varying according to age. Boys were encouraged to say
their own prayers in the dormitory which they did with complete unselfconsciousness taking up whatever position their faith required. It all
seemed much less complicated than in multi-racial Britain today. I put
that down to the fact that we were all boarders and that there were no
grown-ups to put ideas into children's heads. Hindus and Muslims often
find it hard to live together in India, and sometimes impossible. But we
never had even the beginnings of a problem at the school.

Well, we did have just one. But it was Christian. A Roman Catholic
master said his Church would not allow him to attend daily chapel. I
considered it most important that every master should attend, if only that
he might hear any general talk or notice given afterwards. First it was
arranged that he should come to the chapel after the service but then
he had authority from his Church to be present at the service in body
provided he was absent in spirit. Earlier in England I had known of a
Roman Catholic who would leave Anglican groups for the final prayer as
his Church said he must be absent in body, though he could be present
in spirit. Oh Rome, Rome, how I love you, but how exasperating you can
be! Yes, I know you have repented in sackcloth and ashes long since and
moved further in your reformation of thirty years than we did in ours
for nearly three centuries.

{ 83 }

I used to do a fair amount of teaching. It has always seemed right to me that a head should not isolate himself from the classrooms. Fortunately I had a bursar and well-staffed office which relieved me of a tremendous amount of administrative work. Mathematics was my love and I often reflect on how miles ahead were those Indian boys of most English boys of today. Not that they were all brainy. I used to think of them in three classes: those who got their theorems right and knew they got them right (the best); those who got their theorems wrong and knew they got them wrong (the teachable); those who got their theorems wrong and thought they got them right (the near impossible).

In quite early days I felt the need of a chaplain to the school. Moreover I knew whom I wanted, Canon Gilbert Elliot who had recently retired from Calcutta Cathedral. He had been chaplain at Victoria College, Kurseong, and had a real gift for the work. But, alas, there was no money as Government would not allow us to spend school money on this post, this in spite of the fact that the Government grant (later restored) was still being withheld. So there was nothing for it but to raise a fund. We needed anything up to 200,000 rupees, nearly £16,000. I started a fund, but my expectations were low. Then the Lord stepped in.

I was in Kodak's in Bombay in the winter holidays when a fellow customer discovered he had left his money behind and could not buy the film he desperately needed. I asked if I could help and offered him ten rupees which was more than enough. He said he would give me his name but I said it would be better if he had mine if he wished to return the money. Next day it came back through the post with a letter of thanks containing no sender's address and an illegible signature. Some while later I was in Calcutta Cathedral celebrating the Eucharist, and discovered my server to be the man I had met in Kodak's. So in the vestry we introduced ourselves and he turned out to be Lord Craigmyle, head of the large shipping firm McKinnon and Mackenzie. I asked him whether, on the strength of my loan of ten rupees, I might ask him for a donation to the chaplain's fund, and he said that the day before he had had an unexpected cheque for £15,500 and that he would gladly give me that. So there was the money in a single donation. Scarcely can a ten rupee note have been better spent!

Gilbert Elliot came shortly after and was a real father-in-God to boys and staff. He was slow in everything he did but everything was done beautifully, chapel notices most beautifully written out, and so on. He prepared the confirmation candidates, taught Scripture, preached and took services, but unfortunately his health shortly broke down and he had to return to England. Great was our sorrow. Later he grew stronger and became warden of the St Barnabas Homes for retired clergy where I once stayed with him.

Boxing was an early casualty of my time. Sherwood had been a highly competent boxing school and this activity was compulsory at all levels. Apart from the distress this caused to some weaker performers, there was the medical aspect to be considered. Less was known then about the dangers of blows to the head than is known today but looking back it seems that the decision was taken on a right instinct. There was on the whole support from the staff and not a few boys were considerably relieved. Roller-skating later became the rage in the gym.

Sport was a problem in that mountainous country, especially as numbers grew. It was impossible to build more playing space than we already had. The idea of a swimming pool was then hit upon and with the help of the boys who dug and removed the earth and the professionals who dynamited and built the walls, we had within a year two pools, one shallow for beginners, the other serviceable for the proficient. I had long believed that every child should learn to swim, and only a small proportion of Indian children could do so. Class periods, formerly devoted to gymnastics or boxing, were now largely given over to swimming and nearly everyone was enthusiastic about the new sport. I suppose that a swimming pool offers exercise to more people for the space it occupies than any other facility and in our confined conditions that alone was great gain.

The pool was opened by Malcolm Macdonald, the British High Commissioner, who was a delightful guest. He disappointed me slightly in failing to mark the opening ceremony with a dive from the high board, which I had heard he had done on a previous occasion, having donned swimming trunks under his clothing which he had rapidly shed. One advantage in having a pool of our own was that it removed the temptation to swimming in the Government House pool about half a mile away. Apart from the fact that it wasn't our pool, unsupervised swimming plainly has its dangers and, though the attraction was healthy, its indulgence could obviously not be allowed.

Bounds were liberal and with certain restrictions middle and upper school boys were allowed to roam anywhere within about fifteen minutes' walk of the school. But just occasionally we would get a leopard seeking its prey near the school and then bounds had to be drastically restricted.

They are usually harmless to humans but I felt we could not afford to take the risk. Two shock-filled bound breakers once came running to me saying they had bumped right into the leopard which was bothering us at that time. On one occasion the PT master shot a leopard just outside the school grounds. The creature was already ailing and it was kinder and safer to despatch him. At least a hundred were present at the kill, so it made quite a stir.

George Thompson, our Senior Master, later immortalised the incident in satiric verse. George's connection with the school began as a boy and after a brief break he returned to teach music and train the choir. In all he must have served the school for more than fifty years. His integrity inspired the trust of boys and staff. To me he was a loyal friend and colleague and his wisdom often served me well. He was a person of great enthusiasms and having, in my later years, decided to learn to type, he was nearing the hundred words a minute mark when I left the school. This was something of an achievement on an old-fashioned portable, sixty being a highly acceptable secretarial performance and that on an office machine.

My bedroom window at Sherwood looked across the lake on to the Hallett War School, where I had been headmaster during the war years. About six o'clock one morning I looked out to see the school on fire. I knew of the problems getting outside help; there were no roads within almost half an hour of the school. All would depend on extinguishers and on what water could be hosed at that level. I hurried to our senior dormitory and the boys were quickly out picking up every extinguisher they could find and begging others from our sister school, All Saints, and Government House nearby. There was a 500 ft trek down, then another of 700 ft up on the other side of the lake. Some managed to get horses, tethered for the night at the lakeside. Hurricane House, as we had called it on account of its exposure to high winds and in memory of the wartime fighter of the day, was severely damaged, but we did learn later that our efforts had considerably helped, which was encouraging for all concerned. More still, perhaps, it helped our friendship with Birla Vidya Mandir, the Indian school which had taken over the Hallett buildings after we vacated them in 1944.

An interesting visitor to the school was Mr Patel who had a degree in graphology from America. He offered vocational guidance, which he gave from the study of the applicant's handwriting, and wanted to know if he could be of service to older boys. I was cautious when I met him and felt

I should subject him to a trial which I did from three of a hundred or so essays on my windowsill. I then let him see the senior boys who wished to be helped but stipulated that I must be present. I must say he seemed to me to be remarkably accurate though not entirely so. It was difficult to contradict him. Thus, when a boy said that Mr Patel was wrong in saying he had musical talent, he received the reply that it was waiting to be developed. There were one or two outstanding hits. My secretary came in and asked if he would examine her writing. He thought she was a junior school teacher, and told her he thought she would soon want to give up teaching and take up secretarial work.

I happened to have a photograph of the writing of St Francis de Sales and I asked Mr Patel what he could say from it. I made notes at the time and copy below word for word what I wrote. The letter was, of course, in French, a language Mr Patel would not have known, nor would he have been likely to have heard of Francis. It falls far short of describing Francis, but most, it seems to me, fits in well with much of what we know of him.

> Sense of responsibility very strong and he likes to carry burdens (Mr Patel explained that he was speaking figuratively). Has marked literary ability and his characters would be creative. Highly enthusiastic. Idealistic. Intelligent. Has an internal conflict which makes him at times timid and shy and at other times bold and confident. Fond of good food, especially gravies. Has a strong sexual appetite but kept (it) in suppression. Loves the good things of life but denies himself of them very largely. Quick thinker. Drive. Fond of music. Good judgement at end but not at beginning.

Mr Patel was quite open about his art, though he would have called it a science which up to a point I think it is. He gave a blackboard lecture to the senior boys telling them what they might look for and he showed me a number of signs as well. I think that most people of experience and perception can read a good deal into handwriting without having any lessons. For example, the pressure is a good guide to the depth of the emotions and the slope as to whether heart rules head or the reverse, a pronounced forward slope being a sure guide to the former. Microscopic handwriting one naturally associates with the capacity for deep concentration. The one who never dots their i's is usually absent-minded or hurrying their way through life. The few who make a small circle in place of a dot are the unhurried and precise. Anger and aggressiveness, enthusiasm and generosity, are easily revealed in writing. I think most experienced people can form judgements on these things without quite knowing how. But to go into details as an expert would do is another matter. If you are that sort of person, beware. Many of your friends will take to typing.

Numbers at the school were growing, eventually to reach five hundred and it was attracting many boys from East Africa. These were mostly Patels, and at one stage we had over seventy in the school and it was hard to sort them out. They were often weak in English but they were hard workers, as indeed they are known to be in England today. We owed a lot to our Patel clan. Indian boys could, incidentally, be picturesque in English as the eight-year-old who announced apologetically that he had left the room on the floor. But it was a parent who in a state of exhaustion after the climb to the school exclaimed that he was 'all breathless and pantless'. Yet when did I strive at Hindi as those many men and women struggled at English and with what courage and splendid results? And, after all, English is terribly confusing. I once said 'How do you do?' to a student in Cawnpore to be met with the reasonable reply: 'How do I do what?'

A popular innovation was rock climbing, to be followed later by mountaineering. This was to make splendid use of the terrain in which we were situated. There were many rocks of a hundred feet or so near the school which offered excellent practice, all of course under the supervision of a skilled instructor. We did, however, have one accident (to a master) which might well have been fatal, but a rescue party did gallant work and mercifully the injured man made a complete recovery. In mountaineering we really had the advantage over English schools for within thirty miles or so climbs were possible for up to 20,000 feet in the perpetual snows, though 18,000 or rather less would be the usual limit. The party would be away for three weeks in the summer term, out of touch with the world except for a radio (receiver only) on which they could listen to special weather reports from All India Radio, AIR as it was aptly abbreviated. We were fortunate in that our two PT instructors, both ex-Indian Navy, were enthusiastic mountaineers, and in addition we had expert help from outside. The consent of parents had to be obtained, and I still wonder at their courage in letting their boys go, for of course there were no rescue parties, phone or radio communications, helicopters or hospitals to come to their help in case of need. It seems much more dangerous from an English perspective than it did then but we were well served and thankfully never had an accident.

What did the boys do when they left school? Most went on to a university becoming perhaps doctors, businessmen, lawyers, teachers and so on. One, Salman Haider, became India's foreign minister; another, Amitabh Bachchan, became the country's most popular film star. Sanjeev Dhawan became president of the Cambridge Union. Many went to the National Defence Academy near Poona in preparation for a Service career. Others emigrated to England or America or elsewhere. And there must, too, have been the great army of self-employed.

In 1966 I had been over fifteen years at Sherwood. I had been unwell at the end and it seemed time that I should leave. When I was fifty-seven, two letters came by consecutive posts, one from the Bishop of Lucknow asking if he might start negotiations with the Government for me to remain beyond the retiring age of sixty, and the other from Fr Wain of the Cowley Fathers asking if I would be ready to leave Sherwood to go to Poona to be chaplain to the CSMV, a branch house of the Wantage Sisters in England. Apart from the other considerations I felt I had had my fill of schoolmastering and had no doubt which I should accept. I wrote accordingly to explain to the Bishop and gave notice that I would be leaving the school at the end of the year. My successor was already to hand, Derek Beaman, an Oxford graduate in English, who had been such a strength on the staff over the past twelve or so years. There are not a few Sherwoodians who owe it to Derek's patient teaching that, after arriving with little knowledge of English, they now speak it more fluently and grammatically than many brought up in its use. Derek preferred teaching to administration and moved on after four years to teach at Bishop's School, Poona, but died recently in his sixties. He fell in love with India and with Indian friends at every level. I think he would never have wanted to return to England. His deep and simple Christian faith helped, as it should, to unite rather than separate him from other traditions. I personally owed a lot to his friendship and help.

The school, which now includes girls on its roll, flourishes as never before under Mr D. R. A. Mountford who has guided its fortunes for twenty-four years.

On leaving Sherwood I spent six weeks with the Cowley Fathers in Poona (who were all about to leave the country for good) to be introduced to the work and to that of St Mary's Church where I was to be priest-in-charge. And so to England, though not without pausing for a week in Rome and Assisi. But that belongs to another chapter.

13

Travels

❧

O N LEAVING SHERWOOD COLLEGE at the end of 1966 I went to
stay for six weeks with the Cowley Fathers in the Panch Howd
district of Poona. Three or more fathers lived in the large monastic house
which served the district generally and also the Wantage Sisters who lived
in the convent next door. The fathers were due to leave India in a few
months when most of their work would fall on me, and I naturally wanted
to become acquainted with my future duties whilst they themselves were
there. Fr Forbes Bishop was in charge, assisted by Frs Lonsdale Wain and
Alan Bean. I had come to know the last two well when they had spent
two weeks with me on holiday at Sherwood. They spent most of their
free time butterflying, Fr Wain being a world known figure in the field
of lepidoptera, having discovered a new species of Himalayan moth which
was named after him. I recall one lunchtime when in most unCowley-like
fashion they leapt from their chairs, dashed for their nets, and went
chasing after some rare species which had fluttered by the window. Needless to say their main task lay in the hidden life of prayer and in pastoral
work generally. Fr Wain was my confessor and spiritual director over a
period of nearly twenty years and I owe a great deal to his understanding
and counsel. Born in 1900 he died in 1990. Fr Bean lives on in Oxford
(1998) having spent many years in India, the beloved country, as he
always calls it. It was one of my great joys to have them spending two
weeks with me in 1964.

Returning home in February I broke my journey at Rome at the
invitation of a Sherwood parent who worked in the Indian Embassy. After
a few days I took the coach to Assisi to fulfil a long-felt desire to explore
the country made famous by the little poor man whose life heralded a
new era for the Christian faith. I was rather unwell at the time and
probably attempted more than I should but was determined not to let
the opportunity slip by. I was put up by two loving Franciscan sisters who

kept a small boarding house and often had to disappoint them in being unable to do justice to their ample fare.

From Assisi I moved on to La Verna where St Francis received the stigmata, a journey of several hours by train and bus. It was a bitterly cold day and I was glad on arrival to be able to warm myself by the roaring fire in the bar just by the bus stop. The one day pilgrimage completed, I needed to get to the railway station about ten miles away in order to catch the evening train for Florence. The surest way seemed to be to hitch a lift but the road was lonely and perhaps one car every ten minutes was all one could expect. However, almost at once a little sports car with a lone driver came along but my signs went unheeded as it sped by. I suppose I must have been elated and inspired by closeness to St Francis, for I found myself heaping blessings upon the driver as he made his way down the winding road and finally disappeared. A few minutes later I spotted a similar looking car coming back towards me. Sure enough it was indeed the same. The driver must have turned back two or three miles on in order to fetch me. I was overwhelmed by his kindness but language problems made any communication other than by signs impossible. So I wrote him a short letter of thanks as I sat beside him, knowing that he would have little difficulty in getting it translated. Twenty-five years later I was to write a book on praising God in all circumstances, not as a means of bargaining with God to get what one wanted, but as an act of faith that God is in control of every situation and will bring everything to its best end. The sequel that day came as a mighty surprise. I caught the train to Florence and spent the night there and in viewing some of its art treasures the next day. Then it was back to Rome to catch the plane for London.

This was my first time home when my mother had not been there to greet me. She had died in 1962 at the age of 83 after a long and wearisome illness. Strangely her complaint was the same as that of my father, Hodgkin's disease, a relatively rare form of cancer. Her friend Noel Heath, much used in the ministry of healing, who had not been in touch for some time, was led to look in two days before her death. She found her to be 'already half in heaven' as she held converse with my father who had come to meet her. On Noel's departure she was seen by Joan, her face aglow in an ecstasy of joy as she raised herself from her bed and, reaching upwards, cried out 'it is wonderful, it is all so wonderful'. What seemed to be unconsciousness followed until her soul went to God on 21 August as dawn was breaking. I trust that I have not lifted the veil too much in my hope that our own strengthening in the faith may be shared with others. Joan continued to live in my mother's home in Charmouth where she made me more than welcome.

The SPG arranged for me to see their doctor after which I was sent off to the Tropical Diseases Hospital in London for a thorough check. It was my first experience of an English hospital for nearly fifty years. I was amazed by the thoroughness of the examination and of the teamwork which lay behind it. There was one ludicrous moment when we were all sent to bed in the middle of the day because some high-up health authority was visiting the hospital and it was thought to be more impressive if he found us between the sheets. After two weeks the caring and, as it seemed to me, distinctly able consultant came along and said: 'It's all right. You haven't got it'. I quite failed to catch on, realising only later that he was telling me I was free from cancer, the possibility of which had not entered my head. In fact there was nothing wrong which could not be attended to by a low fat diet.

It was a short holiday, and in May I left for India by ship sharing a cabin with a Jesuit priest who was greatly disturbed by advance knowledge of the Pope's encyclical *Humanae Vitae* whereby artificial contraceptive practice was forbidden. It was a surprise verdict, for it was generally known that the committee appointed to consider the question had indicated the other way. I can understand that there is some advantage in Rome holding aloft the ideal, even though it be aware that few will attain it. I have been told that Pope Paul VI once said that if only six couples on earth could live the will of God in this teaching he must uphold it. But my Jesuit companion would reply that against that must be placed the weight of guilt imposed upon the many who find themselves unable to conform. Even though this may in some measure be allayed by pastoral flexibility a heavy burden must remain. I myself believe (for what it may be worth: perhaps I should explain that I write as a life-long celibate) that Rome's position would be right for an unfallen world (though in an unfallen world it would not need to be stated), and that Lambeth's position is right for the world as it is. (And here, in passing, I see a close parallel with divorce.) We are fallen and weak and it seems to me contraceptive provision must be made for those for whom the Christian ideal is unrealistic. In their case sexual intercourse will in any case take place, and if it be without contraceptive protection, abortions will soar, or unwanted children will be born, or husband and wife will become estranged through the weakening of the physical bond, making contraception the desirable alternative. I would say that if a husband and wife decide thoughtfully and prayerfully before God, taking advice if that be indicated, that for them artificial contraception is the right way, then they should proceed in good conscience. This, at least for the time being, is to be their God-given, God-blessed way of celebrating their sexuality. Discipline, of course, is needed as in every other area of life. But I think that it is important that they should not slip into artificial contraceptive practice as though it were as obvious and natural as the eating of their meals. I think this is faithful to the mind of Lambeth. However, what is right today may not be right in a few years, and so there is wisdom in reviewing one's decision from time to time. And in making a decision now or in the future the possible side-effects of artificial contraceptive practices to health should not be overlooked.

Undoubtedly we live in a climate of opinion which makes abstinence a suspect word. I believe we need to affirm that men and women can be raised to complete wholeness in Christ without the experience of genital intercourse in their lives. If it were not so how could Jesus himself have been a complete and whole man? It is untrue to say (as is not uncommonly heard today) that monks and nuns in living out their vows of celibacy are necessarily missing out on something needed to make them fully mature men and women in Christ. All creative work, of which not the least is the daily round of prayer and praise, ministers to the sublimation of the sexual instinct, to what has been called the spreading of sexuality throughout our bodies. I believe myself to have seen more wholeness in monasteries and convents than in that same number of people, chosen at random, in the world outside.

But it may be a warning is needed here. I am not speaking of the abstinence which springs from repression, not of a cold and frigid abstinence, as may sometimes be the case in those whose lives are dedicated to celibacy. I am speaking of the abstinence which is tied to self-control, the abstinence which recognises the beauty of sexuality and is conscious of the creative part it has to play in true spirituality, the abstinence which allows erotic imagery (as, for example, in The Song of Solomon) to be raised to God in praise and delight for the beauty of his creation. It is a part of God's purpose that our sexuality shall be raised into creative channels. That is the sanctification of one's sexuality in the power of the Holy Spirit. There is nothing cold about abstinence, or at least there should not be, there need not be. We may experience the warmth of love every bit as strongly from men and women who, dedicated to celibacy, have learnt to spread their sexuality throughout their bodies, as from those who have been called to commit themselves to the married state.

How is it that our sexuality may be spread throughout our bodies? It is taking place in contemplative prayer when sexual imagery arises unbidden from the unconscious as one of the many distractions which may make themselves known at this time. Such imagery is not to be followed. We are not to get involved in it or to develop it (though we cannot help being aware of it) but we are to allow it to float on the periphery of consciousness, ourselves attending to our centring word (icon or whatever) allowing the distraction to float away when it will of its own accord. In this process a gentle detachment is taking place (just as it would if anger or envy etc. had arisen) and we shall in time be freed from the domination of the imagery which has assailed us. Our sexuality is not lost nor repressed but is raised, spread, shared with the body as a whole (whilst remaining genitally alive) and such people may be remarked upon for their animation, warmth, radiance, joy, as distinct from the lack-lustre quality of life which will accompany repressed sexuality. This same process is, of course, equally open to those in the married state.

Or again, this spreading of sexuality throughout our bodies is taking place in warm and loving friendship where we may or may not be aware of a sexual component involved. If we are so aware – and we cannot influence our feelings any more than we can influence our saliva when cutting a lemon – then we accept them gladly, knowing that 'feelings are meant to be felt', and allowing them to be raised to God in a spirit of praise and thanksgiving. It is a subsidiary element of friendship, the friendship itself being based on lasting spiritual qualities as distinct from this other which may be transitory in nature. A mark of true celibate friendship is not that it is necessarily without a conscious sexual component but that it is non-possessive of the other and always releases the other into their own freedom. It will stop short of genital relationship or of such petting as may lead in that direction. But it will not necessarily exclude embracing or other physical contact. The boundaries cannot be laid down *in absentia* but must remain in each case particular to the couple concerned. What is written applies equally to same sex friendships.

Or once more, the spread of sexuality throughout our bodies is taking place when a man or woman can look upon a piece of erotic art and can lift it in praise to God for the beauty of the human form. This is not pornography in the seedy, downgrading sense that the word carries with it. Pornography is an indulgence in the sexual for its own sake, a wallowing in it, whereas what is being done now is an upraising of it. It may be noted in parenthesis that I am speaking of works of art and not of the pictures commonly presented to our senses which are designed to appeal simply to the erotic and are usually degrading and insulting to womanhood in general. But, even in the realm of which I speak, discipline, which at times will involve denial, is necessary because of the frailty of our nature. Such discipline is necessary in all sense experience – tasting, hearing, smelling – and not simply in the two senses treated here. The important point to grasp is that its need is not because the senses are evil but because they are so supremely good that God cannot ultimately be satisfied with anything less than their full potential. The whole of our discussion is illuminated by St Paul where he writes: 'For every creature of God is good, and nothing to be refused if it be received with thanksgiving; for it is sanctified by the word of God and prayer' (1 Timothy 4:4–5).

Some words of William Blake may be quoted as having bearing on the area on which I have spoken.

> He who bends to himself a joy,
> Doth the winged life destroy.
> He who kisses a joy as it flies,
> Lives in eternity's sunrise.

A further writer who may illuminate our thinking at this point is St John of the Cross in *The Ascent of Mount Carmel*. In chapter 24 of book 3 he writes:

> Whenever a person, on hearing music or other things, seeing agreeable objects, smelling sweet fragrance, or feeling the delight of certain tastes or delicate touches, immediately, at the first movement directs his thought and the affection of his will to God, receiving more satisfaction in the thought of God than in the sensible object that caused it, and finds no gratification in the senses save for this motive, it is a sign that he is profiting by the senses and that the sensory part is a help to the spirit. The senses can then be used because the sensorial objects serve the purpose for which God created them: that He be more known and loved through them.

No doubt the above is a counsel of perfection to which many can do little more than aspire and only the saints come near to attain. But it states with admirable clarity the divinely intended partnership between sense and spirit. It should, however, be added that John offers a warning later, saying in effect that there are those who will suffer more harm than good in looking upon objects which may delight the senses, indulging the appetite without (as yet) the capacity to raise the heart to God ('his will pauses in them and feeds upon them'), and that for them a turning away from the objects presented to them is necessary. ('They assuredly prove more a hindrance than a help.') The whole chapter from St John of the Cross could be read with profit.

So far as I can remember the voyage as a whole was uneventful. I recall, however, a group of eight Catholic nuns who would come to meals as a group and say a rather lengthy grace in the presence of passengers already started. I am sure it was a courageous witness though I wondered if the effect was not more to isolate them than unite them with the rest of us. Is the Christian to see grace in an outward form, whether in the saying of words or the making of the sign of the cross, as a necessary preliminary to a meal? I confess I sat down to my meals without any passenger knowing whether there had been an uplifting of the heart to God. Was this cowardice or a laudable desire not to convey the impression that I might be more holy than those around me? How impossible it can be to fathom our motives!

I cannot resist intruding with an amusing recollection. Twenty years ago and more I was conducting a retreat at the Diocesan House near Canterbury. For some reason I had it in mind that on the last morning we were being given a bumper send-off breakfast. Accordingly, as we stood assembled for our meal, I offered, 'For bacon, egg and buttered toast/ Praise Father, Son and Holy Ghost.' We sat down with keen anticipation only to see passed through the kitchen hatch plates of cornflakes and rolls and butter. Spontaneously the Dean of Canterbury (Ian White-Thomson) revived our drooping spirits: 'For cereal and buttered bun/ Praise Father, Holy Ghost and Son.'

But what of the practice of grace in general? One way of looking at it is to see every meal as an extension of the Eucharist (which it always should be) and to see the eucharistic blessing as covering the whole. It is not my habit necessarily to say a grace when alone (I am stating a fact, not advocating a practice) yet I endeavour to live in a spirit of thanksgiving and to make acts to that end during the day. (This, incidentally, is the way most of us may be helped towards living out the passage quoted from St John of the Cross above.) Yet when it comes to a meal with friends I like a shared grace and especially where it is the only acknow-ledgement of God during our time with one another. It serves to bring us together within the family of Christ. The problem is how, if you live with others, you prevent it from becoming a mere formality, a veneer spread over a meal to give it an air of respectability. In religious communi-ties and other places where the spirit of prayer is maintained this is not likely to be so. In a family household it may well be otherwise. The remedy then seems to be to adjust the frequency to what can be managed in some degree of reality. For some that might mean saying grace at one meal a day, for others at Sunday lunch. For all, I suspect some rationing is desirable. Even our devout Victorian forbears did not say grace at afternoon tea. I was once told that Archbishop Geoffrey Fisher made it a rule only to say grace in his house when potatoes were served. That sounds good common sense to me. Some such rule is a safeguard against the scourge of scrupulosity which, apart from being one of the most self-regarding and painful of faults, is a denial of that liberty of spirit into which Christ would set us free.

14

Poona: Parish and Convent

I ARRIVED IN POONA in early June and was met at the station by Sister Mary Frideswide, the principal of St Mary's School and the sister in charge of the little group of Wantage Sisters who taught at the school. She took me to my flat opposite St Mary's Church in Staveley Road, the two Anglo-Indian schools – Bishop's and St Mary's – lying just beyond. For me it was a luxury flat for, although it lacked both fitted bath and shower, it offered a water closet, a convenience which in Sherwood belonged to the boys alone. In addition to two small bedrooms there was one large room where I could spread my books and papers. Its main drawback was the corrugated iron roof which drew the sun's heat, sometimes in summer raising the room temperature to 113 degrees. In those conditions you stripped as far as you could and wrote with arms resting on blotting paper. But fortunately they were not prolonged and the more normal temperature of around 100 was bearable. Poona, incidentally, was a refuge from the heat in the plains: my roof was the culprit. The Bishop, who had the flat below where he resided for short periods, had a much cooler clime.

My time of arrival in Poona is etched in my mind because my first Sunday was to be St Barnabas Day which falls on 11 June. St Barnabas has always been a favourite saint and has associations with Sherwood whose chapel was dedicated to him, and with two friends Eric and Doreen Bussell with whom I would sometimes stay. Doreen was in charge of the small SPG St Barnabas hospital in Ranchi and what an inspiration she was! The hospital, which catered mainly for the poor, may not always have had the equipment Doreen would have wished for but love and sacrifice were never wanting. Not much is known of St Barnabas, but the New Testament describes him as a good man and full of the Holy Spirit. Could one wish for a better obituary?

My first Sunday on St Barnabas Day was something of an ordeal. For the awful truth was that I had never sung a Eucharist in my life and this was to be the first of many Sundays. That may sound trivial to the reader but the reader has never heard me sing. When I was ordained thirty years before I was sent off to a singing instructor in London to train me in the opening versicles in matins and evensong. After toiling with me he pronounced me fit, but I so botched up the first matins that the vicar called across, 'Say it, man, say it', which I did and have been happier to do so ever since. I had practised for this coming Eucharist for months and somehow got through and, providing the organist never dared to change any of the tunes, I managed tolerably well throughout my time. The organist was a sister, happy to play for the glory of God, which she saw to be better served by being accommodating to my voice rather than indulging in more adventurous tunes of her own liking.

I suppose it is a compensatory device in my unconscious which makes me fond of the story of two elderly monks croaking their way through vespers when they were joined by a boy from the cathedral choir. When it came to the Magnificat they fell to silence that the magic of the young voice might be heard alone. That night an angel came to the senior monk saying that God had sent him to enquire why no Magnificat had been sung that night. The monk told him to go back and tell God it had never been sung so beautifully before. After delivering the message the angel returned to say that God had said that no Magnificat had entered heaven that night. No doubt the story is a bit hard on choirboys but I think it is one their trainers might sometimes do well to bear in mind. There can be in our cathedrals and churches magnificent singing from a technical point of view but if it lacks devotional overtones it is powerless to raise the heart and mind to God. It is the combination of the two which makes for the magic of Master Lough's great aria recorded in my schoolboy years, able to move the heart even on the old wind-up gramophones, which were all that we had in those days.[1]

I had inherited most of the work of three Cowley fathers and was kept busy from the start. To begin with I found myself on about twenty committees and chairman of most. In addition to St Mary's Church and parish there was the chaplaincy to the sisters, the conducting of retreats related to the convent and elsewhere, and a host of lesser duties. I don't know how I managed the first year. After telling the Bishop I had given forty addresses in Lent, he provided me with two curates and it was easier from then on, though shortly I was to become archdeacon as well. This, however, was a small task compared with the same post in England for there were not much more than a dozen clergy, and they all lived close by except one who was an overnight train journey away. I felt myself to be the most inadequate parish priest ever and a complete ignoramus as an archdeacon. What was my amazement when the Bishop told me I was the best archdeacon he had ever had!

My bishop was Christopher Robinson of Bombay who, as Bishop of Lucknow, had invited me to Sherwood College sixteen years before and who, as bishop, had been chairman of its Governing Body during my first ten years. He had come to India as a young priest to join the Cambridge Brotherhood (now the Delhi Brotherhood) and his whole life was to be given to that land. He was largely responsible for the CIPBC (Church of India, Pakistan, Burma and Ceylon) Prayer Book which, with its valuable supplement, was a considerable advance on anything in the Church of England at the time. He worked tirelessly for the establishment of the Church of North India in 1970 to which he belonged until his death in 1988. He was sixty-three when I went to Poona and a true father-in-God to his clergy and people. With Fr Wain's departure from India, he became my confessor and director through my Poona years. He probably had more friends in India than anyone I have known and I am personally deeply grateful to him for friendship, encouragement and frequent hospitality. His graciousness and generosity as a host were well known and after retiring from Bombay he returned to the Brotherhood to become its guest master, for which he was admirably suited. My sister Joan, who came to visit me in Poona, used to describe him, with his shock of thick white hair which he kept to the end, as comely and goodly to look upon and that admirably portrays him. I would just want to add that, like Barnabas, he was a good man and full of the Holy Spirit.

Bishop Christopher had a wonderful story from his early days in India. Shortly after his arrival, a friend of the Brotherhood called to drive him to a meeting twenty miles away. Prayer in India may be offered on all occasions, but Christopher was unprepared for what he now heard: 'Lord, you know the left front wheel is loose. We pray that you will keep it on until we arrive.' Never before had Christopher prayed so fervently. He liked to say that on opening his eyes on arrival he declared to his driver: 'Look, what's that rolling along in front of us?'

A welcome respite from work in Poona were days spent with Fr Alwyn Jones, priest-in-charge of the Seaman's Port Trust in Bombay. He was a great worker and organiser, generous in spirit, and his genial outgoing nature made him a quick contact man and so admirably suited him for visiting ships in the docks which were almost here today and gone tomorrow. He fought hard to get the mission to stay open an extra hour until eleven at night (he would do the supervision) to give the seamen more chance of returning straight to their ships rather than visiting a brothel on the way. I associate him, too, with the perpetual arranging of football matches between one crew and another. On one occasion a Russian and Italian crew met on the grounds of St Peter's School where it was the custom to ring the Angelus bell at six each evening. Alwyn explained to the Russians that play would stop and that they must be silent whilst everyone fell to prayer. But when the moment came it was the Catholics who chatted away happily whilst the atheists stood in awed and reverent silence.

Sermons were always a problem to me and I used to tell the congregation (a fine cop-out, this), that a poor sermon gave them the opportunity of exercising patience which was more fruitful to them than any words I might speak. Patient they indeed were with a parish priest who had had no training and was trying to learn the job as he went along. And yet in spite of my administrative inexperience something did get through and there was a real bond of affection with those who had borne with me when my time was up.

The arrival of two curates set me free for various out-station duties. I went to Delhi to conduct the annual retreat for the Cambridge Brotherhood and to Calcutta for that of the Oxford Mission. At that time I was speaking of the seven signs in St John's Gospel leading up to the great sign, the resurrection itself. I have never minded saying in one place what I have already said in another. If a thing is worth saying once it is worth saying many times. I cannot believe Jesus spoke the parable of the prodigal son on one occasion only and the teaching of the sermon on the mount must have been given to many audiences. A recent obituary in *The Times* speaks of a priest who in the course of thousands of sermons only once preached the same one twice. I marvel from afar, but have no desire to try to emulate him.[2] And those who are like me may claim to have the Beloved Apostle on their side. If tradition be correct his latter-day sermons contained simply the words 'Little children, love one another' repeated over and over again. And when they complained he said simply, 'It is the Lord's command: it is enough.' But, in fairness, that too is not for our imitation, for it presupposes a degree of holiness none of us is likely to reach.

One of my tasks was to visit St Peter's School, Panchgani, each month and take the Sunday services for them and Kimmin's (girls') School nearby. This involved a three-hour drive into the hills amidst beautiful scenery, though sometimes it was too hot to enjoy it. On one occasion, as chairman of the Governors, I had to visit a Muslim member of the staff in connection with some request he had made. On arrival at his house his wife told me that he was at his prayers. She showed me in and I sat on a couch as he did his prostrations on his prayer mat before me. Then after about ten minutes he rose and bowed and made himself ready to attend to our business. I was deeply touched. As chairman of his Governing Body I was a person of some importance to him in relation to the request he had made, but rather than attend to me at once he continued to give all his attention to God, and this in complete unselfconsciousness as though that was the natural and obvious thing to do. I admired his detachment and singleness of heart. And yet I am not saying we should do as he did. There can be a sacrificial offering in leaving one's prayer to attend to another, as well as in remaining at it. But my admiration for that Muslim remains.

On one visit to Panchgani a twelve-year-old girl had run away from her school. Search parties went out everywhere and returned empty-handed. We were really alarmed as the late afternoon drew on. A Bible Christian, as I think he might have called himself, asked me to accompany him in his car for a final search. Off we went on a rainy and misty monsoon day with little hope, on my part at least, of succeeding in our task. My driver stopped at a crossroad and prayed aloud that we would be led to find the child. Then off he went down one of the three roads available to him, and in less than a quarter of a mile there she was dashing across the road a hundred yards ahead. He drove on, leapt out and ran up the hill after her. It was perfect timing on God's part. If my driver's prayer had been that much shorter or longer we would have missed her.

My initial reason for going to Poona was that I might be chaplain to the Wantage Sisters, whose main house was at Panch Howd with branches at St Mary's School and St Crispin's, each within about two miles of the convent. The parish work was added later. It was a valuable experience but I was happiest with the convent work, the daily masses, the occasional retreats, the weekly visit for confessions. Mother Susan Dominica was in charge, and I found in her a good friend and one to whom one could talk on any subject. At a convent everything is done just right. The vestments are beautifully laid out, the altar prepared, the linen spotlessly clean. But the priest is, or in my case was, the servant of the nuns. They set the service and the feast days and the ritual as they liked it. In my case I was grateful for this because I knew little and stood to learn a lot. They were very good to me and made me feel welcome and at home though I must have been raw stuff after the expertise of the Cowley fathers.

There was one mass each week at St Crispin's, a beautiful massively built church with a remarkable atmosphere. Sister Hannah, a former Lancashire policewoman in days when the breed was distinctly rare, was in charge. She once told me that the great Indian Christian mystic, Sadhu Sundar Singh, stood in the church and declared it would stand till the second coming of Christ. I have no doubt he sensed something very special amongst those heavy stones laden with the prayer and devotion of many years.

I was too late to meet Sundar Singh, who is thought to have perished in the snows on one of his visits to Tibet in about 1927. But when at Cambridge I read everything I could find about him and in India his name was much revered and stories abounded. One, told by C.F. Andrews, relates how he was praying one night, seated in the open a few yards from the *dak* bungalow in which he was staying. A friend looking out into the moonlight was horrified to see a leopard moving up behind him. He did not dare shout a warning lest the leopard should take fright and pounce. But as he watched, Sundar Singh looked round, put out his arm, and man and beast sat on together. I recall a friend in Allahabad telling me that, many years before, she was anxious about her young daughter who was very ill in hospital. She could get no news however much she tried. Unexpectedly Sundar Singh walked in and she told him of her distress. He asked to be allowed to retire for a quarter hour and then told her that her daughter had died very peacefully half an hour before. And so it turned out to be. He conversed so often in his ecstasies with people who had crossed over that he may well have spoken with this little girl, but who can say?

My visits to St Mary's would include mass and hearing the sisters' confessions and sometimes that of some of the girls. They made model confessions at confirmation, all read out and well arranged. After hearing them through I sometimes asked them to put the script aside and then just say the three sins which bothered them most. That was when we often got to the heart of the matter.

Once at the Convent an Indian sister went down with Parkinson's disease. The local doctor diagnosed it, and she was then sent off to a specialist in South India who confirmed the diagnosis but said the only possible treatment was through surgery available in the west. So her passage was booked by plane to London where a specialist would examine her. The day before she left, Mother Susan asked if I would lay hands on the sister with prayer in the convent chapel, whilst the other sisters prayed silently around her. It was an ideal setting for healing and the atmosphere was special that night though the convent chapel always carried with it the spirit of prayer. When she got to London the doctor said there must have been a misdiagnosis, and no operation was necessary. His opinion was accepted, though some of us in India felt we knew better.

In those days I did not often lay hands on the sick. I do so quite often now in obedience to a call which I shall explain later, and like to begin with a prayer for myself asking God that he will empower my hands to bless and to heal, as he has promised, in the name of Jesus. Those last words do not, however, imply any limitation of the extent of God's saving grace. One occasion stands out. I was visiting a member of St Mary's congregation in a Poona hospital and laid hands on him with a blessing. Whether he was helped physically or not I do not remember. But as I was leaving his bedside a Hindu, who had seen what happened, called out to ask if there was no blessing for him. He was in a bad way with cancer. I laid hands on him with prayer and by next day his cancer had gone into remission and by all accounts he was a different person. He died of cancer about six months later. But in those extended months of his life God surely had a blessing for him in answer to his faith which leapt across the barrier of creed.

15

Poona: Ashrams

ONE OF MY TASKS was to help build up the Christa Prema Seva ashram in Poona. In the old days this had known such heroes as Jack Winslow, Brother Douglas, Bill Lash and Verrier Elwin, but it had fallen on bad times and was now going to ruin. The Sisters of the Sacred Heart in Bombay with such formidable people as Sister Dhalla, their mother superior (who had almost caused a riot in Bombay when, as a Parsee, she was converted to the faith), and Sister Sarah, an Oxford classical scholar, wanted to form an ecumenical community with some of the Wantage Sisters. At that time I was expecting to be a member of the community after a brief spell in England but that was not to be and my contribution was to the bricks and mortar only. A few months later the ashram became once more a place of prayer and has served the diocese well and also the wider Church.

When you called on Mother Superior Dhalla (now Vandana) you never knew whether she would be standing on her feet or her head. She was an ardent devotee of yoga and was taught most splendidly by Fr Lobo, a Roman Catholic priest who had learnt much at one time from B.K.S. Ayengar who lived in Poona, and has sometimes appeared on English TV. Ayengar is the only person I have met who could lie on his stomach and plant both his feet on the top of his head. Fr Lobo was always a few inches off in those days. Don't ask me the spiritual merits of this for I would be at a loss to answer, but you will agree it has to be a spectacular thing to watch, more especially if you first lie on the floor and see how far you yourself can get. But I can understand that there may be advantage in standing on your head, for it gives the inside organs a different gravity pull for a period and I can well believe it has other benefits as well. Fr Lobo used to do a half-hour headstand every morning before breakfast as part of his meditation period. Even to get there at all was well out of my reach but I did do the easy and beneficial shoulder stand. There were, too, many simple exercises, movements would be the better word, for yoga is all so different from western physical training and, performed in a spirit of recollection, they might well be a benefit to many. So, too, the corpse posture (let it not be said that anyone can do that for it is an art in itself) can give you that relaxation which makes for fruitful prayer. But are such exercises in themselves prayer? I think we may say that as soon as we offer anything up, not evil in itself, for the love of God, which includes yoga exercises and the typing of the pages of this book, it becomes prayer.

For myself, a willing recipient, Fr Lobo concentrated on posture in prayer. He would sit me down on an upright chair (lotus posture on the floor for proficients), and ask me to sit with an easy tension in the back, shoulders down, neck and head straight with the body. This would allow for a counter relaxation on the crown of the head, the forehead, the face, the jaw. Eyes were to be lightly closed, you yourself looking mentally to the level of the heart. He would explain that there were six sets of muscles around the eyes and that they were all to be relaxed. 'Let your eyeballs feel they are dropping out' was a favourite phrase. Your arms were to be relaxed and, too, the hands which were to rest palms downwards on the top of the thighs. In that position you were simply to sit and to sit still, an operation which, we may say, becomes prayer so soon as the desire for prayer is present, just as the sitting of a blind man on the pavement becomes begging as soon as he puts down a bowl, indicating that the desire for money is there. Without that desire the man is resting and not begging. I found Fr Lobo's teaching helpful and have done so ever since.

But equally I have found the teaching of *The Cloud of Unknowing* valuable though it is in contrast to what I have written here. *The Cloud* says in effect that if you are all in a huddle when you begin your prayer then, as the contemplative work you are engaged in proceeds, you will find your body straightening out so that it will take up a position reaching upwards to correspond with the aspiration of the spirit. Anyone who cares to try this may find out for themselves it is true.

As I have said earlier I was expecting to become a member of the ecumenical ashram and, partly for this reason, asked Sister Dhalla (as she then was) if she could arrange for me to spend a while in a Hindu community to help me to get the 'feel' of ashram life. She arranged for me to go to the Brahma Vidya Mandir (Temple of the Knowledge of God) women's ashram, situated near Paunar, which lies about three hundred miles east of Bombay. Their resident guru, who had founded the ashram in 1959, was the renowned Vinobe Bhave who had been one of Gandhi's closest friends and disciples. In his younger days Vinobe had walked the length and breadth of India trying to persuade landowners to give up freely some of their land to the poor, who owned virtually nothing. In this he met with a considerable amount of success being responsible, it is said, for the redistribution of some four million acres. When I met him he was seventy-five and a venerable teacher attracting disciples from far and near. Each evening he would walk around the ashram compound with his guests, picking up leaves which he often said he could not bear to see lying around. Vinobe was a Brahmin and such work in India is usually left to the lowest castes. I think he was trying to teach his disciples the dignity of manual work. Coming from such an exalted person, his action spoke of deep humility. Indians treat their gurus with great respect; the sisters would look to Vinobe for advice in the running of the ashram, but he preferred to remain fairly remote, laying down guiding principles only. He was an ascetic figure, eating sparingly, and later on he spent a full year in silence. Sometimes I would watch, not, I confess, without envy, when he was being oiled and pummelled and massaged by his devotees. Yes, there are some compensations in being an eastern guru!

Life in an ashram is more informal than in a monastery or convent. Here there were two guest rooms, one for each sex. In my room there were four wooden board beds, where you laid out your bedding which would probably include a thin mattress. I was fortunate in finding an empty bed on my arrival but later the room filled up and three or four were having to sleep on the floor. At four each morning we were awakened and would go to Vinobe's room where he sat, lotus fashion, in his night clothes on his bed, while we all sat on the floor singing praises to God. The sisters had none of the reserve of convent nuns and would sing lustily, slapping their thighs mightily as their praises grew. Then we would go back to our beds until about half past six. The sisters had their own devotions during this time.

I would awaken each morning to see a French student standing completely motionless on his head. He would descend after half an hour and turn to his studies which, he told me, he could do with a wonderful clarity of mind. Another man in the guest room who drew my attention was an Indian, whose name I cannot remember and could never pronounce, who had the spirit of an early Franciscan brother. In these pages

I will call him Ramananda (pronounced Rahmununder) which means joy of God. Ramananda possessed nothing except his clothes and a blanket and a portion of the Hindu scriptures. He had a mission to children and each day he would walk to a village, sometimes more than ten miles away and, having gathered a group together, he would teach them and pray with them. In return grateful parents would provide him with a midday meal. One day he came to me to say he was visiting a village where Elizabeth lived, the only Christian child amongst those he met and that he felt distressed because he could not give her anything from her own faith. Did I perhaps have a card or cross he might take her? I happened to have a card showing a crucifix in my prayer book and was glad to pass it on. Later he told me Elizabeth was so pleased to receive it. Ramananda carried with him the spirit of simplicity and joy. He could speak only out of the heart of his own religion but surely he knew Christ more intimately than all but a few Christians who profess his name?

It seems to me there are two ways of knowing Christ. You can know all about him, as did those who were brought up with him in Nazareth, or you can know him, which is the only knowledge which ultimately matters. We Christians have a great start in being able to know about Christ from the Gospels, but if we do not know him it is as nothing. I think of Ramananda as one of those who at the last day will be saying, 'Lord, when did I see you hungry and feed you, or naked and clothe you, or sick and visit you?', and will hear that what he did in love and simplicity of heart to others was unknowingly done to Christ himself. He will discover that he knew Jesus all the time, without knowing that he knew him.

Dr Stanley Jones, a well-known American missionary in India, used to tell how he was once proclaiming Christ to a mixed audience in Bombay. After he had finished, an elderly and venerable Hindu came to the platform and said: 'Sir, I thank you. I have known him all my life, and now you have told me his name.' It is a perfect illustration of the point I am making.

You cannot be long in India without hearing extolled the virtues of non-violence. It always worried me that anyone should try to build up an ethical system on non-violence. Non-violence, unlike love, cannot be an absolute. Make an absolute of non-violence and as soon as you push a child out of the path of an oncoming car your system is in tatters. You cannot say non-violence is right and violence is wrong. What you can say is that controlled violence may be right, and that uncontrolled violence is wrong. Uncontrolled violence is like a forest fire consuming everything in its path. Controlled violence may be likened to a fire in the living-room grate, serving the occupants well. An angry man knocking out your teeth is an example of the first, a dentist extracting them a case of the second. It is here the distinction has to be made. Non-violence was one of the pillars on which ashram life rested and I wondered if there would be a chance of dialogue in this area. But I was after all a guest and here to learn and listen rather than to intrude. As I thought on this it seemed that the Lord himself was supplying an answer. I saw a monkey stealing bananas from the ashram plantation. And over there, as I watched, were two hefty sisters throwing stones at the creature to drive him off. Fine, I thought, and how sensible, but how does one square it with non-violence? I decided to bide my time.

The sisters were delightfully uninhibited and the senior sister thought nothing of visiting the men's guest room in whatever state we might be. One night as I was about to slip into my pyjamas she came along and asked how I was doing. I said all was fine but that I had been worried about talk of non-violence and I told her what I had seen the day before. I said it seemed to me so right and sensible but how did it all fit in? She looked surprised and then laughed merrily at my naïveté. 'Why', she exclaimed, 'it doesn't matter throwing stones at monkeys if you have love in your heart', adding for good measure that it was quite all right for a mother to spank her child if she had love in her heart. So that was it. The base line was after all the same as mine, not non-violence but love.

Vinobe had his next incarnation neatly worked out. He was a Brahmin, highest of the high, and he would come back as a sweeper woman, lowest of the low. Thus, by embracing opposites, he would move towards completeness. But is reincarnation tenable in itself? There are remarkable stories of memory recovery over hundreds of years which to some make reincarnation a proven fact. I personally think the spirit is indestructible and can never come back. But just as the body splits up at death and becomes a part of other bodies (the Ilkley Moor ba t'at syndrome), is it possible for the psyche to split up in the life beyond and become a part of other psyches, carrying fragments of memories with them? As far as I can understand it, Bede Griffiths believed this. But as for the spirit, the core of personality, that, he asserted, could never return: the teaching of Jesus allows for no other view.

After ten days at the ashram my time was up. It had been an interesting experience, not altogether easy, though the sisters could not have done more to make me welcome, and comfortable within the simple pattern of their life. I'm an awkward floor sitter, more so when the floor is stone, and a messy eater with my fingers when it comes to curries and the like. And in those days I did miss tea and coffee which on religious principles were never taken. But with warmth and love abounding it is almost ungenerous to mention these things. I came away thinking what a lot convents might learn from the freedom and informality of the Hindu pattern. Yet I felt sure the Hindu sisters would be enriched through contact with convent life. The Poona Christian ashram appears to combine what is best in both traditions.

My time in Poona was coming to a close. In November 1970 the Church of North India came into being and I duly became a member. I was no longer archdeacon (thankfully!) and lost my place in Crockford's (inconveniently). I was due for six months' leave in 1971. The Indian Government had a rule that no priest could return to India if his leave was extended beyond that period. I left Bombay by Air India in the middle of May accompanied by Fr Alwyn Jones. Joan met us at Heathrow and motored Alwyn to Stockbridge and me on to Charmouth where I was to remain longer than either of us had anticipated.

16

Taizé and Annecy

O N MY RETURN TO ENGLAND I needed a car which the reliable local garage was able to provide at a cost of £150. It doesn't sound much but roaring inflation was still to come. My first official engagement was not till September, when I was booked to give a retreat at St Michael's House at Wantage where some of the elderly sisters lived. I decided that in preparation I would do what I had often wanted to do: visit places in France linked with people I had known through spiritual reading. These could then become the basis of the retreat addresses. Accordingly I set off in August, with a tent packed in the car boot, to visit Taizé and Annecy, Ars and Albi. Annecy was the episcopal home of St Francis de Sales, Ars boasted of the world's most famous curé, and Albi had at times accommodated Jean-Pierre de Caussade, whose writings had held me for many years.

Taizé was first stop. I don't propose to describe it in any detail. It is too well known and its chants have gone round the world. Shortly after the war Père Schultz, who had done valiant work in sheltering escaped prisoners and Jewish refugees on the run during the war, founded a small community open to Christians of all denominations. It has grown greatly, and its ecumenical status is its glory and its strength. It was particularly good to see for once a Christian centre where we older people were so vastly outnumbered by the young. That has to be another of Taizé's great contributions to the Church of today. In the chapel services I especially liked Père Schultz' custom of placing a young child in the midst of the choir. A delight was the little darkened chapel down the road which carried an atmosphere all its own. I didn't speak to Père Schultz personally, but was close to him when he gave individual blessings, and counsel if asked. He carried with him an aura of holiness; there is no need to say more.

Père Schultz spoke to us on several occasions. Five words have remained with me to help me in my prayers. I have often reflected on them. 'For me', said Pere Schultz, 'prayer is waiting'. As my contribution to Taizé let me offer my reflections on those words.

There is much in Scripture to support them. 'The Lord is good to those who wait for him', says Jeremiah. 'They that wait for the Lord shall renew their strength', says Isaiah. 'I waited patiently for the Lord, and he heard my cry', from the Psalms. And more than two thousand years later, and moving beyond the Bible to St John of the Cross, we read that 'in prayer we are to learn to rest with attention in loving waiting upon God.'

And so, when the time for silence comes the need is to wait and to be content to wait as best one can: patiently, expectantly, lovingly, longingly. That is my part and it is all that I can do. The rest belongs to God. I see myself as the parched earth looking upwards, waiting patiently for the rain to fall. I can neither hasten the shower nor determine its intensity when it comes. My only need is to desire God, to desire to pray and then to wait. God wants to heal my broken, wounded spirit. I must let him do the work, handing all the stresses and strains over to him. And then just wait. A short centring word or prayer may help. Simply the word 'Jesus' or the familiar 'Be still and know that I am God' would do well. And it may help to look mentally to the level of the heart.

It may not be long before distracting thoughts intrude. The rule here is that we may acknowledge them or recognise them, but we are not to develop them or encourage them, or in any way to get involved with them. We must let them drop from our consciousness as a stone may drop into the sea. And if they won't drop away but insist on floating on the periphery of consciousness, then we must be content to let them float. We must not attempt to draw them back into ourselves. Rather must we make a renewed act of surrender and seek to re-establish ourselves with our centring prayer. This process is not without pain. If it be offered with patience and perseverance, a dying to self and a rising to new life in Christ is taking place. Here is a part of the Holy Spirit's work of sanctification.

This period of waiting is sure to be demanding. And we will find ourselves asking whether it is of any use, whether we are truly praying. St Augustine has comforting words here: 'Your very desire is itself your prayer; if your desire is continued so is your prayer also. Whatever you are doing, if you are desiring to pray, you are praying. If you do not wish to cease from prayer, do not cease from desire.' And these words are true, the intention or the desire is prayer, whether we are speaking of vocal prayer, eucharistic prayer, office prayer, Jesus prayer, rosary prayer or, as now, the prayer of the silence of the heart before God.

If, then, we are tempted to ask whether we are really praying, all we have to do is to ask ourselves one question. Do I desire to pray? Am I desiring God? And if the answer is yes, then we are truly at prayer. Even if all we can do is to desire to pray that is enough.

It is important to understand this. Sometimes people may speak as if correct posture is prayer. Sitting with a straight back helps partly because it helps us to be attentive and alert, and partly because it assists abdominal breathing. But correct posture in itself is not prayer. And correct breathing is not prayer. What then is prayer? It is the intention or desire to pray.

Or it is sometimes said that relaxation is prayer. Relaxation assists prayer because it helps us to be receptive. But relaxation in itself is not prayer. Prayer is the intention or desire to pray.

Or some may speak as if bodily stillness is prayer. Bodily stillness assists prayer because it helps towards the stilling of the mind. But bodily stillness in itself is not prayer. Again, then, what is prayer? It is the intention or desire to pray.

Or, not uncommonly today, people may speak as if a change of consciousness is prayer. It may happen that in the silence we are taken from the ordinary workaday state of beta consciousness to that of alpha. This is a restful experience, and where it is of the Holy Spirit it will be welcomed. But in itself an altered state of consciousness is not prayer. It can, for example, be induced by drugs or by deep relaxation. What then is prayer? At the risk of being wearisome, let it be said once more that it is the intention to pray, or the desire for God, which determines whether we are praying.

Undoubtedly, in this period of waiting we are sometimes taken hold of. St Antony the Great says that he prays best who does not know he is praying. Watch a group of children at play. They are so engrossed in their game that they do not know they are playing. There is no corner in a child's mind which can allow him to say, 'Now I am playing'. If, perchance, he does say that, then the game for him has at once lost some of its perfection. It is the same at prayer. Periods may pass when there is no corner of the mind which can say, 'Now I am praying'. Just as you cannot say in bed at night, 'Now I am sleeping', but can only say in the morning, 'I slept', so you cannot now say at prayer, 'Now I am praying', but can only say later, 'I prayed'. I am not speaking of any exalted state. If the phone rings we shall hear it at once. These showers of rain, as it were, come and go, and the parched earth cannot determine their time or intensity. So, too, these periods of which I have spoken depend on God and not on us. They may be waited for but not sought, least of all striven after. Striving would, in any case, be in vain.

Prayer is waiting, intending, desiring God. Prayer, we might say, is a holding on to God, until waiting, waiting, waiting, we move into the knowledge that we are being held.

From Taizé I motored to Francis de Sales' country and found a camping site by the Lake of Geneva. Francis, who was born in 1567, was Bishop of Geneva from 1602 until his death twenty years later. He was not able to take up residence in Geneva since it was a Calvinist stronghold, and apart from the possibility of imprisonment, his very life might have been at risk. Hence he resided at Annecy some twenty-five miles to the south. I went to Francis' birthplace, the castle of Thorens, standing amid scenery of breathtaking beauty. Annecy nearby, with its Convent of the Visitation overlooking its picturesque lake nestling in the hills, carries with it, or it did for me, an air of serenity and peace such as one associates with the saint to whom it owes its fame. Well, that is what I thought at the time, but on reflection, how true is it? Is the picture of a calm lake on a still, sunny day, set in beautiful countryside a valid representation of peace as the Christian understands it? I think not. More accurate is the picture of a boat on another lake, with the wind howling and the waters swelling, with twelve troubled men toiling at the oars, and a thirteenth asleep on a cushion. That is a picture of Christian peace, the trustful peace of Jesus in the midst of a raging storm. That is the deep peace Francis must have known as he bore the burdens of his diocese and the travail of its people, not to mention the inner strivings which belong to every Christian soul. That is the peace which passes understanding, and it must truly pass the understanding of any who have not experienced it. I feel wary in the presence of people who set store on a felt peace for it usually means there is a reliance on feelings rather than faith, which alone can take us through the desert patches which must come our way. It is interesting to note that in only one place does the New Testament tell us to seek peace, and that is in a quotation: 'Seek peace, and ensue it'. The Scriptural emphasis is that we are to seek the God of peace rather than the peace of God. If we set our hearts on seeking peace, it may well be we shall find some spurious quality fitly enough represented by a calm lake on a summer day and in doing so we may miss both peace and God. But if our hearts are set on seeking God, it is him we shall find, and because he is the God of peace, his peace must necessarily be ours as well. I have always liked the story of the Cowley novice who, finding himself in the presence of Fr Benson, the great and holy founder of his order, and not knowing quite what to say, inquired tremulously, 'Father, when you go to prayer, do you find peace?' 'No,' came the firm reply, '*war.*'

Francis lives on today through his books and letters. In an age when most religious writing was directed towards the professionally religious, Francis wrote for men and women living in the world, showing how the events of everyday life can be lifted up to God and be made the means of sanctification. His best-known works are *The Introduction to the Devout Life* and *Treatise on the Love of God*, but for the modern reader wishing to capture the spirit of Francis, I would recommend *The Spirit of Francis de Sales* written by Albert Camus, Bishop of Belley. As Boswell was to Johnson so was Camus to Francis. In his book, now reduced from five volumes to one (Camus wrote over two hundred books in all) there are nearly three hundred anecdotes of St Francis, illuminating aspects of his life and teaching: patience, humility, prayer life etc. Camus is nothing if not thorough. He lived but 'three leagues' (25 miles?) from Annecy and employed a young servant who had practically no other duty than to act as postman between Francis and himself. It seems that he wrote to him on the slightest pretext and accepted Francis' replies as infallible. Francis, incidentally, was a prodigious letter writer, sometimes, it is said, writing up to fifty letters a day: in all more than two thousand letters of direction are still extant. Periodically Francis would stay for a few days at Belley, where he was liable to be put through a more thorough examination than he ever knew. We had better learn it from Bishop Camus' own words.

I will own up to a trick I played on him which some might think inexcusable. Every year he used to come and stay with me for a week and on these occasions I used to watch him through little holes which I purposely bored in the walls in order that I might observe what he did when completely alone in his room, whether in study, meditation and prayer, writing, sitting still or moving about going to bed and getting up – in other words, under all those circumstances when men tend to feel themselves quite free from restraint. But I never saw him alter his bearing in the slightest: what he was among others, that he was when alone, and the repose and placidity of his mind were reflected in his bodily movements. He was just as composed when alone as in great gatherings, and when occupied in prayer one would have thought he was in the presence of all the saints and angels. For hours he would remain motionless as a statue and his expression would portray a deep reverence. When he was alone in this way I used to watch whether he crossed his legs, or leant upon his elbows, or the like. But no, the gentle aspect of his posture never changed, and it was this gentleness which inspired all who met him with love and reverence.

Francis was an older contemporary of St Vincent de Paul being fourteen years his senior. Of Francis, Vincent wrote:

His ardent fervour shone through his public preaching as well as his ordinary conversation. When I thought about his words afterwards I admired them so deeply that I felt sure that he was the best living portrait of the Son of God on earth. I remember thinking again and again: How good you must be, my dear God, since Monsieur de Geneve who is but your creature is so wonderfully good and kind.

Francis would gladly have escaped the burdens of office to live in seclusion, as he put it, with 'my rosary and my pen'. But his busy life of administration and preaching, letter writing and counselling continued to the end. The end was in fact unexpected and sudden and on 27 December 1622 his Calvary was begun. The rupture of a cerebral artery left him in a heavy stupor for which the only known remedy was to do everything possible to rouse the patient from sleep. The methods used were painful in the extreme until finally he was cauterised with red hot irons. It is said that he bore this treatment without murmur, a reflex tautening of his shoulders being the only indication of his pain. He then cried gently murmuring 'Jesu Maria'. Hardly surprisingly he lived but a few hours dying at eight o'clock in the night of 28 December.

I append a selection of Francis' sayings taken from various sources.

Try as much as you like but in the end only the language of the heart can reach another heart, while mere words as they slip from your tongue don't get past your listener's ear.

Since, O my soul, thou art capable of God, woe to thee if thou contentest thyself with anything less than God.

Be patient with everyone, but above all with yourself. I mean do not be disturbed because of your imperfections, and always rise up bravely from a fall.

Religious orders are not formed for the purpose of gathering together perfect people, but those who have the courage to aim at perfection.

Moderation is always good in all exercises, excepting that of loving God.

Provided that God is glorified we must not care by whom.

Nothing is as strong as gentleness, nothing so gentle as strength.

Love is the abridgement of all theology.

Every Christian needs a half hour prayer each day, except when he is busy, then he needs an hour.

He who stays not in his littleness, loses his greatness.

Make sickness itself a prayer.

We must never so form our opinions as not to be ready if necessary to give them up.

There was never an angry man that thought his anger unjust.

Our words are a faithful index of the state of our souls.

Flies are attracted by a spoonful of honey more than by a whole barrel of vinegar.

And one saying from St Jeanne de Chantal whom Francis regarded as his spiritual daughter and who founded the Community of the Visitation with him in Annecy.

If, going to prayer one can become pure capacity for receiving the spirit of God, that will suffice for any method. Prayer must happen by grace not by artfulness. Go to prayer by faith, remain there in hope, and go out only by love which requires simply that one act and suffer.

17

Curé d'Ars and Caussade

FROM THE LAKE OF GENEVA I drove to Ars, the little village near Lyons made famous by its parish priest St Jean-Marie Vianney, patron saint of parish priests, known to the world as the Curé d'Ars. The journey took much longer than I had anticipated and it was nearly 11 p.m. when I arrived. Judging it to be too late to seek accommodation in the village I slept in the car. The village had a large parking area and I think I had it to myself. At about 9 o'clock I made my way into the village and enquired in a holy objects' shop if I could get a room for a few days. The sister was concerned to know I had slept rough – though that is a strong word for a slight inconvenience – and hurried off to find me a room in a house for visiting clergy. It was comfortable, friendly, and cheap.

I made my way to the church. It still kept much of its old-world charm. The pulpit from which the Curé preached was still there, and his confessional in which he sat for most of the day and much of the night. Three hours' sleep appears to have been a normal ration. All around the wall were crutches thrown away by those who had been cured through his ministry. He did not usually pray for miracles himself, but asked his penitents to put their requests to a favourite saint Philomena who would attend to their needs. It was said that he would at times dart out of the confessional to snatch someone from the queue in which people might be kept standing for several days, saying they had no time to lose or were perhaps needed for some crisis at home. He had remarkable supernatural gifts which enabled him to reveal to his penitents sins they had overlooked or sometimes, no doubt, wished to hide. Many remarkable miracles are associated with his name, in one case the wheat, which was running low, being multiplied to meet the needs of an orphanage for which he was responsible.

The evidence for this miracle, which invites comparison with the Gospel story of the feeding of the five thousand, is remarkably good. We must remember that the Curé is not some figure of the ancient past. Many who knew him would have lived on to the first twenty or thirty years of the present century. His curate at the end of his life, Abbé Toccanier, received the following account from the Curé's own lips: 'I had a great number of orphans to feed and in the granary there remained only a handful of wheat. It occurred to me that St Francis Regis, who had fed the poor miraculously in his own lifetime, might well do it again after his death. I possessed a relic of this saint; I placed it in amongst the wheat which remained, the children prayed and the granary was full.' There is, too, evidence through the bishop. There is also a well-attested story of the multiplication of the dough three or fourfold in the hands of the one who was making the bread. This was recorded on oath. The cook simply worked on the instructions of the Curé on the little flour she had. These are reassuring stories for numbers of Christians in an age when so many are at pains to explain away the miraculous in the Gospels. We clergy serve our people badly when we start off by asking how much modern men and women will believe. The task of the Church, if I may borrow imagery from Archbishop Temple, is not to ask what Jones will swallow but to declare to Jones what there is to eat.

The Curé was appointed to Ars, considered to be the least important parish in the diocese, in 1818 when he was forty-two, and remained until his death forty-one years later. The diocesan clergy were opposed to the appointment, seeing him as a person of little education and considering he should never have been ordained. The story is told that they prepared a round robin for the bishop, protesting his inadequacy, and that by mistake it got forwarded to the Curé himself who signed it, adding words to the effect that he couldn't agree more. Much relating to his life remains a mystery, his tussles for example with the one he would call 'le grappin', who would throw his furniture around, bang on his doors, and cause mayhem generally. We do not in any way detract from his sanctity if we find explanations for these events in the immense emotional and psychological conflicts arising out of his temperament, early life, and the ceaseless burden of his priestly vocation. These happenings may be seen rather as part of the raw material out of which his sanctity was fashioned. We all have to work with the stuff of life God has given us. Whatever books the reader may wish to read of the Curé d'Ars I believe the one by Lancelot Sheppard (*The Curé d'Ars*, Burns and Oates) should not be missed. His penetrating psychological insights in no way diminish but rather serve to enhance the heroic sanctity of his subject.

Many stories are told of the Curé's capacity to foretell the future. A remarkable one concerns a nineteen-year-old girl who arrived late at one of his church instructions. He stopped his address to tell her she should see him afterwards. He then revealed that he knew she was on her way to Lyons to find work as a domestic servant but she was to be warned as great danger threatened her. Arriving at Lyons she was provisionally engaged by a man who insisted, however, his wife must first see her to confirm the appointment. On presenting herself at his house she found no wife and remembering the Curé's warnings took to her heels and ran for her life; literally so, one may believe, for the man was later convicted of murdering several such employees.

It was obviously necessary for the Curé to be short and incisive in his direction if he were to see all who sought him out. He seems to have been a master of the art. On one occasion a group of young men came on a pilgrimage to Ars. A young man joined them with his gun and his dog saying that whilst duck shooting was his real aim he would like to see the Curé out of curiosity. With many others the group was outside the church awaiting a sight of the Curé as he left the confessional to go to his lunch. There were many he might have spoken to but he went straight to this young man and said: 'It's a pity your soul is not so fine as your dog.' The saying worried the young man through the night and he went to confession next day. After receiving absolution there came the parting shot, 'You must be a Trappist monk.' And so he was, and for a period of thirty-six years, dying in 1888.

It is from Ars that there comes the well-known story concerning the peasant whom the Curé observed frequently sitting in his church before the tabernacle, in which the Blessed Sacrament was reserved. On being questioned, he replied, 'I look at Him, and He looks at me'. The French mystic and locutionist Gabrielle Bossis whose work *He and I* has been translated into many languages, once received the message, 'Give yourself a rest from saying prayers so that you may enjoy my Love'. It would be hard to give a better description of what that peasant villager was doing. Sitting in silent adoration, eyes fixed unstrainedly upon the tabernacle, absorbing unconsciously the virtue which flows from it, may be the most fruitful of all forms of prayer. Most people are unable to bear for long the appearance that they are doing nothing. We must, they feel, be loving him; it is hard to sit down and let him love us. But we forget, of course, that love is a response. Child love is a response to mother love. Children do not primarily set out to love, they find themselves giving back what they receive. So, as the beloved Apostle tells us, we love him because he first loved us and the more we can take that love into ourselves, the more will be our response. I do not mean that we are to be dependent on the presence of the Blessed Sacrament though that will be a great help to many. Every breath we take may be an inbreathing of love, for the Holy Spirit is around us and within us. Spacial images are inadequate but they are all we have.

Robert Hugh Benson has a story known to many of a nun kneeling in silent adoration before the Blessed Sacrament in her convent chapel. To the casual visitor nothing is happening. But to a 'sensitive' who enters, the atmosphere is charged with energy, and the praying figure is linked as by an unseen light with all humankind in its needs. Teilhard de Chardin's retelling of this story is, perhaps, less well known. It runs:

> All at once he [the sensitive] sees the whole world bound up and
> moving and organizing itself around this out-of-the-way spot, in tune
> with the intensity and inflexion of that puny praying figure. The
> convent chapel has become the axis about which the earth revolves.
> The contemplative sensitized and animated all things because she
> believed, and her faith was operative because her very pure soul
> placed her near to God. This piece of fiction is an admirable
> parable. If we could see the light invisible as we could see the clouds
> or lightning or rays of the sun, a pure soul would seem as active
> in this world by its sheer purity, as the snowy summits whose
> impassible peaks breathe in continually for us the roving of the
> high atmosphere.

There are, indeed, sensitives who can see 'the light invisible'. I myself know one who commonly does so; and on occasions the angels who accompany our worship. Being an artist he is able to portray what he sees. We affirm the angelic presence at every Eucharist, but it can be an encouragement to faith when it is made known through 'sight'. That is why I write it down here. Thomas was one who found that encouragement. Rather unfairly we single him out and call him 'doubting Thomas' as though he stood alone. But perhaps we should have had a doubting Peter if he had been absent, as was Thomas, when Jesus first appeared in the Upper Room. It may be that none would have stood the test. What we do have is the assurance of Jesus that those who have not seen and yet have believed are truly blessed.

The Curé spoke from his pulpit mainly of the love of God. We must believe that much is lost as his words are transferred to the printed page. The tears which flowed as he pleaded with his listeners to bathe themselves in that love cannot be recaptured. 'The interior life is like a bath of love wherein one plunges'. He likened the love of God to a flowing torrent sweeping everything in its course. As for our faults they are 'like a grain of sand beside the great mountain of the mercies of God'. And finally, 'A pure soul with God is like a child with its mother. It caresses her, it embraces her, and its mother returns its caresses and embraces'.[1]

From Ars I motored to the cathedral city of Albi in the South of France hoping to pick up some trace of Jean-Pierre de Caussade who, through his great book, *Abandonment to the Divine Providence*, had been a constant friend and companion over the past thirty years.

Caussade, who was born in Toulouse in 1675 and died in 1751, had served at least two periods in Albi, one as chaplain and the other as rector of a Jesuit college there. If I were to be asked which four books, other than the Bible, had most influenced my life, then Caussade's would have to be one of them. Of the other three one would be *The Cloud of Unknowing* written by an anonymous author in the second half of the fourteenth century; another *The Way of a Pilgrim*, the story of the *Jesus Prayer* told by a Russian peasant; and the other, and most of all, Mother Julian's *Revelations of Divine Love*. This, however, I came to much later in life.

Caussade's book is divided into two parts, the first being a treatise on abandonment which takes up little more than a quarter of the book. It is the second part, consisting of letters of spiritual direction to the Sisters of the Visitation at Nancy, which has held special appeal. It is here that Caussade becomes truly and spontaneously alive as heart speaks to heart in a series of about a hundred and fifty letters, all devoted more or less to one theme, yet without wearisome repetition, each letter having an individuality of its own. Unhappily the sisters' side of the correspondence has been lost and we are left to imagine their questions and ordeals through Caussade's replies. He writes warmly and encouragingly and rebukes tenderly when he finds the need to do so. One wonders how the sisters took some of his letters because on many occasions when they might have been expecting sympathy, he expressed undisguised delight at their trials because of the purification he can see God is working through them. They must have become quite accustomed to this and I have wondered whether they may sometimes have shared their letters in rueful merriment when such situations arose. One cannot doubt they loved him dearly and missed him greatly when his chaplaincy ended. I have edited a book for Burns and Oates, *The Fire of Divine Love*, which contains an introduction to Caussade's thoughts, and a hundred one-page extracts from his letters. Readers who relate with the passages below are likely to find that this book serves them well in the absence of the full book, which is out of print and not easy to obtain secondhand.

The cathedral at Albi was a delight but as for memory of Caussade, the reason for my visit, there I drew a blank. None of the few I was able to question had heard of him. He seems to have been a much neglected writer until recent times. And yet an authority such as Dom David Knowles writes that his name would have to appear in any list of the ten greatest spiritual directors since the time of St Bernard.

Here is a piece of wisdom from Caussade in the best tradition of spiritual direction. Is there any 'interior soul' (unfashionable phrase today!) who is not the better for being reminded of it from time to time?

> To be in no way astonished at our wretchedness is a good foundation for humility based upon self-knowledge: whilst to feel that wretchedness keenly and constantly, and yet to be untroubled by it, is a very great grace from which springs distrust of self and true and perfect trust in God.

'To be untroubled by it' – there's the rub, and the test of true humility. Humility encompasses every virtue yet itself is the most elusive of all. If you want it too eagerly you are exercising the very pride you hope to overcome. Francis de Sales has the answer: 'What do you think the bed of tribulation is? It is simply the school of humility.' Efforts to put on humility as a woman puts on a new dress are apt to backfire. It has to be put on for you, and what is more, you can't choose the design! Above all, as St Teresa says, humility is truth.

A favourite illustration of Caussade's has reference to dealing with distractions. I often quote it, but I have to go beyond it and think he would have been pleased. He tells us that we must let go of our distractions in prayer as we would let stones fall from our hands into the sea. We are not to fight them, but simply to let them drop away, and find their own way to the ocean bed. But, if only my distractions were like stones! Too often they are ping-pong balls which float around me, and remain somewhere in the periphery of my mind. Caussade would surely say we are to let them float and at all costs to resist the temptation to pick them up, but simply to wait, with the heart fixed on God, until the tide takes them away, when it will, as it will, if it will.

More than thirty years ago I made out a diary of short extracts from Caussade to cover a period of three months. I find I still have the selections and reproduce some.

> You say you do not know how to pray. Experience has taught me that persons of good will who speak in this way know better than others how to pray, because their prayer is more simple and humble but because of its simplicity it escapes their observation.

> Peace and tranquillity of mind alone give great strength to the soul to enable it to do all that God wishes ... while anxiety and uneasiness make the soul feeble and languid and as though sick.

> To escape the distress caused by regret for the past or fear about the future, this is the rule to follow; leave the past to the infinite mercy of God, the future to his good Providence, give the present wholly to his love by being faithful to his grace.

> These perpetual alternations of light and darkness, of consolation and desolation, are as useful, I should say as indispensable, for the growth and ripening of virtue in our souls, as the atmospheric changes are for the growth and ripening of the harvests.

> God permits your slight infidelities to give you a deeper conviction of your weakness, and gradually to destroy in you that unhappy self-esteem, presumption and secret self-confidence which would never otherwise allow you to acquire true humility of heart.

> We no longer expect anything more from self but only from Him alone. No longer do we count on our good works but solely on the mercy of God and the infinite merits of Jesus Christ; that is the true Christian hope which will be our salvation.

> You seem equally ignorant of this great principle, that usually more progress is made by suffering than by acting, and that to

take things patiently is to do a great deal, and especially to be patient with oneself.

I congratulate you that God has taken away some of your natural vivacity. The loss of your gaiety will only be temporary. It will return but completely changed or rather transformed into spiritual joy; quiet, tranquil and peaceful because it will be like that of the saints, in God and coming from God.

Things often go perfectly and then I return thanks to God for it. But sometimes everything goes wrong and then I bless him for that also and offer it as a sacrifice.

In the eyes of God violent temptations are great graces for those souls which by them suffer an interior martyrdom; they are the great battles in which great victories have made great saints.

You explain yourself in a manner which might be misunderstood by those who have no experience of this state of prayer (of recollection). You say that you do nothing ... but your soul acts so quietly that you do not perceive your own interior acts of assent and adhesion to the impression of the Holy Spirit.

I paid one more visit, this time to the L'Arche community on the site of the former village La Borie Noble in the hills above the south coast of France. The community was founded by a remarkable Italian, Lanzel del Vasto, who became a follower of Gandhi who gave him the name Shanti Das (Lover of peace). He was a fine looking man, a sculptor and musician, an ardent vegetarian and pacifist, and author of many books. In the cause of peace he had once fasted for forty days in Rome, and in protest against torture in Algeria he had fasted twenty days in France. I had interesting talks with him and was made most welcome by the community. There followed the long drive back to Calais which exhausted me as I did it in one day. And so to England, and on to Wantage to conduct a retreat based on my travels.

18

The Anchorhold and Bede House

I RETURNED FROM FRANCE in early September 1971 and, after spending the night with my brother Reg and Juliet in Winchester, I drove to Wantage to conduct the retreat for which my visit to France had prepared me. I then returned to Hilcot, Joan's home at Charmouth, which commanded a beautiful view of the surrounding Dorset country-side. It was a welcome base which Joan had all along made available to me, and her loving hospitality knew no bounds. But not all was well. I was developing back pains, probably brought on by a month's driving and camping in France, and eventually (in early November) it was considered I should see an osteopath, my one and only visit to this brand of healer. A blind man of high reputation was recommended but I was not to be one of his star patients. He felt me down, said 'Man, you've got a bloody back', put me in harness and worked on me with all his considerable strength. His wife appeared later, saw I was in no state to motor home, and together they gave me tea, and he kindly charged me no fee. His last words as I drove away that Friday evening were to be sure I did nothing strenuous over the weekend. But that was impossible. I had a sermon for the USPG (as the SPG was now named) on the Sunday morning, which meant motoring over a hundred miles the next day to spend the Saturday night with Reg and Juliet. In the pulpit I coughed – and slipped a disc. That cough or, more accurately, the events which led to it, surely changed the course of my life for I was due to return to India in a week and that was now out of the question.

As I have mentioned, the Indian Government did not allow clergy to return to India if they exceeded a leave period of six months. However, the Wantage Sisters in Poona were looking for an extension for me on compassionate grounds. Meanwhile the USPG had sent me to be treated as an outpatient at the Westminster Hospital, and the doctor promised that if I were prepared to lie long enough on my back I would get well.

So that is what I did under Joan's care at Charmouth, a masseuse coming in twice a week to help things along. It was during this period that I received a letter from Donald (Canon A.M.) Allchin of Westminster School days, who was now Warden of the Sisters of the Love of God at Fairacres in Oxford. He asked me if I would be free to consider accepting the post of Warden at one of their branch houses, Bede House, near Staplehurst in Kent. This thoroughly appealed to me, but I had to explain that the possibility of returning to India was still open. I think I had no doubt in my mind that the turn of events indicated I should now remain in England and, with the USPG doctor feeling strongly that I had done enough time overseas, I wrote to Wantage to explain and everything was amicably fixed up. Visits to Fairacres followed and the appointment was confirmed. I felt pleased and privileged, but inadequate in the extreme, especially as part of the task was the spiritual direction of two hermit sisters of the community for which I felt totally unequipped. It didn't matter. They looked to the Holy Spirit to do the real work. I just made it look proper and respectable.

By February 1972 I was markedly better and I thought it would be a good plan to ask Fr Slade ssje of the Anchorhold at Haywards Heath if he could accommodate me with the 'family' he had gathered together since his own long sojourn in India. I felt this would be a good preparation for my work at Bede House and so it turned out to be. Accordingly in March I went there, still a bit of an invalid, lying flat on the floor, I remember, during recreation times after lunch and supper. At that time there were about half a dozen people living a loosely knit community life with Fr Slade as their head. Fr Slade had been and still was, and is, my own spiritual director, and men and women would come down to the Anchorhold from all parts of the country to seek his counsel or stay for a few days. There was a balanced life of work and prayer. At that time we had three half-hour periods of silence each day, preceded by a ten-minute Office, and one or two shorter services in the chapel as well. Pottery, woodwork, gardening and work on the allotments nearby, together with domestic chores, took up most of the rest of the day, each working according to his gifts. Each would take it in turn to cook the supper, say the grace and be thanked by the others after the meal. For lunch we had the best homemade bread ever, with cheese and salad and fruit. It was a friendly and welcoming atmosphere and seemed to run without any rules. Although that can hardly have been so, there was nevertheless the freedom and friendship of family life.

June came and I moved to Bede House, taking up the post formerly occupied by Fr Wessinger SSJE of the American Cowley Fathers. He was about to return to the States to be their new superior. I was welcomed by Sister Jocelyn Mary who was Sister in charge. Although I was Warden it was she who, in Fr Wessinger's day, had come to do many of the expected wardenship duties such as the booking in of guests and the day-to-day running of the place. My part was to do the shopping in Staplehurst two miles off, to meet guests at the station a mile beyond and to be generally available to them during their stay. There was also the daily mass at seven o'clock (Sundays at eight together with a homily). How I strove at those homilies, wondering if I would ever have enough to nourish those ardent sisters' souls week after week and, for all I knew, year after year. I would also join the sisters at their daily Offices, except that I didn't attempt their night office for which they rose at two in the morning returning to bed at about three.

After a short while my car packed up and I needed another. I happened to see one advertised in the Staplehurst post office for fourteen pounds and learnt that the notice had only just been put up. So I went at all speed to the owner's house, found what looked to be a real old-fashioned MG, built when leather seats were made of leather (I have no other clue to its age) and asked if I might take it for a spin. As I pressed the self-starter the hooter sounded, but apart from that embarrassing feature it seemed to be in good shape and had an MOT for almost a year. Returning to the house twenty minutes later I found a queue assembling for the bargain of the year. It was now or never, so I handed over the fourteen pounds and drove off. The sisters were shocked, amazed and delighted and one of them leapt into the car and drove it up the road (in the heat of the moment they had forgotten they were an enclosed community) and pronounced it fine. For a mere eight pounds the minor defects were remedied and I would often use it to transport sisters to and from the mother house in Oxford. We all felt so safe and comfortable in that car and it was only when it went for its next MOT that I learnt it might have dropped any of us onto the road at any time. The sisters were, I think, relieved that I was able to invest a little more in the replacement.

Bede House is an idyllic place. It was founded by Mother Mary Clare of Fairacres in conjunction with Father Gilbert Shaw in 1966. Set in the heart of the Kent countryside, its grounds of several acres are dotted with Colt houses, one of which is for the warden, two for the hermit sisters and the others for guests. The 'working' sisters (cenobitic to use the correct word) live in a charming old farmhouse which is close to the chapel and library set in a converted oast house. Not that the hermits were not 'working'. Most of our visitors knew what we were about, but there were the romantic few who would say to me, 'O father, how I'd love to be a hermit'. I would explain what they did, beginning with their rising time at three and their two hours gardening before breakfasting at eight. Before I had gone much further they had decided that their spiritual journey lay elsewhere. I remember our builder, Mr Cramp, saying to me, that if he could find one able-bodied man of forty prepared to work half as hard as 'that old lady over there' (pointing to hermit sister Mary Teresa in her seventies digging indefatigably in the garden) his business worries would be over. Please don't let me ever hear that enclosed sisters have an easy life!

Colt houses are small and, since they are wooden, the inner and outer temperatures almost keep pace with one another. But mine was a comfortable little house and suited my needs ideally at the time. It had a wee kitchenette with a miniature fridge and stove. Lunch was in the farmhouse and a dish for supper was brought over by the sisters. There was an alarm bell in each Colt house for fire or other emergencies. One unenlightened guest thought it was to summon the sisters for his early morning tea and was somewhat embarrassed to hear the whole compound become alive with bells. In monastic circles there is a hoary story of a guest who was awakened with a knock on the door and the customary 'Dominus tecum'. Instead of replying 'And with thy spirit' (in Latin) he called out, 'Leave it on the mat'.

Shortly after taking up my work at Bede House in 1972 I was asked to give the Lenten lectures in Canterbury Cathedral. I took as the subject *Prayer and Contemplation* and this became my first book, published by the SLG Press at Fairacres. Later it became part of a trilogy in America with contributions from Mother Mary Clare and Metropolitan Anthony Bloom and then was taken over by Marshall Pickering who to their embarrassment spelt my name wrongly on the cover. And thus it went back to Fairacres. It never made any headlines and I am not aware that it received a review but I am told it continues to meet a need and one could not wish for more.

There isn't much I can say about my time at Bede House. It doesn't advertise, leaving itself to be discovered by individuals who want a quiet time for reflection and prayer. There were no groups coming for retreat, and in any case it cannot take more than half a dozen night guests at a time. Occasionally there would be Quiet Days and sometimes I would be away conducting a retreat, but for the most part each day went on as the one before. Visitors were, of course, changing all the time, few coming for more than a week, and that meant meeting a number of interesting people throughout the year. I valued it specially for the opportunities it gave for an ordered life of prayer and worship within the setting of community life and for the contacts it provided with Fairacres, where I would often spend a few days. Mother Mary Clare was superior at first, later to be followed by Mother Jane. It was the latter I knew best and many a time I motored her to or from Bede House. These were times of exhilarating conversation and she was a great companion. The Fairacres sisters are holy people and I always felt this to be especially so of Mother Jane. Later she suffered a long-drawn-out and painful illness, borne, I was told, with great patience and courage, until her death several years ago. I used to think I had a special place in her heart, but probably it's like having a special place in the heart of God; you share it with everyone else.

I mentioned just now that I met interesting people and I will talk about two of them. One was Patricia Jenner, a policewoman (now retired) in the Maidstone force. She was pronouncedly psychic, and occasionally would see a monk in medieval garb in the Bede House garden or chapel. One day she was visiting us by bus and I had to meet her at the stop two miles off. That afternoon I had her visit in mind, but dozed off in my armchair. I was awakened by a clear call: 'Father Robert'. The meeting at the bus stop at once came to mind, but to my surprise there was no one in the room who had come to remind me. I looked at my watch and found I was already five minutes late. Ordinarily I would have dashed to the car in the parking area, and driven faster than usual to meet the beleaguered guest. But I looked upon this as something special and told myself everything would be all right if I proceeded at my usual pace. The bus and I arrived at precisely the same moment. Later I wondered if it was a telepathic communication I had received. After all, the Lord would hardly call me father! Either way, the timing was perfect.

One day Patricia told us of a danger spot on Bluebell Hill, a few miles from Maidstone. Several years before, on the day before she was due to be married, a young woman travelling with three friends had met with an accident at this spot and she (with two friends) had been killed. Now she was said to be returning to the scene. She would stand in the path of an oncoming car causing the driver to swerve, and accidents had followed. On one occasion (but I should say I have only a newspaper report for this, though I don't rule out its truth) a driver, seeing the young woman, stopped and gave her a lift, only to find a few miles later that she was no longer there. The police were worried about the whole affair, and Patricia wondered if we could do something about it.

One morning at 6.30 Sister Jocelyn Mary, hermit sister Mary Teresa, Patricia and I set off in my car for the scene of the accident. As dawn was breaking I celebrated a Eucharist, and we prayed that the earthbound ties might be cut and that the young woman might find peace. It was a moving occasion and I think we all felt that what we prayed and hoped for had been done. There were no further reports of appearances during my time at Bede House and, indeed, not for a further fifteen or more years, but then (according to a newspaper report) a lorry driver 'ran over' a young woman at this same spot but could find no trace of a body. If the report is accurate it is a corrective to our hopes and expectations. One can offer no explanation to the recurrence of the events after so long a lapse of time. However, whatever be the truth, one does not need to assume that the young woman has not long since been at peace. Such happenings are often explicable as place memories which may fasten themselves on to and occasionally reveal themselves in places where overwhelmingly strong emotions have been experienced.

Another visitor I recall was Dr Martin Israel. Martin is an immensely psychic person but as, once again, in his case the psychic is wholly subsumed in the spiritual, that can only be for the good. He is a writer of great spiritual depth and one feels he writes as he speaks, the Holy Spirit giving him the necessary power of expression. It seems that he never has to prepare a talk: the words flow for a full hour without notes or hesitation. Apart from his writing and one-to-one pastoral work in his house, Martin is an assiduous retreat conductor and was, until recently, a parish priest. His retreats are fully booked almost as soon as they are announced and if you want an interview you have to put your name down as soon as possible after the list goes up. Beyond all this is the unseen work in prayer, and many a soul who has passed over, and no doubt many who remain, must have cause to be grateful to him. Alas (one speaks in human terms), his health has been sacrificed to his work. His friends now pray that by listening to his doctors he may have many years ahead in which his remarkable gifts may be exercised. I first met Martin when he came to talk to the sisters in (I think) 1973. I was there on Staplehurst station as he arrived on the train from London. Martin is a person of little small talk and it was obvious he wanted to be quiet as I drove him to Bede House. Shortly before we arrived he turned to me, and with great feeling said, 'Those poor people on the train; they had such muddy auras. There must be a lot of suffering ahead.' He meant, of course, the suffering of purging and cleansing, however experienced, before we are ready for the fuller vision of God. Later, I mischievously wondered if I had polished up my own aura that day. Perhaps he had been peeping at it before he spoke. Certainly, when I next met him he had taken a look, as he told it to a friend who told me. We all have these auras and they reveal whether we throw out gold or garbage for others to feed on in the atmosphere around us. Since none of us are saints or demons it must necessarily be somewhere in between and the proportion in which the ingredients are mixed raises or lowers the temperature of the spiritual climate in which we live. I expect we all know the difference between the 'spiritual temperature' in, say, the Holy House at Walsingham and a London railway station in the rush hour. Animals, too, pick up this psychic atmosphere. Tail-wagging and welcoming dogs usually come from happy and friendly homes, whereas those which slink furtively down the street at their master's heels are likely to have quite a different background.

For about twenty years I used to sleep on the floor. I got into the habit after slipping a disc, it being the only place where I was moderately pain-free. Then I found it gave me such good relaxation that I decided not to take to a bed again (though I am grateful for one now). Sleeping on the floor has many unexpected advantages. You get a good relaxation, you save the space of a bed, you have a bedside table all around you from which nothing can fall off, and when anyone says they're sorry they haven't a bed, you simply say that you don't need one. But it did mean taking one's bedding round, which included a light roll-up type mattress. However, it gave one's hosts no problem.

Speaking of relaxation, it was at Fairacres that I met Ursula Fleming whose work lay in teaching the art to numerous groups throughout the country. Once we did a day in St Alban's Cathedral together, she doing the relaxation part and I the worship and address. I think about fifty came. The chairs were cleared and all lay down on the cathedral floor, having brought their own rugs. Ursula supplied broom handles which relaxees laid beneath their spines, often with many mock protests and groans. This allowed the shoulders and other overlapping bits of the body to fall down to the floor. After ten minutes the broom sticks were removed, marking the end of the preparation stage. There was another half-hour to come whilst Ursula encouraged the group to let go more and more. Everyone would get up looking wonderfully refreshed. I had come across this practice in India (without the broom handles) and Ursula taught me more. For those who want to know more, Geoffrey Harding's book *On lying down in Church*[1] could be a good teacher. The author was, in his later years, vicar of a City of London church and used to teach businessmen in their lunch hour how to enjoy a relaxed twenty minutes on his church floor.

Relaxation is not itself prayer but it may be an admirable preparation for prayer. In itself it is neutral, a-moral as the moralists call it. A relaxed fireman on the roof will be better equipped to enter the skylight and rescue the old lady than his tense colleague. A relaxed cat-burglar will likewise be better equipped to steal her purse. But there has to be a degree of tension in all we do. The art of relaxation is to gather the tension only into the muscles we need for the work before us. When you lie flat on your back on a hard surface then, short of using drugs, the deepest relaxation may be achieved. If instead you lie on a soft bed then, to quote Ursula Fleming, the bed relaxes and not you. However, a firm bed can give you a good relaxation though not quite as good as the floor.

Although relaxation is not itself prayer, it becomes prayer as soon as the intention to pray is present. There can be no prayer apart from the desire for God, and when in a modest way I teach people to relax, I like them to use prayers of surrender which correspond with what they are doing with the body. 'Casting all your care upon him', 'Underneath are the everlasting arms', 'Into your hands I commend my spirit', suggest themselves for this purpose. It is interesting to note that St Ignatius of Loyola and the Benedictine Father Augustine Baker both give lying flat on the back as one possible posture for prayer. No doubt they recognised the value of the relaxing component in such a position.

Some people need a low pillow to help them but it is important that it is the neck which is supported, the head then lying back on the pillow. Or a neck pillow does well. A cushion under the knees raising them just slightly is also a help.

It looks so simple but there is an art in relaxation and it needs practice. You lie down on your back and just let all your muscles go limp. Two or three deep breaths may help to make a good start but after that you let the body look after its own breathing. Some teachers advise tightening various muscles one by one and then suddenly releasing them. I will not attempt to speak of it as I have not used it much. I was taught to talk gently to my muscles, not harshly or they will rebel. They have to be coaxed. You say to the muscles in your right arm, 'Let go, that's good, yes just go on slowly, slowly letting go'. And you feel them doing so. Then you attend to the hands and the fingers one by one in the same way. You do the same for the other arm. After this you may go through the whole body putting your awareness into one point after another and shifting the point of focus every two or three seconds. You go right down to the toes and then up again to the neck, the jaw, the facial muscles, the eyes, the brow and the crown of the head. (The exercise can be done at any time but a ten-minute period as you get into bed at night can make an excellent preparation for a good night's sleep. Those who suffer from insomnia could be greatly helped here.) Signs of relaxation are that the body feels warmer and heavier and as if wanting to sink into the floor or bed. Another sign: raise your arm keeping your elbow on the floor. Let it fall freely and see if the hand bounces which shows the relaxation is good. The bounce tests the freedom of the fall.

After a while thoughts will float into the consciousness: amongst them may be fears, memories, very likely painful ones because those are the ones we tend to repress in waking life. This is the demanding part. You don't argue with them, you don't reject them, you don't encourage them, you don't follow them, you drop them into the arms of God and, if they insist on floating on the periphery of the mind, you let them float. Here you can say prayers such as I have suggested. You may very well want to get up at this point. The way forward is to see it through. Each session like this is a healing experience and, as you relax day after day, the situation will change and what used to trouble you will bother you less and, hopefully, in the end not at all. But if you simply *have* to get involved with your thoughts, and fear and agitation are winning it is best to cut the period short and go to it another time. You haven't lost; something will have been gained. If all goes well, you will rise from a half-hour period wonderfully refreshed and prepared for the task ahead of you. Ursula Fleming was in her early days an accomplished pianist, but became so overcome with fright before an audience that she became quite incapacitated. She used to tell her relaxation pupils that she simply had to take to the practice if her work was to continue. In the latter part of her life she became a keen student of Meister Eckhart. Her relatively early death a few years ago was a shock to all who knew her.

Whilst on the subject, the flat back position is an excellent moment for dropping thoughts or affirmations into the unconscious. Relaxation helps them to penetrate the superficial layers of consciousness and to take root deeply within. Julian of Norwich is rich in thoughts suited to this time as the final chapter of this book will reveal.

After three years I felt it right to move on from Bede House. I thought that my hundred and fifty or so homilies had given the sisters all that I was capable of giving. They were wonderfully patient: I must have repeated myself so often. I am not at all good at talking to set subjects as one has to do through the liturgical year. Sometimes it was easy; sometimes I toiled all night (almost) and caught nothing. But they usually seemed to catch something, breathing life into my inadequate words or perhaps just exercising patience. They knew in their bones one of life's deepest secrets: that all failures and contradictions, sufferings and disappointments, even sins and evils, can be turned to good account if only we can accept them patiently and, yet more, thankfully, offering them with such love and devotion as may be given us. It has been well said that the tragedy of life is not suffering but that we fail to use suffering creatively. Patience is not that passive virtue we sometimes assume it to be, but is that heroic quality of life which makes suffering creative. Whereas impatience, by contrast, is that which makes suffering a destructive force. To write these things is not difficult but to make them one's own in the deepest layers of the personality is the work of a lifetime. One might truthfully add that it is for this, above all else, that a lifetime is given.

19

Ibiza and the Rosary

THIS CHAPTER WILL BE short on memory and long on reflection. I want to talk of the rosary which is a form of prayer I believe many Catholics would do well to get back to and many Anglicans and others would be glad to discover. It was shortly after leaving Bede House in 1975 that I discovered the rosary and not until several years later that I began to use it. I have found it to be what Austin Farrar used to call it, a heaven-sent blessing, especially where I can say it with others, devoting perhaps twenty minutes to its use and then fifteen minutes to the silence before God to which it leads.

After leaving Bede House I felt in need of a sabbatical year and this was kindly arranged for me by Lady Hyde Parker whom I had known as an oblate of the Sisters of the Love of God during my time at Bede House. Ulla invited me to spend a year at Melford Hall in Long Melford, offering me accommodation in the central wing of this National Trust country house. She herself lived in a second wing and her son Sir Richard Hyde Parker with his wife Jean in the third. So we weren't exactly crowded! The chapel was in my wing and Ulla and I would meet there daily for Eucharist or Office. The downstairs part of my wing was open to visitors and I would have to pass in full view of them as I took my afternoon tea on a tray from Ulla's pantry to my rooms. I was amused to see them stop and stare and murmur that that must be the butler.

The butler had in fact left shortly before I came. I was much relieved as I did not think I would have been able to live up to his high standards. I should, perhaps, explain that sartorially I have never been a great success and my choice in ties might have been as erratic as Wooster's under the eye of the ever-watchful Jeeves. Moreover my table etiquette had been modified by many years in India. Burton, if I may so call him, once came to Ulla in a state of shock after discovering Richard and Jeannie behaving in distinctly dubious taste during afternoon tea. 'My lady,' he said, in visible distress, 'do you know what I saw Sir Richard and Lady Hyde Parker doing?', reminding her one way and another, in mounting concern, that all through the years they had stood only for the highest standards of propriety. It was not long before Ulla herself was in shock, wondering what dreadful scandal was about to descend on that hallowed seat. Eventually, after much prompting, Burton yielded up the awful truth. 'They were eating doughnuts.'

Ulla had a spacious house in Ibiza and in August 1975 I spent several weeks there with her, her daughter Beth with her husband Thomas, and their family of four. Ulla and I used sometimes to go to evening mass at the church serving a small fishing port a few miles from her house. We would arrive perhaps ten minutes before the service to find the men on one side and the women on the other reciting the rosary, each side answering the other. I was so ignorant, even at that stage in my life, that I did not know what was happening. But this I did know: that a deep reverence prevailed in that simple peasant church and that the mass which followed was a contemplative experience for most of us. It was that which drew me to the rosary and later I was instructed in its use. I have written a book on the rosary, given talks to Catholics, Anglicans and Methodists about it, and I run two ecumenical rosary groups so that most people think it has been with me all my life. But that is not so. It all began in that faraway fishing port in Ibiza.

Space allows me to speak here only in general terms. I think that what I write will be intelligible to those who are not acquainted with the rosary, but for a description of its use I would ask them to turn to a friend or buy one of the many small books or cards available in Catholic shops and sometimes elsewhere. There they will find simple instructions on the rosary and the fifteen mysteries (biblical scenes) associated with it. Here I will just write down the Hail Mary, which is a prayer said fifty-three times in a chaplet of the rosary, fifty of which are in groups of ten said on the five decades. The Hail Mary runs: 'Hail Mary, full of grace, the Lord is with thee; blessed art thou among women and blessed is the fruit of thy womb, Jesus. Holy Mary, Mother of God, pray for us sinners, now, and at the hour of our death.'

Let me begin by saying that there is only one way in which we can pray and that is to pray with the heart. By the heart I mean the innermost core of the personality. It cannot be described but I think the reader will understand what I mean. Call it the will or the desire if you like. But, you will say, surely we can pray with the lips. No, we can't. Or with the eyes, looking at icons, for example. Again, no. Or with the ears, listening to the choir singing an anthem? No, once again. Or with the nose, as when incense is used in a church service? Wrong again. Or with the touch such as when we finger rosary beads? Absolutely not. Let me repeat: there is only one way to pray and that is with the heart. The lips, the eyes and the ears, the nose and the touch, may be a great help to prayer because, and only because, they help to move the heart. But no opening and closing of the lips, no movements of the tongue, no looking upon icons or listening to music, no smelling of incense or fingering of beads, are in themselves prayer. Their value lies entirely on their capacity to arouse the heart. Computers can be programmed to say the Hail Mary but, since they have no heart, they cannot pray.

The rosary is a means by which the lips and the touch and the ears (when in a group), and in varying degrees, the imagination (as in meditating upon the mysteries) are used to move the heart to prayer. Other instruments may be used as a means of stirring the heart: icons, architecture, flowers, scenery, music, chants, silence, Office, the list could go on and on. The rosary is simply one instrument, but one which I believe many would be glad to discover. There are many ways of saying it. You can say it aloud or silently or simply by moving the beads meditatively through your fingers. You can say it by listening to a tape. That is the way I often use when alone. Some people say that that is the lazy person's way of using the rosary. You get it said for you. Not a bit of it. The best way to say the rosary is the way in which it most effectively moves the heart to prayer. And for many people listening to a rosary tape assists that more than reciting the words. So in saying the rosary ask only: Which way helps most to move the heart to prayer?

Once, on the radio, I said that you can say the rosary, if you wished, with your feet, and I went on to explain what I meant. Unfortunately the editor cut out that last bit and left listeners wondering how they could manipulate the rosary beads on their toes. I must have seemed a right ninny. But I was talking sense. I was thinking, as I explained, of a Catholic priest who had come to see me, who said he had been praying an abridged rosary with his feet from the railway station to the Julian Cell. In each set of eight paces he said, Ho-ly Je-sus, Ho-ly Ma-ry. As he put down each foot, saying in his mind the corresponding syllable, he was uniting his heart again to God, living in a succession of present moments. That is a very good way of saying the rosary, or for that matter of using many other prayers. If the heart is moved to prayer that is all that matters.

It is an exercise in celebrating the sacrament of the present moment, a phrase which was, so far as I know, first used by Jean-Pierre de Caussade. That is what I meant when I said on *Woman's Hour* that you can say the rosary with your feet.

In early Christian days pebbles were often used to count the number of prayers recited and from that custom a string of knots or beads evolved. Today we have the mass produced machine-made product conforming to an accepted pattern, easily available, at least in the western world. The instrument of the rosary keeps the prayer on course, divides it into elements which can be handled one by one as the mysteries are covered, and acts as an encouragement to see the prayer through until the end.

This is important. But important, too, is the help the rosary may give in enlisting the sense of touch as an aid to prayer. Probably most readers have experienced how sight or sound may be a help to prayer. Touch, too, may help, but for many that is a discovery yet to be made.

I recall a psychiatrist writing how he would sometimes prescribe for his patients an exercise in awareness to be practised for five or ten minutes several times a day. For this period the patient would consciously reflect on everything he was doing. 'Now I am getting up from my chair, now I am walking to the door, I am opening it, I am taking steps into the kitchen, one, two, three, four, five, I am turning on the tap, warm water is flowing over my hands', and so on. This was to help the person to become centred, to gather in the dissipated energies of the mind. There are probably times when most of us would be helped by an exercise of this sort and the rosary offers just such an exercise. Leaving aside the recitation of the Hail Mary, which we shall come to shortly, we may be helped to the recollection of our scattered minds, simply by moving gently round the rosary, holding the beads one by one, and allowing our awareness to go into what we are doing. For this particular moment my whole consciousness is gathered into the holding of this particular bead with such devotion and attention as may be given me. As my fingers pass through each successive bead I am drawn into the action, the distractions of the outer world lose their hold, the mind is stilled, and gradually I become receptive to what God may have for me. Often this can be done, not at the set times of prayer but, for example, when out walking, allowing the rosary in the pocket to slip through the fingers, each new bead being a new point of awareness. Sometimes we may combine the action with prayer on each bead, at other times it may be the intention alone which is sufficient.

Let us now turn to the saying of the Hail Mary. For some not brought up in the Catholic tradition this can be a problem. Let it be noted, however, that the first part of the Hail Mary is purely scriptural. The words are a combination of the words of the angel of the annunciation to Mary, and of those of Elizabeth to Mary when Mary visited her in the hill country near Jerusalem. To these words the Church has added only the word *Jesus*. So, whatever our background, there can be no problem there.

It is the second half which may present a difficulty. 'Holy Mary, mother of God, pray for us sinners, now, and at the hour of our death.' The words 'mother of God' are intended to say something about Jesus, not about Mary. They mean, simply, 'mother of Jesus, Son of God' and so witness to the divinity as well as the humanity of Jesus. But the words are offered directly to Mary which raises the theological question of whether we may call upon the saints directly for their prayers. By far the larger part of the Church (the Roman Catholic and the Orthodox) have answered yes, and would claim that experience shows that it makes for an enrichment of the doctrine of the communion of saints expressed in all our creeds.

However, for those for whom the direct invocation of Mary is insuperable, the rosary in its traditional form has to be ruled out. But all is not lost. I ask them to bear with me until the end of the chapter. The instrument of the rosary remains and may still be enlisted as a help to prayer. I see the instrument of the rosary as a piano and the Hail Mary as a tune. If you are uneasy with any particular tune you do not get rid of your piano. An infinite number of tunes may be prayed on the instrument of the rosary, and the same pattern of Creed, Our Fathers, and Glory be-s may be used as before. For example, you could use this Jesus rosary, 'Blessed be Jesus, true God and true man; blessed be the name of Jesus. Jesus, son of Mary, have mercy on us, now, and at the hour of our death.' It can be used with the traditional mysteries, apart from the last two for which might be substituted the Transfiguration and the second coming of Christ; our own transfiguration into the likeness of Christ is what the rosary is ultimately about.[1]

I speak now to those who do not have a problem with the Hail Mary. The first part is an act of blessing, which is closely linked to praise and thanksgiving, all of which are of such importance in prayer. In another chapter I hope to talk more about that. And the second part is a prayer of intercession for ourselves and others. We simply ask Mary, who can see our needs so much more clearly than we can ourselves, to pray for us, or the person or cause we have at heart. How easy it is for the element of condescension or patronage to creep into intercessory prayers! The Hail Mary cuts through all that. 'Pray for us sinners', we say, putting ourselves down at the same level of dependence and need as the one for whom we pray. None of us can know where we would be without our advantages, our upbringing, our opportunities and especially the grace of God. If we like, instead of using the mysteries for the rosary we can name one person for intercession on each bead before the Hail Mary is said. I myself believe that God is using Mary very much in these days as a helper and intercessor throughout the world. In the next chapter we shall come to a powerful example of this.

Repetition in prayer is a problem for some people and the rosary can present a difficulty on that account. They recall how Jesus said we were not to use vain repetitions. But the operative word is *vain*. Life is full of repetitions. The steps when we walk, the rotation of the wheels of a car, the stitch after stitch in knitting are obvious examples. The question to ask is whether they are vain. If the wheels of the car are on an uphill icy road and just race round and round you could say that the rotations are indeed vain, and the driver will soon give up. If I walk step after step to church, then the steps are not vain, for each takes me closer to the altar of God: which is an easily translatable parable in the realm of prayer. As I go round the rosary, each Hail Mary serves ever so little to deepen the uniting of my heart with God. And strictly speaking there is no repetition, for each prayer is made from a slightly different vantage point from the one before. At the end of a round (known as a chaplet) of the rosary you are prepared for a silence before God, which you were not ready for when the prayer began. It is the frequent repetitions (as we call them) which have done this.

I have found it helpful to see vocal prayer like this. See the words as the banks of a river and the prayer, that is to say the inclination of the heart to God, as the river itself. The banks are very important because they keep the river deep, and they keep it flowing. But it is the river which really matters. So, too, it is the uniting of the heart with God in prayer which really matters; the words simply help to that end. The parable may be taken further. When the river reaches the sea the banks are no longer needed and drop away, and we are left in the silence in the ocean of God's love.

So we should not be afraid of repetitions. So long as we are saying the rosary with such sincerity of heart as God may give us, all is well. He asks no more.

Now I would like to say a word to those who are more experienced in the saying of the rosary. Do not be alarmed if the mysteries tend to drop away. This means that the rosary is becoming what it should be, namely an instrument of contemplative prayer. The rosary is a wonderful instrument because it meets us where we are. If we are in the way of discursive meditation, it meets us there as we let our minds rest lightly on the mysteries as we pass through them. If we are in the way of affective prayer, which is the bridge between meditation and contemplation, it meets us there as we pour out our devotion before God. And if we are in the way of contemplation it again meets us as we let go of the mysteries, being simply dimly aware of the mystery we are passing through. By this time the material of the mysteries has so soaked into our beings that we can't help receiving the virtue of them, even if we have little or no consciousness in the mind. So it is good to remember that rosary prayer works first at the relatively superficial level in holding before the mind material for meditative reflection but that later, and more importantly, it frees the mind for engagement at a deeper level. At this stage the emerging, unfolding and deeper self is encountered and new energies of the spirit are released.

A final word of advice. Allow the prayer to do its own work. At first you must pray. But later you may allow yourself 'to be prayed'. At the beginning of prayer our consciousness is in holding on to God. Later we are enabled to rest in the knowledge that he is holding on to us. And that is the better part of prayer.

I began with the help I received from peasant folk. Let me end with this beautiful description from the French writer, Maréchal, of a peasant woman telling her beads before the cottage hearth.

> The monotony of these repetitions clothes [her] with physical peace
> and recollection, and her soul already directed on high, almost
> mechanically, by her habitual gesture of drawing out the rosary,
> immediately opens up with increasing serenity on unlimited
> perspectives, felt rather than analysed, which converge on God.
> What does it matter then if the [humble soul] does not concern
> herself with living over and over again the exact meaning of the
> formula which she is repeating. Often she does better; she allows
> herself to rise freely into a true contemplation, well worn and

obscure, uncomplicated, unsystematized, alternated with a return of attention to the words she is muttering, but building up in the long run, on the mechanical basis they afford, a higher purified personal prayer.

20

Medjugorje (1)

MEDJUGORJE (Mej-oo-gori-ay) is a small village of about four hundred houses situated in the former Yugoslavia some fifteen miles south of Mostar. Until recent times it was scarcely known outside its own mountainous area towards the south of Bosnia-Hercegovina. Then in the summer of 1981 an event took place on one of its surrounding hills which has put the village into the history book for ever. Since then it is estimated that twenty million people from virtually every country in the world have flown or driven or trekked to Medjugorje, some no doubt out of curiosity, but most in search of a closer walk with God. As with Lourdes in 1858 and Fatima in 1917, the Virgin Mary visited and, at the time of writing, still visits this remote little village.

Mary is said to have appeared first on St John the Baptist's Day, 24 June 1981. (I shall in what follows drop the term 'is said', and the like, because it is tedious, and in any case I write as a firm believer that the claims of Medjugorje are true.) 'I have come', Mary explained, 'to tell the world that God exists and that he loves you. He is fullness of life, and to enjoy this fullness and obtain peace, you must return to God.'

On that special day in 1981, Ivanka, then a girl of fifteen, was walking with her sixteen-year-old friend Mirjana towards Podbrdo Hill, the pasture ground for the sheep. All of a sudden she looked up and, seeing the form of a young woman, cried out, 'Look, the Gospa', Gospa being the Croatian for Our Lady. 'Why should the Gospa appear to us?' asks Mirjana, who also sees the figure. Nevertheless they are shaken and tell their parents of what they have seen.

That same evening the two girls return to fetch the sheep and once again the Gospa is there. In bewilderment they stand and stare. At that moment sixteen-year-old Vicka (Vitska) comes along the path, and the girls summon her excitedly. Vicka, supposing they have seen a snake, runs to join them. She then sees the shining figure, panics, kicks off her shoes and runs for dear life. However, she soon recovers her composure and rejoins her friends. Just then, sixteen-year-old Ivan passes by carrying a bag of apples. Seeing the apparition, he drops the apples and takes to his heels. These four are so shaken and excited that that evening they cannot but tell their families and neighbours. Not surprisingly, no one takes them seriously, and many laugh at them.

Their convictions, however, are not shaken, and on the next day the four teenagers return to the same place accompanied by a few friends who believed their story. Among them were Marija, a girl of sixteen, and Jacov, a boy of ten. The Gospa is waiting for them though it is only the six whose names I have mentioned who are able to see her. Her arms are outstretched in a gesture of welcome. They run to her at great speed and on reaching her they weep with emotion and then kneel down to pray. Ivanka, whose mother died two months before, ventures to ask how she is. The lady assures her she is well and happy. On the Gospa being asked if she will return the next day she says that she will.

On the third day, Friday, Vicka, ever practical, sprinkles the vision with holy water, saying, 'If you are the Mother of God, stay; if not, go.' The lady smiles.

On the fourth day, the Yugoslavian Communist authorities, greatly worried by the rumours in circulation, take the children off for interrogation and medical examination. They are declared healthy and well.

On the fifth day, police and soldiers are present when the six see the apparition, which is not visible to others. Fifteen thousand people have assembled and the police are powerless.

On the sixth day, a plot is hatched. The authorities decide to give the children a 'treat'. They are taken for a long drive by two social workers so that they won't be back in time for the apparition. The ruse fails as the lady is seen coming towards the children. At their insistence, surprisingly, the car is stopped, and the children bundle out and drop to their knees. The escorting women see nothing and light their cigarettes, quickly to be extinguished when a light envelops them all. When Fr Jozo questions them all later he says the stunned expression on the faces of the communist women made them more eloquent witnesses than the children themselves.

So it all began. Fr Jozo was parish priest at the time but was away conducting a retreat during those first few days. On his return he interviewed the children extensively and was unable to believe their story. Crowds were increasing all the time and the police believed it was all a put-up show, a camouflage to disguise a coming revolution. Finally Jozo came to believe. On 2 July he was sitting praying in the parish church when he suddenly heard a voice telling him to go outside and protect the children. He went immediately to the church door, and while his hand was still on the handle the children rushed up, grabbed hold of him and begged for help, calling out that the police were after them. He took them inside and hid them until the danger had passed. After that he came to believe absolutely in the visions and has since been one of the visionaries' staunchest supporters. A month or so later he was sent for by the Communist police at Sarajevo and warned that if he did not denounce the apparitions as spurious he would be sent to prison. He remained faithful and was sentenced to a term of three and a half years, but served less than two years after wide international protest.

The remarkable thing about the Medjugorje visions is their extent. They have already continued virtually daily to four of the visionaries, which means that each has received more than five thousand apparitions. In the course of the apparitions the visionaries are each being given ten secrets, relating partly to themselves and partly to future events in the world. Some warn of disasters which must overtake the world apart from a radical return to God. That much is known. But Mary also warns that we are not to dwell on these horrors for 'the only attitude of the Christian toward the future is hope of salvation.' If we think about evil and war, she tells us, we are on the way towards them. 'Your task is to accept divine peace, to live it and to spread it.' Mirjana and Ivanka received all ten secrets in about the first two years and after that their daily visions ceased, though Mary still comes to them at special times. The other four have each received nine secrets. It is generally assumed that the visions will end when all have received the full ten. The visionaries are extraordinarily adroit in keeping the secrets, which people try to wheedle out of them. One has, in fact, given her nine secrets away in a moment of helplessness under hypnotism, to which she agreed in the interest of the investigations. The hypnotist, when rebuked for invading another's conscience, said the secrets were as safe with him as those received in the confessional. It is hard to justify his action but it does add evidence to the existence of the secrets, if that be needed.

The manner of the visions appears to be similar to the way in which the apostles saw the risen Christ in the forty days after the resurrection. The visionaries hear Mary speak in the same way as we hear one another speak and at first they were surprised that no one else could hear Mary.

They speak to her as they speak to one another. You can see their lips moving during an apparition but you hear nothing. They report that they see Mary as they see anybody else. They touch her on occasions and, with her permission, have sometimes embraced her. They ask her questions and receive her replies. Once in the early days, ten-year-old Jakov asked her if Zagreb Dynamos would win their football match; on which occasion she simply smiled.

The visionaries have been medically examined by teams from all over the world. The most recent report of which I have knowledge was published in 1993 recording the findings of Michael Petrides, director of a psychiatric clinic in Connecticut. It is of sufficient interest to quote in full. I have taken it from *The Children of Medjugorje* of February 1997. It runs:

> Five alleged visionaries tested were found to simultaneously look at precisely the same spot (even though no reference point was visible) within one-fifth of a second of each other when the Blessed Virgin Mary allegedly appears. Such synchronization can only be explained by some external 'object' holding their gaze – but one which those around them could not see. During the same one-fifth of a second there are simultaneous kneeling and succession of eye movements. There is no eye movement during the entire apparition (from 3 to 45 minutes). There is also the simultaneous raising of their heads and gazing upwards while remaining fixated on a spot moving upwards when the apparition is finishing.
>
> Two of the alleged visionaries do not blink at all during the apparition. The eyeball normally dries when there is no regular blinking (15–20 times a minute) to moisten the cornea, but lacrymal secretion does not seem necessary during the apparition. The other alleged visionaries blink at about half the normal rate. None of them blinks in response to the touching of the eye during the apparition (cornea sensitivity to varying pressures is completely absent), although they blink normally at other times.
>
> There is no reaction to pain during the apparition. When touched with an algometer, which causes a cutaneous lesion or skin burn, there was complete absence of sensitivity. The alleged visionaries react normally to pain at other times.
>
> The interesting results of a hearing test before and during an apparition showed normal hearing, but during an apparition

an input of ninety decibels (equivalent to a loud explosion) showed *no* reaction. Auditory evoked potential measurement (electrical activity of the ear) indicates normal ear activity with no transmission to the inner ear during the apparition. It is a measurable inhibition of hearing that is involuntary and inexplicable physiologically.

Electroencephalographic (EEG) tests confirm that the alleged visionaries' brain functioning is normal and healthy. EEG tests rule out the possibility of epilepsy or psychotic hallucinations. The alleged visionaries are not asleep or dreaming either. Hysterical neurotic reaction or pathological ecstasy is also ruled out by the EEG testing. What EEG testing showed was that before the apparition, the brain waves are predominantly beta rhythm interspersed by alpha rhythm (normal conscious attentiveness). At the start of the apparition the beta rhythm remains for a short time and then is replaced by an almost uninterrupted alpha rhythm. Alpha rhythm is most observed during relaxation, in a state of expectation, or engaged in meditation. It also usually requires practice to achieve such a diffuse response. Because most of the brain is devoted to visual processing, it is noteworthy that the alpha rhythm over the entire cranium was exhibited while the alleged visionaries had their eyes wide open throughout the apparition. Closed eyes would be expected with alpha rhythm because visual stimulation usually produces interference with alpha rhythm.

To test visual stimulation further a 1000 watt light bulb was placed in front of the eyes of the alleged visionaries during the apparition. There was no blinking movement of the eyelids to the 1000 watt stimulus. There was an interesting pupillary response. The pupil contracted as one would have expected in bright light but there was no change in alpha rhythm to the 1000 watt light. This is scientifically inexplicable and never seen before. *For the pupil to respond the brain must register the light but no brain wave took place.* Additionally such intense stimulation normally causes a significant cortical response, but none occurred during the apparition period.

During the apparition period another scientifically inexplicable event takes place. The alleged visionaries' voices stop during the time that they are having the vision. Even though all the muscles involved in speech continue (all mouth, jaw and throat muscles), the larynx (voice box) shuts off. This is physically impossible. The laryngeal function cannot be physically isolated from the rest of the muscles of speech. The larynx ceases to omit sound during the apparition – except for one exception. In unison, during the apparition the alleged visionaries will be heard simultaneously praying, 'Who art in heaven, hallowed be Thy name . . .' When asked, they report Mary is leading them in the Lord's Prayer.

In summary, the unique aspects of the results of the scientific investigation point to the conclusion that nothing in the physical realm is allowed to interfere with the apparition experience. Scientific experts have defined the phenomena 'as a state of active intense prayer, partially disconnected from the external world, a state of contemplation with a separate person whom they alone can see, hear and touch.'

No medical team has been able to discredit the visionaries. A remarkable feature is that the visions take place wherever the visionaries may be, whether in their own country, or abroad.

It has seemed best to describe the background of Medjugorje before coming to my own four visits, the first being in the early summer of 1989. We were a party of eleven, brought together by my friend Jean Dale who had asked me to act as chaplain. Together we flew from Luton to Split, where we boarded the waiting coach for Medjugorje, about three hours away. Our journey took us through breathtaking scenery along the coast road which sometimes rose several hundred feet above the sea. The drop could be almost sheer, and if you were at the back of the coach you could at times see it directly below you as the driver made his way along the winding road. The barriers at the edge looked distinctly frail and although our driver was as careful as could be wished, I must say my heart leapt from time to time, as did other hearts, too, as I was to learn later. After about sixty miles we turned inland, the drops now into the valley became less precipitous, and we were soon on the narrower roads which led to our destination.

Two features of every conducted drive to Medjugorje are a lecture from your guide and a saying of the rosary. A full chaplet of the rosary takes perhaps twenty minutes, and in this way we are prepared for the pilgrimage and the miles are soon eaten up. The guide's lecture is always much the same, a little bit about the history of the place and the events in which we shall be invited to join, together with a warning, or perhaps it is just an advice, that we should never try to make things happen in

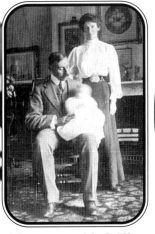

My parents with Griff at
St Lawrence (1908)

Father, aged 60

Myself with Griff (left) and
Dick (centre) (1913)

School days (1926)

Cambridge (1931)

Hallett War School (1944)

Mother, aged 70

Griff (killed in action 1940)
with his retriever Bill

St John's, Nassau with
George Sherman (1950)

Sherwood College (1966)

Rosendal, the family home near Exmouth

Juliet and Reg

Diana and Dick

Gabrielle and Joan (1983)

Outside my flat at 80A King Street, Norwich
(1995)

Griff, Barbara and baby Jill (1939)

Founder's Day Physical
Training display,
Sherwood College

Mountaineering expedition,
Sherwood College

The scattered buildings of the Hallett War School

With Bishop Christopher Robinson and Brigadier Gyan Singh, leader of Indian Everest expedition. Founder's Day, Sherwood College (1961)

With Doreen Bussell at Sherwood (1964)

My sister Joan (*c.* 1982)

The Julian Cell, St Julian's Church, off Rouen Road, Norwich

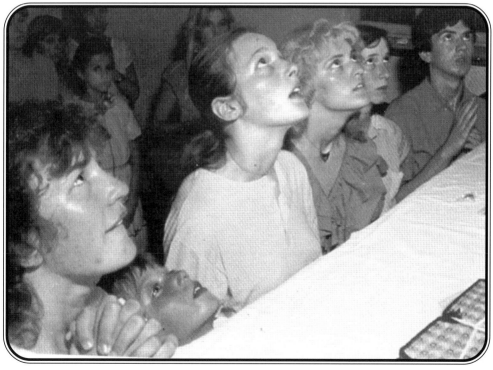

The Medjugorje visionaries:(left to right) Vicka, Jacov, Ivanka, Mirjana, Marija and Ivan (1981)

With (left to right) Edna Jones, Mary Crist, Denise Treissman and Richard Crist (1993)

Holding the UK Templeton Award with (left to right)Ros and Richard Ellwood, Edna Jones and Geoffrey Treissman (1994)

With June Blythe, blowing out the candles on 88th birthday cake

With Richard and Jean Herschel (formerly Furness) after wedding Eucharist in Norwich Cathedral (1997)

With (left to right) Sheila Waller, Jean Dale and Medjugorje hostess (1992)

Outside St Julian's Church following ceremony marking my retirement
from the chaplaincy at the Julian Shrine (1990)

Medjugorje. We are to leave it all to Mary, or to Jesus, or to God to work everything out for the best. I must say I have found that an excellent recipe, and on each of my four visits have been surprised at how things have worked out whilst I seemed to be no more than a watcher of the events which overtook me.

It was dark and past nine o'clock when we arrived. We changed from our luxurious coach into two taxis which took us to our lodgings, an old farmhouse to which an annexe for visitors had recently been built. Ivan Vasilj was our host, a family man with a friendly and caring wife with three lovely children, Andrea, a boy of five, and his two sisters who were a little older.

Here I must say something about Medjugorje hosts in general. There are many of them, for several thousand people may be staying at one time in this small village. From my own experience, and from what I have heard from others, they are a witness to the claims of what has been happening in this place. They don't look out for money, other than the modest sums the travel agencies may pay them, and no kindness is too much for them. To give but one example. On one visit my companion, on arrival, broke his spectacles on which he absolutely depended. Our host motored fifteen miles into Mostar to get them mended next day and, finding the optician closed for the weekend, made a second journey on the Monday, all at his own expense and ready to take nothing but the cost of the repair. That is typical of the kindness and generosity we found. Moreover we always found our hosts to be prayer companions. We felt we could invite them in to share in the rosaries we said in the house, and a bond of fellowship between ourselves and the family would be built up in that way. Medjugorje itself is enveloped in the atmosphere created by the apparitions. That is the beauty of it. It has often been called the nearest place to heaven on earth, and many are the visitors who would find no problem with that.

On that first visit we were fortunate in that four visionaries, Vicka, Marija, Ivan and Jakov were in Medjugorje at the time. The first three were then approaching their middle twenties and Jakov was nearly eighteen. Mirjana, whose daily visions had ceased some years before, was also there, but not Ivanka whose daily visions had also ended. These last two were married but the other four were then single. At the time of writing, all are married excepting Vicka. Our guide called each morning to announce the programme. On that first day we walked across the fields to Angelina's rosary shop at the foot of the hill of apparitions. The attraction here is that Angelina, a gracious lady, fully in tune with the events of the place, makes many of the rosaries herself. As we walked the mile or so to her shop we said the rosary, each taking it in turn to lead whilst the others made the response. This is an entirely natural thing to do in Medjugorje and you would be sure to meet other groups doing the same thing. We moved on from the shop towards Vicka's house which is less than a hundred yards away. Vicka was speaking from the steps which led from the balcony of her house to a large gathering of Americans crowding her small garden and the road beyond. Vicka is immensely good-humoured as she speaks to one group after another, different interpreters coming forward to enable her message to be understood. This particular group was wanting not only her handshake but her autograph and had to be restrained by her interpreter, who said that Vicka did not like her talks to be clapped and that she was not a film star but just an ordinary young woman of the village.

Vicka was answering questions when we arrived. She had been asked of the nature of hell and was in full flow with her reply. One of the things you notice when the visionaries answer questions is that they do not give their own opinions, but invariably preface their remarks with some such remark as, 'What our Lady says is . . .'. So it was now. I cannot quote her exact words but they went something like this: 'Our Lady says that God sends no one to hell. It is possible for us to choose our own hell in this life and we may go on making that choice, and then when we die we find ourselves in the hell we have chosen. But God has not sent us there. It has been our choice.' What I recall vividly is my reflection that Vicka, who could never have heard of Julian of Norwich, was speaking pure Julian at this point. Julian firmly believed in hell but that it is our wrath which may send us there (defined as all that opposes peace and love), the wrath which we are not allowing God's all-compassionate love to quench.

That night, soon after nine o'clock, we climbed the mount of apparitions, a rocky and difficult climb especially in the dark, to be with Ivan and his prayer group who meet every Monday night on this hill, to pray and to await the coming of Mary. Nothing is allowed to prevent this weekly rendezvous, neither rain nor snow. We said the rosary with the others for a while and then Mary appeared to Ivan with a message for his group. She came alone, unlike the previous Monday when three angels were with her. Afterwards she rose above us all, smiled and held out her hands in blessing. All this we were told later in several languages by the interpreters present.

Our party were in a somewhat unusual position for we had with us Geoffrey Treissman who is a person of quite remarkable psychic sensitivity. Geoff is often aware of the spirit world around us in a way which is hidden from others. As Mary came to visit Ivan that night Geoff, too, saw her and was able to tell us that she had come alone, which is by no means always so. He was also able to describe how she rose over us and was pleased and held out her hands in blessing, all of which was later corroborated through the interpreter. For any who think the young people are not speaking truthfully (which is unthinkable to me), here is interesting confirmatory evidence from a disinterested witness. I put it down as an additional testimony to what has been recorded elsewhere.

Since our arrival in Medjugorje we had been joined by my friend Jim Nicholls, an Episcopalian priest from America, and his wife Betsy. On the Tuesday of our week, Jim and I had the privilege of concelebrating the Eucharist in the room in which earlier visions had occurred. It is a place with a remarkable atmosphere and, not surprisingly, it was a Eucharist we shall all remember.

A further privilege came that evening when I was allowed to be present with a small group when Marija and Ivan were receiving their nightly apparition. At these times the visionaries are (according to medical reports) unaware of sensory experiences of pain or hearing, or even of being lifted from the ground. I could on this occasion only see the back of Marija's head, but Ivan's lips were clearly visible as he spoke to Mary. The message on this occasion was for the young people themselves. This is almost always the case, the exception being that on the twenty-fifth of each month a message is given for the world. On our visit, which included 25 May, Mary spoke as follows:

> 'I invite you, now, to be open to God. You see, children, all Nature is opening herself to God and is giving light and fruits. This same way, I invite you to live with God and to surrender completely to him. Children, I am with you and I want to introduce you continuously to the joy of life. I desire that everyone may discover the joy and life which can be found only in God and which only God can give. God does not want anything from you – only your surrender. Therefore, children, decide seriously for God because everything else passes. Only God remains. Pray to be able to

discover the greatness of joy and life which God gives you. Thank
you for having responded to my call.'

It was through Marija that the message was given. She is the most contemplative of the group, a young woman of serenity and quiet dignity
but, too, with an ample sense of fun. Each time I was taken to see her
she was out; it was rumoured she had a hide-out in the hills: sensible
indeed. She had only recently returned from America, where she had
donated one of her kidneys to save her brother's life. The visions continued in Alabama where she was staying and attracted a good deal
of attention. She also tells us that Mary appeared to her during the
operation.

It is often said by critics of Medjugorje that the monthly (formerly
weekly) messages to the world given by Mary are banal and repetitive in
the extreme. I see nothing banal in the message I have quoted. At the
same time it is true that Mary speaks in very ordinary terms. But so
does any mother to her children. So did Jesus to the apostles after the
resurrection. There is nothing particularly startling in words like, 'Peace
be with you'. But they bear endless repetition and we repeat them to one
another at every Eucharist. As does any good teacher, Mary repeats herself
often, saying in one way or another the same things over and over again.
In every message you will find a call to prayer, or surrender, or fasting,
or holiness, or conversion of heart, or love of God or neighbour, and
often several of these themes will be in one message. One of Mary's
messages is simply, 'Pray, pray, pray'. In another we find, 'Listen to my
Son'. Spiritual writers like St John of the Cross or Julian of Norwich take
us to more complex depths of spirituality than that. And yet, if we left
them unread (Peter and Paul never had them), and obeyed Mary's simple
words we would one and all be reconciled with God and one another,
civil strifes and wars between nations would cease. For myself, if we had
messages of high-flown spirituality such as one may find in many of the
textbooks available today, I would be asking if there were not someone
behind the scenes who was making them up. I see the simplicity and
repetition as evidence for the genuineness of the messages and not the
other way round, as disbelievers have so often suggested. And if anyone
cares to mull over the message I have quoted, daily for a month, I do
not doubt they will be the richer for it.

During the week I went with a small party to meet Mirjana who, with
Ivanka, was the first of the six to see Mary in 1981. She recounted the

event to us. I cannot remember if she said that she and Ivanka were out for a quiet and forbidden smoke, but that is certainly how it has often been reported. She certainly said that Mary chose her because she was so ordinary. Mirjana (I last saw her six years later when she was thirty) is a beautiful young woman, quietly spoken and of impressive poise. I reminded her (on the first occasion) that Mary often spoke of the rosary, but did she ever speak of silence? She replied, 'There must always be silence.' That was it and what I had wanted to know. To be fully effective, the rosary must take you beyond itself to the silence of the heart before God.

Last time I heard Mirjana speak she told us she had been given by Mary the special task of emphasising the importance of family life. The importance of prayer together from the earliest years is basic to her message. Recently in answer to a question she told this delightful story:

> Our Lady expects little children to pray. The most important thing is for parents to pray in front of their children. Children are not too young to understand what is going on in prayer. I will give you an example. My eldest daughter is five years old now. When she was three I had not spoken to her about my apparitions because I thought she would not be able to understand. One day when she was playing with her friends, I went to check on her. I heard one of her friends say to her, 'My mum is now driving a car'. My daughter was quiet for a while, and then she said, 'Well that's not so great – *my* mum is talking with Our Lady!'

21

Medjugorje (2)

⮜⳺⳺⮞

T HE HIGHLIGHT OF THE pilgrim's visit to Medjugorje is the climbing
of Krizevak, known to many as the holy mountain. On our fifth day
we set out together, starting off soon after half past five in the morning.
Krizevak is about 700 feet above Medjugorje, a steep and rocky climb,
though some like to make it barefooted. At altitudes of every fifty feet or
so are the fourteen stations of the cross, where a pause was made for
prayer and recollection. At the top is a large stone cross set up by
the villagers in 1933 to commemorate nineteen hundred years since the
crucifixion of Jesus. We had chosen a good day and enjoyed a magnificent
view of the plains and hills around. After twenty minutes or so we began
the descent, much more difficult in that rocky and uneven terrain than
going up. We were back for breakfast at nine, perhaps the most welcome
meal of the week.

Our meals were full of fun and laughter all mixed up with the serious
subjects which had occupied us that week. An unforgettable meal took
place on the Friday, beginning with a Eucharist which Jim celebrated for
us as we sat round the table. We used the home-baked bread of our hosts
and a little of the wine they had provided, and passed the consecrated
elements around the table as we communicated one another. It seemed
as though that was the way the Eucharist was intended. We certainly have
an excellent precedent. This particular celebration took place at breakfast
time, and since it was Friday it was followed by a fast of bread and water.
Many of the pilgrims take bread and water only on the Fridays of their
stay (and a few on the Wednesdays as well) uniting themselves with the
request Mary asks of the visionaries that they fast in this way on these
two days in the week. The Franciscan priests in the village are strict in
the observance of this fast. When I made my fourth visit to Medjugorje
in 1994, this time as representative of the Archbishop of Canterbury,
Father Barbaric (in charge) said to me at Friday lunch that I must tell

the Archbishop he must come himself next time and that he promised not to ask him to lunch on a Friday! Though there was, in fact, a Canadian bishop there that day and he and I were allowed a little watery soup in which to dip our bread. Medjugorje is very sure, through Mary, that prayer and fasting go together, but allows that fasting may be performed by a combination of denial in food in such measure as is both sacrificial and reasonable, together with other forms of discipline such as moderation in watching television. For people who think Medjugorje is all about seeing the sun spin and rosaries turning to a golden colour and Mary appearing to pilgrims here and there, all of which is common enough, a rude awakening awaits them when they learn its teaching on prayer and fasting and sacramental confession. Prayer, conversion of heart, love of God and one another, that is the message of Medjugorje. The accompanying signs and miracles of healing (over three hundred have been reported) are there to confirm the word of God as in the Acts of the Apostles.

Talking of Mary appearing and the sun spinning, the following was added to my files a few months ago by a friend in his sixties visiting Medjugorje for the first time, and not at the beginning much in sympathy with what he had heard.

> The sky was laden with unshed rain and quite dark when my companion said, 'Look, look!' – and as if stage-managed the clouds parted and a most brilliant sun shone forth for the first time that day. It immediately began to spin and hurtle towards us and return. When the 'show' was over, the clouds closed again, the rain fell in sheets and night had suddenly fallen. It was quite alarming as I really thought we would never find our way down [the hill Podbrdo] . . . we slipped and crawled back to the road. We were drenched and very grateful to be on the 'flat' when suddenly the whole area was illuminated by a most brilliant light and I noticed what I thought to be a statue of Our Lady at the back of Vicka's house . . . We then realised that it was truly Our Lady as the vision began to move and we watched it as it 'floated' into Vicka's house; and then, total darkness again. Her mantle was shimmering grey, Her veil white, and a halo of stars circled Her head. We were overcome and slowly made our way past the house and back to the main road leading to the church, as it was still pouring with rain. Suddenly a car came, stopped by us, and a lady invited us to have

a lift back to the church. We then discovered that she was a Canadian who had been given permission to visit Vicka's house during her apparition; she, herself, had not witnessed our vision. You can imagine our prayers of thanksgiving when we reached the church.

I have spoken, too, of rosaries turning to a golden colour. I would like to give a little space to this as the phenomenon is so often dismissed as being no more than the tarnish which may come over metal when exposed to the atmosphere. There are too many reports of the real thing taking place for any reasonable person to remain in doubt. And yet I do not know that I have ever seen a (turned) glittering golden rosary (as distinct from one of the colour of a pound coin) unless it be one of my own as I shall tell later. But reports are numerous and some come from friends whom I cannot doubt. Wayne Weible, formerly a Lutheran and now a Roman Catholic, speaks of several of his own rosaries turning to the colour of gold. On another occasion on giving a rosary to a friend sceptical of Medjugorje, he said: 'I've never done this before but I'm going to ask the Blessed Virgin Mary to turn this rosary chain from its silver colour to gold, and then I'm going to give it to you.' He then put it in his pocket, forgot about it until a few hours later by which time the change had taken place. But now to my own story. On my second visit to Medjugorje Marija offered to take my rosaries to her apparition for Mary's blessing. I gladly agreed. I was wondering at that time whether to advertise Medjugorje in *The Church Times* for the benefit of Anglican readers. Two articles I had written for the paper had been turned down and advertisement was the only way through. When I got home to England I unwrapped the packages and found that two of the rosaries and two crucifixes were of a golden colour, the rosaries bright and sparkling, the crucifixes nearer to a bronze. So sure was I that all were silvery grey when I had bought them at Medjugorje that I asked a professional photographer to photograph them which he did, good man, without billing for his services. I took the change of colour as a sign, inserted twelve advertisements in the paper over a year, costing £2,500 in all, the total being supplied by grateful readers. The photographer wrote later to say this had been one of the influences which had led him to become a Catholic. Could I have been mistaken? Perhaps so. It was an overcast day when I bought the rosaries and the lights in the shop were not on. Yet I felt sure at the time of opening the packet that I would have noticed if they had been golden in the shop. And I felt sure I had bought grey crucifixes though there were golden ones on sale. The incident acted as a sign to me and to the photographer so, wherever the truth may lie, God used the event to his glory.

On 26 May 1990, *The Tablet,* in the course of a correspondence on golden (coloured) rosaries, published a letter from me on this subject. In it I quoted a letter to the Medjugorje *Messenger* from Mr Robert Brophy, manager of Irish Precious Metal Ltd, 39 Lower Ormond Quay, Dublin. Speaking of a 'turned' Medjugorje rosary it read as follows:

> I have very carefully examined the rosary beads in question. Between each decade the metal in two short links has changed to a gold colour. They are definitely not gold; but the change in the colour is very surprising. I expected to find just the surface had changed. But in fact, the gold colour has fused right through the metal, making it, of course, a different metal. What has happened near the cross is even more unusual. The same two links have changed to a gold colour – but between them and the cross, four smaller links have changed to a copper colour. Only sections of these links changed to a copper colour. Again, the colour is not just on the surface but goes right through until it meets the other original surface of metal. What has occurred with the metal of these rosary beads is most unusual, and in my opinion would be very difficult, if not impossible, to forge. I have spent many years examining and testing metals and have never seen anything like it.

But what does it matter? Is it important? So people talk. I suppose the answer must be that anything which God chooses to do must matter, must be important, even though we can see no reason for it. But let it be said again that Medjugorje is about conversion and change of heart. All the rest is subsidiary to that. Furthermore, Medjugorje is about sacrifice and not about the modern urge for self-fulfilment. God certainly wants us to be fulfilled, but it is only in sacrifice that that fulfilment will take place.

In one of my rejected articles to *The Church Times* I spoke of a miracle which Fr Barbaric (to be more fully introduced later) had recently related to a group of which I was a member in London. Whilst walking to an evening apparition Fr Barbaric met a blind man being led by a companion. He invited them both to join him. During the vision the man's sight was restored. There was an interesting sequel. The man was rather deaf and wore a hearing aid. Waking up next morning (without the aid) he found he could hear. At what point his deafness was cured must remain unknown. The blindness (perhaps not total though at least sufficient to necessitate a guide) was caused by a thick cataract which was due to be removed. Why God used his own laser rather than the doctor's, who can say? Fr Barbaric said the man could see clearly into the surrounding hills.

One morning Jim Nicholls had an appointment with Vicka and took me with him. He wanted to ask Vicka if she would be open to an invitation to visit Britain, saying that he had already to some extent prepared the way through conversations with Lord Lauderdale who has a deep interest in Medjugorje. Vicka's reply was direct and to the point: Our Lady had given her no indication that she wished her to go; if such direction were given she would naturally go at once. So far no such direction has been received, though I have met both Marija and Ivan briefly on visits to England. And, too, Fr Jozo when he conducted a service at St Martin-in-the-Fields. I had a brief talk to Vicka about the rosary, and told her it was not much in the Anglican tradition. She said that I must teach the Church of England the rosary, since when I have been trying to do just that. And not only the C of E. One of my treasured invitations is to give five talks on the rosary in the Norwich Roman Catholic cathedral. It ought to be a case of coals to Newcastle but, alas, it no longer is. For the record, two weekly ecumenical rosary groups meet in my flat each week, with members of the C of E being in the majority.

Jim then took me to meet Fr Barbaric who has guided the visionaries for many years. If there is a key person around which Medjugorje revolves then that person is Fr Barbaric. He is a priest with a degree in social psychology which must be a great help in his position, having to deal with the visionaries and their frequent examination by medical teams. He is a deeply godly man, sparse and ascetic in his looks and his ways, intelligent, well informed, and with an ever-ready twinkle in his eye. During a later visit when I was sitting with him at the airport I told him how one of my party of two hundred Roman Catholics, who had invited me to join them on their pilgrimage, had said that some of them were praying for my conversion to Rome. Fr Barbaric at once went to one of the RC priests and said they must stop praying in that way as it was against the spirit of Medjugorje, since Mary had expressly said she had not come that people might change their allegiance, but that they might all be deepened in whatever denomination they were.

It was Fr Barbaric who generally presided at the daily evening service which began at half past five and ended almost three hours later. This included the recitation of the joyful and sorrowful mysteries of the rosary during the apparition of Mary, the mass concelebrated by anything up to forty priests, a homily and finally the glorious mysteries and the blessing of religious objects. The church would be packed, making it almost impossible for anyone to leave and there would be a huge overflow outside who heard the service through loudspeakers. Many of the villagers came night after night to what is, of course, their parish church and they were not slow to offer their seats to any more needy than themselves. It seemed a shame to accept, but I did once or twice feeling that what was offered in love should be accepted in the same spirit.

I think we all made our confessions that week. There were queues for confessions wherever a priest was seated, each with a sign before him to announce his language. I found a priest who, distrusting the validity of an Anglican absolution, decided to absolve me from every sin committed since baptism: an unexpected bonus!

On our last day we went to see Jelena. Jelena is one of two young people (Marianna being the other) who have interior locutions, that is to say the words of Mary are not heard with their ears but silently in the heart. Nor is she able to see Mary as the others do. It seems that Mary is working in a very special way through Jelena. 'My heart is burning for you; conversion, conversion, say this to every one of my children, to all my children.' Mary has expressed a wish to Jelena for a group of volunteers who will be completely dedicated to the service of God. Jelena was seventeen when we met her, having received her call at school at the age of eleven. To Jelena, Mary has said, 'Try not to worry too much about earthly matters, for a lack of peace is not conducive to prayer. If we stand first to God, he will supply our earthly needs, and all will be well.' And 'When I say pray, pray, pray, do not understand it as meaning only an increase in the number of your prayers. I want to bring you to a deep desire for God; a continual desire for God.'

We retired to Jelena's beautiful little garden chapel where the very walls seemed soaked with prayer. We prayed in silence and then said a decade of the rosary together. Geoff told me later that Mary shared that peace (bestowed it, might be better) and that she had smiled upon us. I don't know whether Jelena was aware of it or not.

Our last evening had come. Denise Treissman felt the impulse to climb Krizevak – the holy mountain – once more before leaving. Time was short and before supper she dashed up, spent a few minutes there, and dashed down again. Her trouser suit was soaked with sweat and smelt strongly – of roses. There were none on Krizevak. It had dried out next morning and she wore it home to England. Friends there remarked on the smell of roses which remained. I don't think Denise needed any final confirmation about Medjugorje, but in case she did this was it. Roses are closely associated with Mary.

We invited our hosts and their children to share a rosary with us after supper, which they gladly did. Thus was created a bond between us which remained when I went to visit this same house several years later. We were off at four the next morning, our ever-faithful hosts being up to cook breakfast for us. And so to Split and Luton, though my baggage, alas, went to Liverpool. Happily it was soon recovered.

Is there another side to what I have written? Yes, there is, and it comes from Bishop Zanic of Mostar in whose diocese Medjugorje used to lie. (He has since retired.) The Bishop was one of the first to be convinced of the authenticity of the apparitions, stating categorically: 'The children are not lying.'[1] Later he did a complete about turn, doing his best to dismiss the apparitions as nonsense. Wayne Weible writes that the Bishop had been threatened with imprisonment[2] and we must try to understand the fears and pressures upon him under a communist regime. There was another major factor which related to messages from Mary which were critical of his judgement in the transference of two priests. The visionaries had been asked to pass these on to him. No doubt this was difficult to bear. He became determined to denounce the validity of the visions. He circulated bishops throughout the world and made his opinions available to the world press who were swift to print them. The children became 'little liars'.[3] The pilgrims, of whom many were from the professional classes, theologians, doctors, scientists of international fame and the like, became 'naive, deluded and totally blind'.[4] The scientific teams, who had established the mental health and good faith of the visionaries, were flatly contradicted. A much revered and trusted priest became a 'confidence trickster'[5] and 'charismatic sorcerer'.[6] Of this priest, Hans Urs von Balthasar (known as the Pope's favourite theologian) had written that he seemed to him to be 'a model of humility, of deep wisdom, of discretion, a man whose obedience is nothing less than heroic. He is a true Christian man of God.'[7] And of this same priest, Delia Smith, the television cook, had said that the way in which he said the mass did more than anything else to convince her of the genuineness of the apparitions.[8] There can, however, be no doubt that by the violence of his language the Bishop scored many 'own goals' for the truth of Medjugorje. And it is not difficult to see how his behaviour was caught up in the providence of God, for if he had not been on hand to put down the visions, the communists might have done it themselves and made a more thorough job of it. Though, to tell the fuller truth, the communists came to have a love-hate relationship with Medjugorje, for the vast number of visitors, said to be between fifteen and twenty million in the first ten years, was making it a great money-spinner for an impoverished land. When the visionaries spoke to Mary about the Bishop she would tell them to pray for him, adding at least on one occasion, 'for he bears many burdens'. It is not difficult to understand what some of those burdens might have been in a land ruled by a government which had no place for God. I write this in the hope that people throughout the world, so deeply influenced by Bishop Zanic's circular, may try to understand the pressures to which he was subjected. The Bishop's behaviour drew the following strong but dignified rebuke from Hans Urs von Balthazar.

> Monsignor. What a sorry document you have sent throughout the
> world! I have been deeply pained to see the episcopal office
> degraded in this manner. Instead of abiding your time, as you were
> advised to do by high authority, you thunder and hurl
> thunderbolts like Jupiter. While you denigrate people who are
> renowned and innocent, deserving your respect and protection, you
> bring out accusations which have been refuted a hundred times ...
> I hope you sincerely pray to God and His Mother to lead this sad
> drama, one so important, to an outcome which will be fruitful for
> the whole Church. Join with all those who pray with such fervour
> in Medjugorje. Yours in the Lord, Hans Urs von Balthasar.[9]

Although I do not hesitate to consider the Bishop's judgement as being conceived in passion rather than reason I have, nevertheless, areas of concern in relationship to Medjugorje. Thus, I find myself sympathetic (though not ultimately in agreement) with the Jesuit priest who wrote: 'My own reservation about Medjugorje is that I feel uncomfortable, not with the call to prayer and fasting, but of the prescribing of very precise practices in these areas which seem to me not sufficiently to allow for spiritual freedom – the way the Holy Spirit works in so many diverse ways in the lives of different people and at different stages of the Christian life.' The reason I say that I am not ultimately in agreement with that statement is because, although I think Medjugorje lays itself open to that criticism, I don't think it will stand up to careful scrutiny.

Let us look at the Gospels. Jesus gave us principles, and left us to work these out in our lives according to our capacities and needs. There was no specific length for prayer (except 'always'), no rule of fasting (except 'cheerfully'), no rule of almsgiving (except 'secretly'), no commandments (except 'love one another'), no instructions on confession (except 'be reconciled quickly').

By contrast Mary gives rules on the extent of fasting, the hours to be given to prayer, the frequency of confession. But unquestionably she does not intend to contradict the freedom allowed by Jesus. In regard to rules Mary is always 'I invite', and never 'you must'. Mary has come to direct a chosen group ('I have chosen this parish in a special way'). She begins with the wide principles ('Surrender yourselves completely', 'open your hearts and give your lives to Jesus', and much more), and works forward to the rules, and then backwards to a reminder of the principles ('I urge you to offer all your acts of self-denial with love', 'I invite you to the love of your neighbours and especially those who hurt you', 'I want you to love everyone, the good and the bad'). But undeniably in this whole area we are right to be on our guard. If we opt for rules and leave it there, we are in for a barren legalistic religion which will undo what Jesus did to break through the tradition of the Scribes and Pharisees. It would be ridiculous to assert that Mary of Medjugorje is not as alive to this, and more so, than the most watchful of her critics. 'Listen to my Son' is basic to all her messages.

Again, I am uncomfortable with the tendency of Medjugorje to see things in black and white. Many committed Christians will consider this to be its strength. Moral relativism clearly has its dangers lest 'anything goes', yet when everything is white or black and there is no room for the grey, widespread discouragement will set in, and many who might have made it in the end will give up the struggle. It is some of the interpreters of Medjugorje who arouse my concern. Mary is nothing if she is not the great encourager. Whatever the shortcomings she feels the need to point out, every message ends with, 'Thank you for responding to my call'.

Notwithstanding these reservations I do not doubt that it is Medjugorje rather than Lourdes (which I was to visit later) which has the greater power to speak to the needs of our troubled world. Lourdes is prudent, moderate and somewhat set in its ways. You rest comfortably in its reassuring presence. Medjugorje has the ardour and dynamism of youth. The potential for world change is there.

Let the last words be with Jean Dale who brought us together and did so much to prosper our visit. She is writing especially in relation to a later visit I made with her and our friend Sheila Waller in wartime Medjugorje, but her sentiments encompass the whole scene.

> We arrived at our destination at two-thirty in the morning to find our hosts waiting for us with a smile and a three course hot meal! This was the kind of hospitality two of us had experienced before but it still left us speechless. Those dear people giving of their time and substance in such generous abundance epitomize the spirit of Medjugorje. For a pilgrimage to Medjugorje is not a journey to a shrine; it is a journey to a valley and its people, their homes, their land, their mountains, their way of life. It is impossible to separate these elements . . .The messages speak of peace and call for a radical conversion of heart . . .Medjugorje is an oasis of peace in a desolate land. We heard prayers for the Chetniks [historical enemies] 'who are our brothers, children of the same Father.' We heard prayers for the Muslims and witnessed the joyful reunion of our host with his Muslim friends. If the messages of Medjugorje had been accepted and lived all over the former Yugoslavia we would not now be witnessing the blood bath and outpouring of hate. In Medjugorje six very ordinary young people came face to face with Love and Beauty, which has transformed them. Whatever the final outcome, a visit to Medjugorje is a holistic experience of the beauty of the commonplace, of the ordinary people, of the witness of love and reconciliation. It is for me and for many a pilgrimage to the heart of our Christian faith, to Nazareth.

Post script. August 1997. Drug Rehabilitation Centre. Since the typescript of this book was completed a friend (Mrs Fiona Arnold) has written for me her recent experience of a little-known side of Medjugorje.

> Other visitors were standing around drinking glasses of orange juice when we arrived at the wooden gate of Cenacolo, the drug rehabili- tation centre near Medjugorje. The gate was opened by a young man and we were offered refreshment while we waited for our guide, a remarkable man called Kenny: remarkable in appearance, a good six

foot five, strongly built, dark-skinned American; remarkable in the strength and gentleness of personality; remarkable in his own life history, being a rehabilitated drug dependant himself and now the senior member of the centre.

We learnt that the youngest member was 15 and he, Kenny, was the 'old man' at 40. Admittance was not automatic; when a young man turned up at the gates he was given lodgings in Medjugorje (a few miles away) and told to be back at the gates at 8.00 the following morning. If he turned up he would be invited to spend the day in the community, sharing in the work, meals etc. and then asked to return to his town lodgings for the night. This pattern would be repeated for a week or two, and if the youngster could maintain the commitment, reappearing outside the gate each morning, he'd be taken in as a member of the community. 'It's a very tough road to walk,' Kenny told us. 'We can't do it for them, they have to want it enough for themselves. Being at the gate each day is just the first small test.'

Next comes the 'cold turkey' when all drugs are withdrawn from the new member. 'It's a very hard time', was Kenny's understatement of the physical pain and fear that accompanies the withdrawal. But through it all, staying by your side for the twenty-four hours of every day, is the 'brother' you have been appointed. 'He washes you, brings you food, holds you when you're sick, he lives for you. When you are able to share a little of the work you will push one of the barrow loads and your brother will push the other five. For many of us it's our first experience of unconditional love.'

If you survive the 'cold turkey' then comes the really terrible bit ' . . . when you begin to realise what you've done, to your families and friends, the violence and crimes you've caused and been involved in, the lives you've ruined. It's a terrible thing you have to face and you feel unable to forgive yourself.'

The hub of this hard-working, largely self-supporting, centre is the chapel and the Mass and the Eucharist. 'For us the Holy Sacrament and our Lord's love means literally a new life'. A huge painting covering one wall of the chapel, depicting the risen Christ drawing humanity to Himself, is in itself a witness to Kenny's words. Saints are represented and among them stands the figure of a rehabilitated drug addict. The tabernacle containing the Holy Sacrament is located not in the glorious colours of the heavens, but in the intense blackness of the world which lies beneath Christ's feet. The mural is the work of two young members who, having never done a painting in their lives, fell under the spell of a visitor who taught them icon painting and directed them in their work.

Our tour round the compound revealed a community of young men (about thirty, it seemed to me) that worked hard to be as self-sufficient as possible: a few farm animals, vegetable plots, stacked brushwood for fires, bakery, kitchens and laundry and so on. There was also time for creative skills of a more specialist nature: icon painting on quite an extensive scale and woodcrafts (the products being sold in a small gift shop) . . . And then the plaintive, wistfulness of music by the artist Enya reached my ears and drew me into a large makeshift studio. There moving with the grace and controlled poise of ballet dancers, were two young men, travelling smoothly across the floor and watching themselves in the several huge plate glass mirrors propped against a wall. I delighted in their grace and the complicated footwork. As soon as I was noticed by the dancers they came to an embarrassed stop and began bandying wisecracks at each other. Their stance, language and behaviour became that of the tough street-wise youngster, loud, strutting, defensively macho. But I had had the privilege of seeing another side to them, a side which, I believe, would never have had expression but for the power of Cenacolo.

22

Lourdes

L OURDES WAS A HEARTENING experience. Particularly impressive is its care for the sick who flock to this unique town of eighteen thousand people, with its nine hospitals, thirty convents, twenty camping sites and four hundred hotels. They come in their thousands seeking healing, whether spiritual or physical, through the prayers of its pilgrims or the waters of its spring, uncovered under the direction of the Blessed Virgin Mary by a fourteen-year-old girl, Bernadette Soubirous, whom now Lourdes delights to honour. Every year 70,000 doctors, nurses, and helpers give their services voluntarily to care for an equal number of sick people, helping with the nursing, the feeding, the clothing, the pushing of wheelchairs, and the many other needs of those who often can do little or virtually nothing for themselves.

I went to Lourdes by coach (a twenty-four hour journey) in August 1996, one of a mixed group of thirty-five young people, some not yet out of school, and perhaps twenty grown-ups of middle or senior age. The young had come to spend a week caring for the needy. They came at their own expense, one of them (though maybe not in this group) having raised the necessary funds through a sponsored first parachute jump. Later I was to learn how helpful and caring they were in the arduous work they had volunteered to do.

We were but one coachload of four and many others had gone by plane. In all, I was told, there were seven hundred and fifty of us, drawn from five Roman Catholic dioceses, ours being that of East Anglia. I say 'ours' but that, of course, is not quite correct since I am an Anglican, the only non-Roman Catholic in the party. I had for a long time wanted to go to Lourdes, and when I heard that this party had been arranged I asked if I might join it, and to my joy was accepted and, yet more, welcomed. I am most grateful to my Catholic hosts, chief among them

Bishop Peter Smith, Roman Catholic Bishop of East Anglia, who led the whole party.

My most moving memory of Lourdes is of the procession of the hundreds of sick being pushed or pulled (or both) in their wheelchairs, amidst the thousands who made up the half-mile-long processions of the Blessed Sacrament or the rosary. I am not easily moved to tears but this was an occasion when they were near. I was at the side watching whilst thousands came past until I could join in at the end. It was a reversal of the values of the world from which I had come, so much love and caring, all voluntary and unpaid, to meet the needs of those who could not but depend on the good will of others. I went with my friend Richard Ellwood, now of nearly retiring age who, like me, was on his first visit, he as a volunteer to help with the needs of the sick. Pushing a wheelchair can be an arduous business, for although the Shrine (sometimes known as the Domain) where the processions take place is flat, the roads to the hotels can be steep and narrow, and rendered even more difficult by the ceaseless thronging crowds. Richard spoke movingly of the work behind the scenes, and especially in the Shrine hospital in which he worked and visited. It was he who told me of the attentive and caring ministrations of the young people which moved him greatly. I think that in all the world there can be nothing to match this outgoing concern on such an ongoing and impressive scale.

Lourdes lies in the south of France at the foot of the Pyrenees, the mountain peaks to the south rising to 10,000 feet and more. The town itself is surrounded by country of great natural beauty. It is here that Bernadette was born in 1844 when the town was less than a quarter of the size it is today. Her father, François Soubirous, was a stone cutter. He was never prosperous, but after an accident which left him blind in his left eye when Bernadette was five, combined with the coming of steam power, he and his wife Louise and their five children fell on bad days and became known as the poorest family in the town. Eventually they were housed in the cachot, the punishment place of a disused prison, a broken down and delapidated place, still viewable by visitors today, and pronounced by Pope John XXIII on his visit to Lourdes as carrying the heart of its message. Here was not only abject poverty but a measure of disgrace as well, as François had been arrested for stealing in an endeavour to keep his family warm in the bitter winter days. There was, our guide told us, no evidence against him, other than his extreme poverty which might well have led to theft, and he was soon discharged.

It was in 1858 while the family were living at the cachot that Bernadette was granted a series of eighteen visions of the Virgin Mary. They were received in a small cave (known as the grotto) at the rock of Massabielle lying to the north of the River Gave about half a mile from her home. She was disbelieved at first, interrogated by minor officials and threatened with punishment, but she stuck to her story and emerged unshaken. She was a simple and poorly educated child but it came to be seen that her truthfulness and integrity were beyond question. Asked why Mary had chosen her of all people, she replied quite simply that she supposed it was because she was the poorest child in the town.

The first vision took place on 11 February when Bernadette and her sister Toinette, together with a young companion, went to the banks of the River Gave in the hope of finding firewood for the family, who had sold their last log in order to buy food. Spotting wood in the grotto, Toinette and her friend crossed the small mill stream (now no longer there) to enter the cave. Bernadette was preparing to follow them when her attention was drawn to a luminous figure in the hollow of the rock. We had better continue in Bernadette's own words:

> I was taken aback. I couldn't believe it. I rubbed my eyes and I looked again and could still see the same lady. I took my rosary from my pocket. I wanted to bless myself with it, but I couldn't raise my hand to my forehead. It fell back down. Then fear took hold of me. My hand was shaking. Yet I remained where I was. The lady took the rosary which was wrapped around her wrist and made the sign of the cross. I tried to do the same and this time managed to. As soon as I had made the sign of the cross my fear disappeared. I knelt down and said my rosary with the beautiful lady. The Vision passed the beads through her hands but she did not move her lips. After I had finished my rosary she begged me to come closer but I didn't dare to. Then she disappeared suddenly.

Toinette and her friend saw nothing but they coaxed the story out of Bernadette on the way home, promising to tell no one. But the temptation was too great. The story was blurted out at home and both children were told off smartly and forbidden to visit the grotto again.

Mother, however, was persuaded to relent and further visits followed. At the third, on 18 February, the lady asked Bernadette to come to the grotto every day for the next two weeks. At the seventh apparition on 23 February Dr Dozous, a scientist and firm disbeliever was present, determined to put down this nonsense once and for all. It was the beginning of his own conversion to the truth of Bernadette's witness. At the ninth apparition, on 25 February Bernadette was bidden to remove the earth above an undiscovered spring. It is from here that the famous healing waters have flowed ever since. The spring now pours out many thousands of gallons of water each day, which may be drawn by pilgrims from the taps which lie close to the grotto. At the thirteenth vision on 2 March, Mary told Bernadette that she wished a church to be built above the grotto. This is the famous Church of the Immaculate Conception, the name by which Mary eventually revealed herself. It stands today high up on the rock with a beautiful crypt chapel below, and lower still the famous Church of the Rosary. These buildings were for me, architecturally speaking, the beauty spots of Lourdes.

There were eighteen apparitions in all, the last being on 16 July. Each time Bernadette was in a state of ecstasy, this time for a quarter of an hour, during which time Mary bade her final goodbye. There followed four years of study and the hearing of many witnesses. Reported cures were examined and seven declared to be miracles. Finally, on 18 January 1862, the Church declared that 'the Blessed Virgin Mary, Mother of God, truly appeared to Bernadette Soubirous'.

The grotto is the centre for most pilgrims. They come to drink the water or to bathe in it in the baths close by, or to collect it in bottles, as I did myself, to take away for myself and as gifts to friends. Each day I bathed my eyes with the water for reading was becoming an increasing problem. There is nothing magical about the water but God sometimes uses a humble instrument as a means to health, as the waters of Jordan were used for the healing of Naaman. Undoubtedly, the waters of Lourdes have often been used as the instrument of God's healing love.

The first four miracles – the water being the instrument in each case – took place during the period of the apparitions. In all there have been some two thousand recorded unexplained healings from Lourdes, but only sixty-five have been classified as miracles by the very strict medical bureau. To qualify as a miracle a cure has to be instant and complete and of a lasting nature, and effected without any medication or treatment. They thus correspond very closely to the miracles of the New Testament. It can be said with confidence that most sick people visit Lourdes today seeking strength and blessing in their suffering, rather than in the expectation of a cure. Though, naturally, the hope must be usually there. By far the majority of the five million pilgrims who visit Lourdes each year are not sick in a medical sense, but are aware that they need healing at a deeper level than the physical and look to Lourdes for the grace they need.

Bernadette did not herself become involved with the future life of Lourdes. In 1864 she decided to ask if she might test her vocation with the Sisters of Charity. She was accepted but it was soon considered best for her to move to the mother house in Nevers which lies about a hundred miles south of Paris. There was one last prayer at the grotto, and an evening with her family on 3 July 1866, and then she left Lourdes never to return. In her later years she suffered terribly from tuberculosis and the asthma which had been with her from early days but with great fortitude and patience. The end came on 16 April 1879. After repeating twice, 'Holy Mary, Mother of God, pray for me, a poor sinner', she asked for water, took a few sips, made the sign of the cross, and died. Her body, which is remarkably preserved, lies clothed in the chapel of the Sisters of Charity in Nevers. Bernadette, holding her rosary, her face resting in serene repose, may still be seen by visitors to the convent.

Bernadette was canonised in 1933, not (it is often stressed) for her ecstasies and visions, but because of her 'total commitment in simplicity, integrity and trust'.

Beauty is said to be in the eyes of the beholder. For this beholder, at least, all the beauty of Lourdes, architecturally speaking, belongs to the churches of the last century. There is one exception to this, the new Chapel of Adoration reserved for those who want to make extended periods of silent prayer before the Blessed Sacrament. This is a beautifully designed building holding about a hundred people and it is undoubtedly, with the Crypt Chapel (to be mentioned later), the heartbeat of Lourdes. Not many use it, as a percentage of the vast numbers of visitors, but those who do may well find all they want without seeking further. Each of the three churches to which I have referred has its special features. The top one, that of the Immaculate Conception, consecrated in 1876, stands on the rock of Massabielle over two hundred feet above the grotto. Surrounding the nave and chancel are fifteen chapels which between them carry twenty-three windows depicting the history of Lourdes. The Crypt Chapel underneath, if my estimate from memory is correct, holds barely a hundred and fifty people. It carries the atmosphere of prayer, for many visit it for extended periods of silence before the tabernacle. It was formerly the Chapel of Adoration, and it seems that many who have become accustomed to it have not yet found their way to the new chapel.

It was only after I left Lourdes that I discovered that the rosary was said at 4.30 each afternoon in this chapel. I would have so liked to have been there. The lowest church, known as the Rosary Basilica, is remarkable for its fifteen chapels each dedicated to a mystery of the rosary. Over and behind each altar are large and beautifully worked mosaics relating to the relevant mystery. The rosary may well be said by sitting in silence before each mosaic in turn making it the icon of the mystery concerned.

The Shrine is the name given to the whole complex of churches and chapels and walks. It is one of the largest in the world, about half a million square metres, which may be pictured by imagining a rectangle a kilometre long by half a kilometre wide. The most notable construction is the underground basilica of Pius X which was consecrated in 1958. It may be a noteworthy feat in engineering and design but, apart from the altar in the middle and paintings on the walls, it is as uninviting as a car park which, indeed, with its huge concrete structures it closely resembles. But I mustn't be too superior. On Father R.M. Benson ssje being asked by two young priests wanting to show off the extent of their travels, which was the most beautiful church in the world, he replied that it was the church in which the Holy Eucharist was celebrated. The Church of Pius X celebrates the Holy Eucharist for tens of thousands every week. There were more than ten thousand when I was there. It occupies a vast space and can hold twenty-seven thousand people. Elliptical in shape its circumference is about six hundred yards.

A highlight of my visit to Lourdes, and worth all the eight pounds of my less than two miles taxi drive, was not linked with the Shrine but with my visit to the Convent of the Dominicans. Sister Jean Marie had read my book *Our Duty and Our Joy*, and had written to me from the convent hoping that one day we might meet. I was able to reply from Norwich by return to say I would be in Lourdes within a few weeks. And so the visit was fixed up. I found she knew very little English, but her friend, Sister Paschale, was equally fluent in English and French and also interested in the book, which I found she was translating into French. They were both overflowing in the life of the Spirit and we had an animated conversation on what the book was all about, the virtue of praise in all circumstances. I told them two stories which pleased them greatly. Especially in view of what comes later, allow me to share them here.

The first story comes from Merlin Carothers who writes extensively on the subject of praise and thanksgiving. His book *Prison to Praise*[1] has run into several million copies, and at one time used to be placed in every prison cell in California. Merlin tells elsewhere[2] how he was at a posh dinner party with cutlery extending in all directions, a spotless white tablecloth before him and his hostess at his side in a beautiful cream dress. No sooner is his tomato juice placed before him than he upsets it, and watches it roll down the cloth into his hostess' lap. In the hushed silence which follows the only words are from Merlin himself: 'Thank you, Lord, for allowing me to upset my tomato juice.' 'What did you say?' cries the outraged hostess. 'I said, Thank you, Lord, for allowing me to upset my tomato juice.' 'And what made you say that?' 'I have learnt to thank and praise God for everything that happens to me.' A pause, and then, 'Oh, I *am* interested. Do please stay behind afterwards and talk with me.' Well, you've guessed it. She became a convert, and one of his trusted workers.

I retell the above for our delight rather than our imitation. Speaking for myself I need much more practice on the nursery slopes before I attempt the mountain peaks. But the story which follows is a reminder of the possibilities within the range of many and, too, of the opportunities we are so likely to miss. I owe it to Bryan Green of whom I spoke in chapter five. His good and pious aunt had also learnt the secret of praising God for everything. One day, when hurrying for a train from Paddington station, the porter on the platform gate slammed it in her face. Quite unperturbed she walked off to get herself a cup of tea and then returned for the next train. The same porter was at the gate. 'Excuse me, madam, but when I shut the gate in your face, did I hear you thank and praise God?' 'Why, I don't really remember, but that is the sort of thing I would usually do.' 'Madam, you've missed one train. Would you mind missing another? I have a tea break and I have some problems and would like to talk them over with you.' And so his story came out, the problem of his marriage and all the rest, in which she was able to help.

Both stories illustrate the same point about praise. It is an act of faith, acknowledging that God is in control of every situation. And it keeps the lines of communication open with God. Grumbling and discontent, on the other hand, implicitly declare that God has lost his grip on things, and close down communication, thus making one useless to be of help to anyone else. If the grumbler is the most destructive influence in any community, it seems to follow that the one who praises, whatever happens, is the most creative. Of course we cannot always make our feelings go with the praise, nor should we try much to do so. It is what happens at the level of the will which counts. The feelings will follow in due course. Nor can we praise God for evil, but we can praise him for allowing evil, thus honouring the free will he has given us.

Having told the sisters these stories, and had much laughter and discussion, they then wanted to know about Julian who is a scarcely known figure in France. So more lively conversation followed until all too quickly it was my time to go. Here, more than anywhere else, I met life and spontaneity in Lourdes and the most real and lively interest in the things of the Spirit.

This is perhaps the place to mention (whilst speaking of praise and thanksgiving) an extraordinary thing which happened to me on the way to Lourdes. I should explain that some of the young people had brought with them the audio and video cassettes they wished to be played on the coach loudspeakers which were perched just above our heads with no switch by which they might be turned off. We older ones (and perhaps it applies to some of the young too) had already endured two cassettes of what came across to me as meaningless noise when a video cassette of the same ilk was presented to us. And, quite apart from the noise, a fresh punch or kick seemed to be on offer each time I glanced at the screen. Well, I was trying to put into practice what I have just written about, that God is to be praised in all circumstances. I argued with myself lightheartedly that if martyrdom could be a preparation for heaven, then this unholy din could, if endured patiently, be a preparation for holy things ahead. But whatever the will and the mind were doing, the emotions were in revolt. Moreover, I was wondering if this was going to happen all the way to Lourdes which was still fourteen hours ahead. Suddenly, out of the loudspeaker, in the very midst of this senseless film, there came the words, 'Julian of Norwich, Julian of Norwich, Julian of Norwich', spoken loud and clear in a pleasant voice and repeated at least six times. I turned to Richard and asked what Julian could have to do with this film. He had no idea what I was talking about. He had heard nothing unusual, nor had the person just in front of me. They said I must have misheard. Ten minutes later the same words were repeated, equally clearly and in the same voice, though on this occasion just three times. I again turned to Richard, but once again was told I had made a mistake. Well, supposing I had, and that the words were, say, 'beautiful knowledge' (not very sensible, but as sensible as anything else in the film) Richard and the other person would surely have heard it if it were repeated six times. A priest whom I spoke to later told me these words were a voice from the Lord to give me encouragement and hope. I had said I thought they were words thrown out by my unconscious which by some mysterious mechanism became audible to me alone as if through the ordinary channel of hearing. But the two views may surely be reconciled. In so far as one's life is 'hid with Christ in God' the Lord must be in the unconscious and what is thrown out will to that extent be his words. The same psychological mechanism may be at work, as I see it, in the realm of the visual. I shall never know for certain, nor does it matter that I should. The incident helped. For the record I hadn't been thinking of Julian at any time on the journey; nor am I accustomed to hearing such things.

I opted for no more martyrdom and took the precaution of arming myself with earplugs for the return journey. That, however, turned out to be better and before we ended the driver was presented with a Rachmaninov concerto which was, I suspect, as much relief to many of the younger members as it would have been to the older ones among us. To a large extent the young are the victims of the culture the mass media inflicts upon them. There was a good deal of latent talent on our coach as I learnt on the outward journey when the Lourdes hymn was sung as we approached the town and rendered strikingly beautiful with the help of a choir of young male voices from the back.

This was my first visit to Lourdes and I often found myself comparing it with Medjugorje which I had visited four times. I met a lady who loved Lourdes and had made the journey more than a hundred times working for the sick. She had also been to Medjugorje four times. She said she regarded Lourdes as her working place and Medjugorje as her praying place. I thought that was fair comment, and said I had come to think of Lourdes as the Martha of the Church and of Medjugorje as its Mary. I do not, of course, mean there is little prayer in Lourdes. Far from it. But whereas Lourdes is 'in prayer', Medjugorje is 'instant in prayer' as the apostle bids us be. It is an interesting reflection that it is possible for a pilgrim (as in my case) to go through a whole week in Lourdes without seeing a single rosary in action, not even in the quarter mile torchlight rosary procession as it passed me by. It is true that for the many who were carrying torches a rosary would have been impracticable. But there were hundreds who were not. It may, of course, be that in the hotel bedrooms the beads are rattling in the night but I suspect it would be in only a few. In Medjugorje the rosary is prayed constantly and everywhere by groups of pilgrims and by individuals wherever they may be – in the fields, on the roads, in the church or in any quiet spot. There was nothing to correspond with this in Lourdes. Wherever Mary comes, whether at Lourdes or Fatima or Medjugorje, it is the rosary she asks for. And it is interesting to note that in each place she asks (most frequently) for quantity not quality. Quality is, of course, important and Mary often stresses that. But it belongs primarily to God and it is not up to the one who prays to do very much about it. However hard we may try, or however much we may desire it, it is probably not open to any of us to pray the rosary with the same love and devotion as, say, Bernadette. What is open to us in rosary or any other form of prayer is to persevere, to go on and on with such love and devotion as may be given us. Even though that be very little, God will build on it and in his time the quality will grow.

Medjugorje reminded me of the Acts of the Apostles, whereas Lourdes struck me more as being the extension of the home parish church with devotion quickened, no doubt, in most cases. I felt Lourdes, renowned for miracles, would be surprised if one took place, whereas Medjugorje has become accustomed to taking a healing miracle, a vision of Mary, a spinning sun, a goldened rosary and a good deal more, quietly in its stride.

But is it fair to make such comparisons? Is it like comparing the forty days after the resurrection, when Jesus might appear at any time, with the Church in its later days? It is, after all, well over a century since Mary appeared at Lourdes and the Lourdes of that day may well have exhibited the sense of expectation and devotional fervour one finds in Medjugorje today. How will it be in Medjugorje a century after the visions cease? It's a fair question. And yet, in another sense, it may be a foolish one for there are those who see Medjugorje as a preparation for the gathering together of all things in Christ. Or may it be instead a visitation bracing us to meet in faith and hope the calamitous events which must overtake our world apart from a fundamental turning to God? There are spiritual laws as well as physical and to ignore either category is to invite disaster.

But the comparison has been made, and I am inclined to let it stand. I emerged enriched and refreshed by my experience of Lourdes and I believe that every Medjugorje person would acknowledge that without Lourdes the Church would be immeasurably impoverished. And yet I believe I stand for many Medjugorje people in a sadness that not more of the Lourdes persuasion would reciprocate that view. A Passionist priest with whom I spoke in Lourdes (and he is representative of many) told me he did not like Medjugorje. When I asked him why, he said it was because his bishop did not approve of it. I reminded him that his chief bishop was very forward in encouraging and blessing pilgrims visiting that place, and I might have added that in a light moment he had once remarked that but for the fact that he was pope he would be living there himself.[3]

23

The Julian Cell, Retreats and Books

I HAVE THOUGHT IT BEST to place together the visits to the two Marian Shrines though that has meant breaking with the chronological order of events. I must now return to my time at Melford Hall where Ulla Hyde Parker had kindly allowed me a twelve months' breathing space to decide on how my retirement years should be spent. Priests, of course, never retire; we merely draw retirement pensions and I had begun to draw mine at Bede House two years before. I had thought and prayed much at Long Melford on the question of future ministry but without any positive lead so there was nothing for it but to sit back and wait for God to open the way.

Canon Michael McLean was rector of the parish in Norwich of which St Julian's was one of its three churches. It had been badly damaged in the war having received a direct hit which demolished the tower and the roof and the greater part of its walls. After the war Government money was available for reconstruction and it was decided, with the active encouragement of the sisters at All Hallows, Ditchingham, and especially of their beloved and influential Mother Flora, to raise money to rebuild the Julian Cell on the site it occupied in Julian's day. No one knows how long after Julian's time her cell remained but one can be fairly sure that it would not have survived the Reformation. In due course the cell was ready. It occupied, probably, twice the area of earlier days and was now furnished as a chapel which would comfortably accommodate a dozen people. It was consecrated in 1951.

I first met Michael McLean at Bede House and we renewed our acquaintance at Melford Hall where on two occasions he came to lunch. I then learnt that he was anxious to find a priest who could be closely attached to the cell. The building was there but it needed, he considered, a praying presence. The day came when I received a letter asking if I would fulfil this role. It seemed to me to be the way God was drawing in answer to my prayers and I felt honoured and privileged to be asked. The Bishop had been consulted and was happy to license me for work in the diocese. The only possible hindrance was in the matter of accommodation. But fortunately, though I would prefer to say providentially, a house in King Street within a quarter of a mile of the cell was being dismantled to make two flats and Michael quickly arranged I should have one of them. To this I came in 1976 and as I write I have been here ever since.

The work which Michael asked of me was to be a presence at the cell and available to any visitors who wanted to speak with me. But not many came in those days and it was a full month before I spoke with anyone. I was also to consider myself available for the conducting of retreats and this involved visiting a number of religious communities. I think the men's were the easiest because they didn't want overmuch talking; the message from Cowley was that the fathers couldn't bear more than one short address a day. All honour to them. And in my experience men never took notes nor wanted a recording. They just sat back and listened or prayed or went to sleep. Women are more conscientious so it was not surprising that they wanted to miss none of the pearls which dropped from the conductor's mouth. Notebooks and, much more so, microphones put the conductor on his mettle and in my case any pearls which might have been in my heart were apt to vanish before they reached my lips. This, of course, is a personal matter and says more of me than my audience: many speakers probably get added inspiration with a cassette recorder before them. For me, even if it had not made me edgy, it would have upset the intimacy which should exist between the retreatants and the conductor. One can be fairly sure that if a family decided to tape the Christmas dinner conversation for an absent audience the talk would be much less lively and more self-conscious than it would otherwise have been. I found the same principle operative in a retreat.

Most people who visited the Julian Cell came because they wanted to spend a period of silence on the spot where Julian herself had lived and prayed. So as the number of visitors grew, and in the early years it was never much more than a trickle, one would find oneself increasingly sharing the silence with others. It was often out of the silence that questions arose, usually on some aspect of prayer or spirituality, less often on some personal or family problem the visitor was experiencing. Thus when one was alone with someone, talking and silence would often alternate and this could make an ideal setting for a fruitful encounter.

However, as numbers grew, we opened a counselling room in what was the vestry and this gave the opportunity for more formal meetings. I have no training as a counsellor and would never use that word of myself except with the very small c suited to most of us. But one tried to listen in the power of the Holy Spirit and to offer such help as one could. Sometimes people would say they had been wonderfully helped and one would realise one had said just about nothing, but that the sharing of the problem had given them the help they were needing. On St Anselm being asked to help another, he said, 'I shall try to the best of my ability, not so much to show you something as to search with you – with the help of God and your prayers'. That seemed to set a model for our meetings though I once gave a lady the advice of St Thomas Aquinas: 'If you are in a stew there are four things you can do; you can have a hot bath ("I've had that"); you can talk to a friend ("I'm doing that"); you can have a good cry ("I've done that"); you can contemplate truth.' The last has to be an unfailing remedy though we may need the preliminaries first.

Early in my time at the Julian Cell I met Jean Furness,[1] who would visit it most days with her four-year-old child Craig and spend half an hour or more in prayer. This led to a friendship between us and a bonding with her family which has continued ever since. For the past twelve years Jean has lived in the flat above me and she has had an important part to play in helping to make Julian better known. She helped in no small way to create the Julian Centre which is almost adjacent to St Julian's and which sells books and objects of interest to visitors. It has also a well-stocked Julian library which many use for research. Jean is a person who makes friends quickly with people in every walk of life and there are many who are grateful to her for her warm hospitality at the centre. She moved on two years ago having laid a good foundation for her successors. We have two assistants now, Margaret and Mary, who are doing great work in the further development of the centre.

When Jean's son, Craig, was five years old I taught him to play chess and he became quite keen. A little later the Bishop of Norwich (Maurice Wood) came to St Julian's to dedicate the counselling room. Jean and Craig were in church together. After watching the bishop Craig said to his mother in a loud whisper. 'The Bishop's moving wrongly. He is moving up and down and sideways like a castle. A bishop is only allowed to move diagonally.' Later he asked if he could write to the Bishop to tell him of

his mistake and I said he would be delighted to receive a letter. In due
course the Bishop replied as follows.

23 October 1981

Dear Craig,

I was so glad to have your letter and it was kind of Father Robert
to say that it was alright for you to send a letter to your Bishop,
who is an under-shepherd, under Jesus, the Good Shepherd, and
has to look after not only elderly sheep, but frisky lambs like you!

My Great Uncle Willie taught me to play chess when I was your
age, but I have not played for a long time, but I still remember
that even a small pawn like Craig, if supported by a diagonal bishop,
can be a powerful attacking weapon against the black king.

In the same way, we may not be very strong, but with the help
of the Lord Jesus, the Good Shepherd, we can win battles against
sin and evil, and know that when we are on the side of Jesus, the
King of Kings, we are on the winning side.

God bless you.

It is only in comparatively recent years that Julian has become widely
known in the Church. Grace Warrack's translation of her great book, *The
Revelations of Divine Love*, at the turn of the century served to introduce
her to an inner circle, perhaps largely members of religious communities.
I think there were no further landmarks until the rebuilding of her cell
after the war and then, in 1973, the celebrations in Norwich of the six-
hundredth anniversary of her visions. Dean Alan Webster of Norwich
(later to become Dean of St Paul's), staunchly encouraged by Mr Frank
Sayer, librarian and local historian, inaugurated the event. The occasion
included a high-powered four days' symposium, planned by Canon A.M.
(Donald) Allchin, bringing together students and lovers of Julian from
many countries. The celebrations also included an impressive and joyous
procession to St Julian's Church and her cell.

A further milestone came seven years later with the publication from
the cell of *Enfolded in Love*, a small book for the pocket which gathered
together some two hundred of Julian's sayings. The speed with which this
little book took off amazed the publishers who had offered a mere few
hundred pounds for the manuscript. I had more faith in it myself and
asked for five per cent on the first 10,000, seven and a half per cent on
the next, and thereafter ten per cent. As the royalties went to the work
of the cell I felt free to bargain unashamedly. The ten per cent figure

was, however, refused. The book rapidly reached the ten thousand mark and has gone on steadily ever since. The English edition is now approaching a hundred thousand. It was separately published in America and in several European languages. All this testifies to the power of Julian's words. Among the many appreciative reviews and comments, the one we treasured most came from an elderly lady who said she hadn't slept for several years but had only to pick up this little book and she dropped off at once. So I used to tell people that it was much better and more economical than what the doctor ordered for it sent you to sleep in the love of God and that way you would wake up in the love of God as well. The book began a series of which I was asked to be general editor known as the *Enfolded in Love* series which was highly popular for a while. It included a second Julian book *In Love Enclosed,* which contained an excellent introduction by Canon Michael McLean and which I think to be the better book though its sales are but a quarter of the other. This was theological whereas the first was devotional. But they stood together, the second as the cake and the first as the icing. Neither, of course, is a substitute for *The Revelations* itself.

I came to the cell with very little knowledge of Julian but I quickly realised what riches she had to bring to me as to many others and my retreat addresses were largely based on her writings. I was much better acquainted with *The Cloud of Unknowing,* a very different but complementary book written by an anonymous author of Julian's day. My first book after moving to the cell was *With Pity not with Blame* subtitled as *The spirituality of Julian and The Cloud.* I am a populariser and in no sense a scholar and it may be because Julian needed to be made popular and brought within the grasp of ordinary people that it received the acclaim it did. After fifteen years I think it need no longer be a secret that it missed the Collins' biennial book prize 'by a whisker'. The award went to Professor Maurice Wiles, the Regius Professor of Divinity in Oxford, for his *Faith and the Mystery of God,* a book for the trained theologian, thus somewhat limiting its readership. Numbers of better books on Julian have been written since my own but they have tended to be for students rather than the non-academic person searching for a deeper knowledge of God. Mine was greatly helped by sympathetic reviewers. The most memorable comment came from an Archbishop who said, 'I did so like your book. I thought the quotations were so good.' Having realised he had dropped something of a clanger he did not, to his credit, attempt to pick it up.

There is a saying that some write because they have something to say, others because they have to say something. I quoted it to Lesley Riddle, editorial director of Darton, Longman and Todd, when she asked for a second book, telling her that unlike the first it would be in danger of coming in the second category. Lesley was my unfailing encourager over several years and I am glad to have this chance of paying tribute. She had more confidence in me than I had in myself and more than once I allowed myself to be persuaded by her. In the world of books I am more grateful to her than to anyone else. At the time of her approaching me I was about to give the Lenten talks in Norwich Cathedral and I accepted her request thinking they might be expanded into a book. The outcome was *Love Bade Me Welcome* written in two sections: God's love and our response. It was a bit of a 'curate's egg' book but the good parts spoke deeply to some so I think it was worthwhile. The first part endeavoured to show how God's love always exceeds our expectations. The returning prodigal hoped for forgiveness but was met with a father running towards him and hugging him to himself. He hoped for serviceable clothing to replace his tattered rags but received the best outfit his father could supply. He looked for a meal to stem his gnawing hunger but a feast was declared in his honour. He hoped to be allowed to work and earn as a servant but found his sonship had never been lost. The second part dealt with prayer as a response to the beckoning, calling and yearning love of God. Here 'in the healing power of love to which the prayer life lays [us] open, resistances are broken down, prejudices are overcome, passions are subdued, fears are dissolved, memories are healed, relationships are enlarged and a new spirit comes to irradiate our lives which become increasingly marked with the note of trustfulness and thanksgiving'. This crafted sentence from the book gives none the less the plain truth of what the Holy Spirit works in us, as day by day our offering is renewed in the work of prayer. Although this second book sold nearly as many as the first it has, understandably, not been chosen for reprinting. But I have often thought it would bear revising and perhaps may undertake this if any publisher thinks it would meet a need.

A Doorway to Silence, subtitled *The contemplative use of the rosary*, is one of two books I have attempted in the style of the *Enfolded in Love* series. Each of its eighty-two chapters occupies a single page or less. This style is not for everyone but there are a large number of readers (it is now in its sixth impression) who like to have a book they can take up, read for a few minutes something complete in itself and then lay the book down for thought or silence. One reason for its popularity probably lies in the fact that it assumes no prior knowledge of the rosary; another reason may be that it sees the rosary itself as an excellent instrument for prayer and seeks to extend its use well beyond the 'Hail Mary'. It also seeks to offer a rationale for the rosary and explain why this 'monotonous and boring relic of past ages when few could read' (a Roman Catholic paper said that) may be as a sword which can pierce the heart of God. The rosary is seen as a little Office, using neither books nor psalms, but fulfilling in the end the same function as the greater Offices, as it leads the beginner through the way of meditation and affective prayer into the contemplative dimension of vocal prayer and so to the contemplative silence which lies beyond. St Antony of Egypt once spoke of himself as psalming down the devil. The rosary fulfils the same function.

The other book written on the same pattern is *Our Duty and Our Joy.* The words are taken from the ASB Eucharistic liturgy: 'it is our duty and our joy at all times and in all places to give you thanks and praise...' The Roman liturgy is yet more emphatic, speaking of our duty and our salvation. It is the last book I shall mention and because of the importance of its theme I should like to write of it at greater length. The book is largely governed by its prologue which is taken from the writings of William Law. A part of this reads:

> Would you know who is the greatest saint in all the world? It is not
> he who prays most or fasts most. It is not he who gives most alms
> or is most eminent for temperance, chastity or justice; but it is he
> who is always thankful to God, who wills everything that God
> wills, who receives everything as an instance of God's goodness and
> has a heart always ready to praise God for it... If anyone would
> tell you the shortest, surest way to all happiness and perfection, he
> must tell you to make it a rule to yourself to thank and praise God
> for everything that happens to you. For it is certain that whatever
> seeming calamity happens to you, if you thank and praise God for
> it you turn it into a blessing.

We are not, of course, to thank and praise God in order that we may be blessed. God is not open to bribery. But in thanking and praising him with such purity of intention as is given us we shall find blessing follows, though its manner belongs to God and not to us.

There is a story (not told in the book) of a Chinese farmer who was poor but who had one precious possession, a beautiful white horse. One day his horse was stolen and his friends came to commiserate with him. But all he would say was, 'Good luck, bad luck, who knows?' A week or two later the horse came running back bringing five fine wild horses with him. So now his friends came to offer their congratulations. But he would only say, 'Good luck, bad luck, who knows?' In attempting to break in one of the horses the farmer fell and broke his leg. More commiseration followed with the same reply as before. Just then war broke out and soldiers arrived to conscript the men in the neighbourhood. The farmer with his broken leg was passed over and this time, when the others congratulated him, he answered, 'Good luck, bad luck, God knows'.

So the great good fortune of winning the national lottery may be our deepest misfortune, and the misfortune of falling down a well, necessitating the amputation of a leg, may be declared to be (a true example from life) 'the deepest blessing of my lifetime'. This declaration, it is true, came in the evening of life when the person concerned could look back on the enrichment in the things of the spirit which had followed upon his accident. It would have been a giant of a man who could have praised God at the time. But so it often happens, that what seems to us to be our deepest misfortunes, are as the wings of a bird, not dead weights holding us down but, put to right use, the means by which we learn to fly. I recall being told of a father and mother who, knowing their child could live not more than a year, yet thanked and praised God throughout for the 'loan' which was given them. That must be the difference between the saints and ourselves.

The book is a modest attempt at a theology of praise. It is based on Paul's teaching that we should give thanks in and for everything. The theological justification for this is found in the saying of Julian who, following the traditional teaching of the Church, writes that nothing happens by chance but by the sure providence of God. As for evil, whilst we cannot consider it to be praiseworthy, we can consider God's allowing of evil to be praiseworthy, for thus he honours the free will he has given us. This, too, is a Julian thought. The argument is undergirded by St Augustine's declaration that God allows evil only to the extent to which it can be turned to good. A saying of Father R.M. Benson is also sharply relevant to the whole: 'We do not praise God because he has caused us to triumph but because to praise God is to triumph.' The triumph is in the praise. The triumph of the lady at Paddington station (chapter 22) was not in missing her train but in praising God in that situation. For, as there explained, praise is an acknowledgement that God is in control, whereas grumbling expresses the belief that something has passed him by. Praise keeps the lines open with God, whereas grumbling and discontent closes them down.

After writing the book I was interested and pleased to find the following in the new Roman Catholic catechism.

> We firmly believe that God is master of the world and its history. But the ways of his Providence are often unknown to us. Only at the end when our partial knowledge ceases, when we see God 'face to face' will we fully know the ways by which – even through the drama of evil and sin – God has guided his creation to that definitive 'sabbath-rest' for which he created heaven and earth.

And again, St Catherine of Siena is quoted with approval when she says to those who rebel against what happens to them: 'Everything comes from love; all is ordained for the salvation of man. God does nothing without this goal in mind.' But what faith if we can make that our own!

The theme has (as cited) strong New Testament support from Jesus and the Epistle of St James. But the strongest scriptural support (not cited) comes from the last three verses of the book of the prophet Habbakuk. It is a remarkable passage. Contemplating the complete failure of the fruit and the crops, the cattle and the sheep, all there is to live on, the prophet affirms, 'Yet I will rejoice in the Lord, I will joy in the God of my salvation.'

Unlike the three books last mentioned this one has failed to find sympathy with an American publisher. And whereas the others have averaged about 12,000 copies this one has barely exceeded 2,000. But that statement needs qualifying. In 1995 an elderly man, a stranger to me, came along clutching the book which he said went with him everywhere and asked if he might present *The Friends of Julian* with some copies to be given away in memory of his late wife, Joy. He made two gifts allowing us eventually to buy over 15,000 books. We wrote off to theological colleges, retreat houses and religious communities offering up to a hundred for them to give away to their personnel or friends or visitors and at the time of writing they have just about all been allocated. So, through one purchaser, the two thousand was increased to seventeen.

Understandably the book has aroused strong emotions. It has helped and encouraged some, bothered others and angered a few. The weakness of the book is that it fails to indicate that ultimately prayer and praise must dance together as in the Scriptures. Its strength is that it helps to restore the partnership where prayer has largely danced alone. Yet, in spite of its limitations, it will, I believe, continue to be a stimulus to many and not least to myself.

Whatever the verdict, if the prevailing argument of the book is unsound it seems to me to follow that the eucharistic liturgy of the Church must be rewritten. The whole part about thanks and praise at all times and in all places would have to be omitted because you couldn't possibly allow it and then qualify it by an exception clause at the discretion of the celebrant to exclude the events which appeared to be unmitigated and irredeemable tragedies and disasters. The liturgy can only stand in the knowledge (as the book says) that our life here is an unfinished symphony and the final movements are yet to be revealed.

24

A Zen Retreat

DURING MY TIME AT Bede House and later at the Julian Shrine I became interested in Zen-Buddhism, wondering if its meditational practice might not bring important insights to Christian prayer. I came to hear through Ursula Fleming that there was an annual Zen retreat at Spode House in Staffordshire. Spode House, standing in spacious grounds on the outskirts of the coal-mining town of Rugeley, was a well-known Catholic ecumenical centre administered at that time by the widely acclaimed and scholarly Dominican Father Conrad Pepler. In July 1979 I drove from Norwich to join the Zen retreat.

'Whatever has taken you to a Buddhist retreat?' 'Is not Christ sufficient for you?' They were inevitable questions. Yes, indeed, Christ is sufficient, for I believe, with St Paul, that in him all the fullness of the Godhead dwells. But it is not possible for me to confine his guidance and illumination to Christians. He is, as St John reminds us, and at a time when there were a very few Christians on earth, the light that lights everyone coming into the world. 'All that is noble in non-Christian systems of thought or conduct or worship', comments Archbishop William Temple, 'is the work of Christ upon them. By the word of God – that is to say by Jesus Christ – Isaiah and Plato and Zoroaster and Buddha and Confucius conceived and uttered such truths as they declared.' In the end, when all things are gathered together in Christ, it must surely be true that all who will be saved will joyfully acknowledge Christ as their Lord and Saviour however consciously unaware they may have been of his lordship and saving grace in this life.

We were to be in retreat for six days under the direction of two Zen-Buddhists, husband and wife, a monk and a nun. I had not known that marriage could be a part of the monastic life. Although our roshis had Japanese names, Koshi and Hegetsu, they were in fact Americans trained in their mother house, Shasta Abbey, in California. A link with Japan was forged through their Abbess Roshi Jiyu Kennett who, herself an American, had undergone extensive training in Japanese monasteries. Our two leaders were surprisingly young: Koshi told us he had just reached the age of thirty and that his wife was a little younger. It was she who started the retreat, her husband taking over a few days later. It must have been a daunting experience for these two young people to find themselves as leaders of a group in general much older than themselves, of whom not a few were obviously of mature and solid spirituality. However, outwardly at least they were confident and assured, and seemed in no doubt that Zen would offer us a growth we would not find in our own traditions. We learnt later that their pre-Zen background had been that of biblical fundamentalism in America, which would have virtually ruled out the possibility of contact with the range and depth of Catholic tradition.

There were about twenty of us in retreat of whom only two were Buddhists. There were perhaps half-a-dozen Roman Catholic sisters, one or two Catholic priests, some Catholic and Anglican laity, and one Anglican priest besides myself. Given that mixture you can imagine my surprise when confronted with the rules on the noticeboard. We were asked not to bring into the retreat any furniture, pots, plants, drugs, tobacco or chewing gum. We were informed that we might not practise I Ching, tarot, divination or occult practices of any kind. Clothing was to be seemly, no mini-skirts for women nor shorts for men. Other rules were strict but less bewildering. Reading matter other than that assigned was forbidden, and no one might leave the grounds without permission. Social conversation would be limited to teas, and loud talk and laughter were to be avoided. Later I was to discover that these rules had not been composed for our party but were the rules governing retreats at the Throssall Hall Priory from which our roshis had come, where presumably the retreatants would have been either Zen-Buddhists or aspirants. The rules referred to the Priory and its grounds and I had somewhat naturally thought that that meant Hawkshead Priory standing within a hundred yards and in the same grounds as Spode House. However, they were to be our rules as well, unnecessary though many might be.

Supper time came and silence descended on us. Grace was said and Roshi Hegetsu outlined the procedure we were to adopt at meals. First we must learn how to make the *gasho* for this was an important part of the ritual of every meal. The *gasho* is not unlike the more familiar Indian greeting known as the *namaste* (na-mus-tay) in which the palms of the hands are placed together with the fingers pointing upwards and a gentle bow is made from the waist. It is a graceful gesture conveying reverence and respect and, unlike our western practice of shaking hands, lends itself to be used prayerfully, each conveying a blessing on the other. The difference in the *gasho* is that the forearms are now horizontal, one or two inches from the body, the elbows pointing outwards. The dishes were to be passed round the table and we were to make a *gasho* towards our neighbour each time we received a dish and each time we passed one on. It was most important that the whole being should be poured into the *gasho* for it was something far more than an external positioning of arms and hands. The *gasho* was to help us recollect our scattered minds, to help make us present, fully present, in what we were doing. It was the symbol and instrument of awareness. I reflected how usefully much of this teaching could be directly applied to us Christians in the making of the sign of the cross.

We were told that the dishes were to be passed round once; and again, later, for second helpings. These were not in themselves desirable, but were to be seen as a concession to those who were unable to estimate accurately their requirements on the first time round. Ever since I had read those rules I had felt myself growing smaller and by now I was once again an eleven-year-old in boarding school. On no account, Roshi continued, as I shrank yet more, was any food to be left on our plates. I found myself inwardly protesting for, although I shared our roshi's dislike of waste, I believe that if food has to be wasted it is better done outside the body than within. We were then advised to take enough but not too much. Had not a Zen master declared that six parts of the stomach support the man whilst the other two support the doctor? With this pleasantry the tension was eased and we relaxed a little.

Most important, Roshi explained, was the keeping down of noise. Cutlery was to be placed on the table as quietly as possible and dishes were to be moved silently. This was not just a courtesy we owed to one another but a part of the compassion we owed to all created things.

After the meal would come the washing up. Each was to wash their own dishes as they sat at table. A jug of hot water would be passed round and we were to fill our drinking cups three-quarters full. With the help of a paper table napkin we were to cleanse and dry our cups and plates. In real Zen, the roshi explained, we would drink the washing-up water but as a concession to our inexperience we would be spared this rite. Instead, the dirty water in our cups would be poured into a bowl which we would circulate, not forgetting to make the *gasho* as we received it and passed it on. A scarcely audible sigh of relief came from my companions on either side. The full rite, which we were being spared, serves, we were told, to express the principle of conservation.

We then began our meal but it was shortly interrupted by the arrival of a latecomer. She made her *gasho* to the roshi – she had attended Zen retreats under other roshis – and explained that owing to problems with her car she had been delayed on her way. Roshi told her that lateness could not be allowed and that she must take her food into the kitchen and eat it there.

I knew this (middle-aged) lady slightly and had a great regard for her and was not a little upset at this cavalier treatment. After the meal I went to the kitchen and expressed my concern. It was then that I realised how much better prepared for the retreat she was than I. Was not a purpose of her coming to the retreat to have her own will contradicted and accept it gladly? True, she didn't express it in those words, but she sat there cheerfully and contentedly finishing her meal, with no sense of ill-will to our roshi, which I must myself have revealed, and that was the message which her response conveyed. In Zen terms here was the chance for the transcendence of the ego, the letting go of the false and superficial self that the deeper Self might emerge. In Pauline Christian terms we would say it was a putting off of the old man that the new man in Christ might be made alive. The injustice (as it seemed to me) of the penalty created the opportunity for sacrifice, and what to a lesser person might have been disastrous became for her an occasion for growth.

Later we assembled in the lecture room where we were given a talk on the rules. We were, Roshi explained, at a Zen retreat, and we were being paid the very real compliment of being given Zen as undilutedly as we could take it. We must on no account confuse Zen with Za-Zen, this simply being that part of Zen which occupied us in the meditation hall. Za-Zen, or sitting meditation, was simply one part of the whole structure. To have made that mistake – my comment, not hers – would have been like identifying Christianity with formal times of prayer and worship. Zen, she continued, embraced everything we did: working, walking, eating, talking, resting or sleeping. Za-Zen was an important and basic aspect of the whole but we must rid ourselves of any thought that we could pick out things as we liked. Most important was it that we should learn to do things together. It was not for each to go their own way during this retreat; in togetherness would be our strength. Thus, we must all get up together precisely as the rising bell rang and we would be allowed fifteen minutes to dress, wash, make our beds and be in the meditation hall. No one was to leave their bed before the bell and if there were problems of nature we might reflect how they might be overcome by drinking less at night. Similarly, going to bed must be prompt and we would be allowed just twenty minutes and then lights would be out. We were to take a full eight hours in bed as the day's work was heavy and we must be fully rested before the start.

We were shortly sent off to bed in the knowledge that we had just twenty minutes to be between the sheets. Bathing presented a problem for me as there was one bath for about eight of us and my room was some way down the corridor. Each night I set off valiantly, soap and towel in hand, only to discover that, like the man at Bethesda, someone had stepped into the pool before me.

Next morning we leapt from our beds with the bell at six o'clock and once again my Pangbourne training served me well. At a quarter past the hour those who made it were settled on Zen cushions, prayer stools or chairs and, having made a corporate *gasho* to the wall, Za-Zen was begun. From now on silence and stillness reigned.

At the time of the retreat the position I normally adopted for prayer made use of a prayer stool. This is of Buddhist origin but is now widely known in the Christian west. Turned upside down it looks like a book rest with shelving space of about fifteen inches. To use it you kneel down and turning the stool the other way up (i.e. the non bookshelf way) you place it over your calves and sit back on the bridge. Leaving prayer apart, physiotherapists delight in this position as being good for the back, and the stool can of course be used for reading or other occupations. I think most of us used a prayer stool at the retreat but some used the half lotus position aided by a Zen cushion (I think no one was equal to the full lotus) and two people had upright chairs. We took up our positions about five feet from the wall and adopted the posture described for yoga in chapter 15. We were instructed to keep our eyes open and look steadily though relaxedly at the wall. And we were to keep absolutely still.

The type of Zen we were taught bore the name *shikan-taza*, said to be the purest and the most demanding form of Za-Zen (*za* simply means sitting). In *shikan-taza* you allow thoughts to die down of their own accord by saying gently to yourself two sentences. 'Do not try to think. Do not try not to think.' Notice that each begins with the words 'Do not try'. That is to say, energy is to be withdrawn from the concept of thinking and energy is to be withdrawn from the concept of non-thinking. (Note that 'Do not try to think' is very different from 'Try not to think' and 'Do not try not to think' is very different from 'Try to think'. 'Try to think' and 'Try not to think' both put mental energy in, the first into the concept of thinking and the second into the concept of non-thinking. This is what must be avoided.)

So there we are looking gently at the wall and saying to ourselves from time to time 'Do not try to think' and 'Do not try not to think'. And this idea we may expand to cover all the senses. A pattern from the wallpaper, we suppose, holds our attention. (Ideally the wall should be plain.) We say to ourselves, 'Do not try to see the pattern' and 'Do not try not to see the pattern'. We must just let it lie in the line of vision. The smell of a meal comes in from the kitchen. Then do not try to smell it and do not try not to smell it. A dog barks in the garden. Then do not try to hear it and do not try not to hear it. An itch makes itself known on the back. Then do not try to feel it and do not try not to feel it. This can be a demanding exercise and one of the Zen masters says that this form of Zen should never be attempted for more than half an hour.

What happens when distractions come across the mind as they surely will? The answer is that quite simply we are to let them be, paying no attention to them, neither developing them nor getting involved with them, but going calmly on with our work. These distractions, painful though they be, are, said the roshi, for our healing. I was reminded here of something I had read from the Jesuit writer William Johnston who for many years has studied Zen in relation to Christian prayer. In his book, *The Still Point*, he draws attention to C.J. Jung's interest in Zen as a means of bringing healing to the psyche. He writes:

> As a therapist Jung was chiefly attracted by the healing powers of Zen. He often speaks of psychic wholeness accruing from its practice. As conflict was caused by disharmony between the conscious and unconscious mind so this was solved by the rising up of unconscious elements. For this eruption is not an indiscriminate something popping up from the mysterious depths, but is rather (Jung's words) 'the unexpected, comprehensive completely illuminating answer to the problems of one's psychic life'. Hence the resulting equilibrium and peace. Zen helps the development of healthy psychic growth, since in its silent darkness the unconscious is allowed to rise up thus creating a deep and wealthy conscious life.

William Johnston is a Christian contemplative and finds, of course, in the practice of contemplative prayer, as we all do, precisely the same psychological process at work as is here described in Zen. There are differences at the theological and spiritual levels but at the psychological level it is all one and the integration of the conscious with the unconscious proceeds in either case. Jung calls this the process of individuation, which has been described as the conscious realisation and integration of all the possibilities in the individual. It is this which is taking place in the silence I have described.

Shikan-taza was followed by *kin-hin* or meditational walking. We were instructed to form a single line around the room and to follow one another in a very slow walk, being mindful or fully aware of each step, or part of each step we were taking. Everything to do with the body in Zen is prescribed in the smallest detail. Thus in the prayers we recited together each morning we were told of the precise way in which we were to hold our books. So now in *kin-hin* the way in which we held our hands was important. We were to make a fist of the left hand with the fingers closing over the thumb. The right hand was then to be laid around the clenched left fist. The fingers of the left hand would thus be in the palm of the right. The hands were to be held at waist level just away from the body, forearms horizontal, elbows pointing outwards. The walking was to be done very slowly. With each step one knee would be raised so that the thigh became horizontal. The step took you forward about a foot and occupied perhaps ten seconds. Mindfulness was essential. As the textbook put it: 'Walking meditation must be done with awareness: it should never be done mechanically or in a zombie-like fashion. The eyes must not wander. Each step should be done carefully.'

All through the retreat it was impressed upon us that we should be mindful or aware. If we were gardening or eating our meals, or passing round the dishes, our full awareness was to flow into the action. The great aid to mindfulness was the *gasho* which has already been described. Always you made a *gasho* before beginning or ending an occupation. You made it when you spoke to someone and that was to remind you to give your full attention to what they were saying. And you made it when you had finished your conversation which was to remind you that you were now to gather your attention into the next occupation. The story is told of two Zen monks, both of them young men, who were returning to their monastery which lay some miles back from the banks of a river they had to cross. When they reached the ford they saw a beautiful young woman who feared to make the crossing lest the waters were too strong for her. Young Zen monks are not supposed to have dealings with young women but the elder one, seeing her plight, put her on his shoulders and carried her to the opposite bank. The two monks walked in silence for a mile or two after which the younger one exclaimed petulantly: 'Whatever made you carry that young woman across the river?' 'Good gracious,' came the reply, 'are you still carrying her?'

As you move from one occupation to another Zen has a series of brief prayers to recall the mind to what it is about to do. Thus at the beginning of a meal we said grace which included such phrases as 'The first bite is to discard all evil, the second bite is so that we may train in perfection, the third bite is to help all beings'; 'we must think deeply of the ways and means by which this food has come'; 'we must protect ourselves from error by excluding greed from our minds'. During the meal, every chew, and there should be many before we swallowed our mouthful, was to be done in full awareness of what we were doing. Zen has a verse for shaving, a verse before taking a bath ('I must cleanse my body and my heart'), a verse following the bath ('I have cleansed my body, I pray that I may cleanse my heart'), and a stirring verse on the lavatory seat ('Adoration to all Buddhas. Adoration to the limitless teaching. Peace! Speak! Blaze up! Open! To the glorious peaceful one for whom there is no disaster while upon the water closet, hail!'). These are but a few examples of prayers to help us to be mindful throughout the day.

Every major religion has its prayers for set occasions and often these are of great beauty. The Jews have prayers to be said through the day, short prayers set in the form of thanksgiving. Muslims, too, have a great variety of petitions seeking to bring all life under the protection of God. The Christian tradition is no less rich. The danger of such prayers becoming merely a formality is obvious, and where they simply serve to invest a profane event with the appearance of godliness the cause of religion is ill served. Zen, no doubt, is as much alive to these dangers as the rest of us. Its principles cannot be contested. Thus we were told:

> Every attitude of the body expresses a spiritual state whether we like it or not. Western religion has tended to divide body and mind. Make a *gasho* with the hand if you can but if not at least make it with the heart. To learn to bow to all things is the way to find the truth.

And again: 'The hands are very important to the body as the expression of spiritual attitudes.' Every priest at the altar, indeed everyone who has truly learnt to pray, would relate to that. The danger comes when mere formalism sets in. Ceremonial actions are important only in so far as they help the mind and spirit to rise to their proper functions.

We were given a number of aphorisms to ponder. 'Whatever happens to me I will take it for my good' (quoting a Zen master). 'Give up a sense of justice when you come into religion'. What a valuable corrective to our times when litigation is in danger of becoming the national sport!

We were reminded that fear had its proper function and we were not to belittle its value. 'Get the fire under your bum and you know when to get off the stove!'

Of prayer, we were told:

> Some people get scared with what they see in meditation and give it up. But what they see doesn't go away, they carry it with them. We are only given as much to see about ourselves as we can handle. We have to go through some tangled mess, some pretty messy stuff, what St John of the Cross calls 'The Dark Night of the Soul'. Don't think the dark night is reserved for Spanish mystics. We all have to go through it. Having a rough time spiritually does not mean you are on the wrong track, it means you are on the right track. A person who is in the midst of hell, who has bowed to suffering and not run away from it, is already moving away from hell. Suffering without despair is not hell...Our offering to God is sitting. We do a few basic things and God does all the work. Everything which arises in meditation is allowed to go on to God where it is cleansed in love. It is dealt with through the love which is moving through you.

And finally of God speaking in the heart. ' "I simply speak. I'm not going to clobber. If you want to listen do. If not there will be consequences." God will not force anything on us. We say we don't like it. He says, "That's all right. I can wait for ever" '.

It was arranged before the retreat that we should have a Catholic mass each day. I heard this was (understandably) a little difficult for the roshis to accept. But we were ninety per cent Christians and I think everyone looked forward to it. Indeed for most of us it was, I suspect, the highlight of the day. Not that we failed to value the rest. It would be more true to say that the mass served to breathe extra life into our other activities.

It should be understood that what I have set out to do in this chapter is to describe one particular retreat, not to advocate any one way of prayer or even of eating one's meals! Zen offers other ways of prayer, (and perhaps of eating), the use of a mantra, for example, and this is well established in the Christian tradition. Readers who are not familiar with the mantric way and want to learn it can hardly do better than buy *The Way of a Pilgrim* in one of several translations from the Russian. The book has become a spiritual classic and as we follow the pilgrim on his journeys we are likely to become identified with him in his quest for unceasing prayer which the mantra (in his case, the *Jesus Prayer*) may help to establish in our hearts.

There is a story of a holy bishop visiting three monks on an otherwise deserted island. They had been there for more years than they could remember. They had no Bible, no liturgy, no books. The bishop asked them how they prayed and they said: 'We just say: "Father, you are three. We are three. Have mercy on us." ' The bishop thought it would be a good thing to teach them the Lord's Prayer and he spent several days with them for the purpose. Then he bade them goodbye and set sail for another shore. But soon the monks signalled to him to come back. Try as they might they had forgotten the prayer. Could he please teach it to them again? The good bishop returned and laboured with them once more. But then, realising he was getting nowhere and seeing their simplicity and holiness, he decided to leave them to it and assured them that their simple mantric prayer would take them all the way to heaven. Thanks be to God!

25

America, Norway, Tongues and Healing

ON MY EIGHTIETH BIRTHDAY (1989) the Bishop of Norwich (Peter Nott) came to spend part of the morning with me. I was moved that he should spare the time from his busy life. But I was glad as well because it gave me the chance to raise the question of my resignation from the chaplaincy at the Julian Cell which I had been considering for some while. Several years before I was torn by doubt and on the verge of retiring but was given a remarkable sign that I should stay on. I am not easily given to asking for signs being mindful of the words of Jesus that it is an evil and adulterous generation which seeks them. But I believe there are occasions when we may ask for them and I thought this to be one. I had a lump on the back of my neck of about the size of a hemisphere of one centimetre diameter which I had often been told I should show to the doctor. It had been with me for at least fifteen years. I recall stopping one day in the street and saying, 'Lord, if you make this lump go down I shall take that as a sign that I should continue my work at the Julian Cell.' Within a few days it had disappeared and I am told no trace of it remained. I know this sort of story is irritating to some but I see it as a witness that things do happen to the body in answer to prayer (and I would classify this as prayer) which are outside the working of nature as we understand it. I have no explanation. I was relieved to have the sign and continued my work with new assurance. However, now on my eightieth birthday it seemed that the time for resignation had come and I suggested to the Bishop that I should give a year's notice in order to give plenty of time for a successor to be found. This was agreeable and accordingly I left my work in the summer of 1990. No successor was forthcoming nor has been since. It is not a work to which a salary or accommodation is attached and probably only an unmarried priest drawing a retirement pension, such as myself, could afford to take it on.

I continued to live in King Street about a quarter of a mile from the cell and the Julian Centre and, without being tied as before, endeavoured to make myself available for meeting people who wished to see me. There were some who had read my books and wanted to learn more about Julian, others who were looking for pastoral help, and not a few who liked to come simply to share a saying of the rosary or silent prayer. Two rosary groups developed, one on Tuesday mornings and the other on Friday evenings. These are friendly and informal occasions and our prayer time of thirty-five minutes on Tuesdays or sixty minutes on Fridays is followed by chatter and refreshments. Chatter may suggest something rather superficial but the simplest conversations are sanctified by prayer and in our experience often lead on naturally to the consideration of deeper things.

In the spring of 1991 Fr Richard Crist, rector of the Episcopalian Church of St Hilary's, Prospect Heights, near Chicago, came to see me to ask if I would conduct a quiet weekend in his parish in the following autumn. With typical American generosity he offered to pay for a companion to travel with me if I felt the journey to be too much on my own. That was not necessary; indeed I had a very comfortable journey, travelling in club class as economy was overbooked. I am jumping ahead a little when I say that I told this to some of the St Hilary's parish and they said they would pray for the same thing to happen on the return flight. I said I couldn't possibly pray for that as someone else might need the seat more than myself. They quickly brushed that aside. 'Don't worry, father, we'll be praying.' Not only did I get the seat but sat next to a man who was complaining that his son had had to travel economy because all the club seats were booked. He and his disappointed son would swap seats during the flight. I didn't dare let on! I am not trying to make any theological point but it is odd how things worked out. And I won't try to disguise my pleasure at being called to the desk shortly before departure to be told my good fortune.

I prayed a lot about this visit but left England without any idea of what I should talk to the parish about. I had a day to acclimatise and went to bed the night before the talks without knowing what I should be saying. And then it dawned that I had to talk on the rosary. It was just as well that the forty or fifty who were there had no advance knowledge as they told me later that half of them would not have come if they had known the subject. As it was, many surprised themselves by the ease they took to this way of prayer and I was told that two rosary groups were formed after I had left. There were already an extraordinary number of societies in the parish – more than thirty I later discovered – but they tended to be 'active' and another prayer group helped to assure a proper balance.

It is impossible to go to the States without talks developing. Americans have a way of thinking that English people have a considerable share of the amazing energy with which they themselves have been endowed. They also have the strange habit of assuming that if you have been to Oxford or Cambridge you are quite remarkably learned. So if you aren't Professor when you mount the podium you are at least Doctor and you do your best to wear the mantle naturally, and fervently hope there will be no time for questions afterwards. And then, after it is all over, when you have done your feeble best, a substantial cheque arrives with an assurance of the helpfulness of your talk.

One of the joys of this visit was in being able to stay with the Order of Julian of Norwich in Waukesha in the state of Wisconsin. Here is a small but flourishing company of men and women living under vows in a monastic community founded in the autumn of 1982 by Fr John-Julian who was their guardian for the first thirteen years. Fr John-Julian is a man of unusual theological insight and a gifted writer. Moreover, he is wholly devoted to Julian and is able to expound her teaching with verve and passion. He is responsible for an excellent translation of Julian's Revelations[1] but at the time of writing has never written a book. One must hope that that lack will be remedied. His penetrating articles in *JuliaNews* make exciting reading. Sister Scholastica Marie succeeded as guardian in September 1995 and under her the community continues to build up its strength. I am not alone in believing that more is being done in America than in England in making Julian known.

My main hosts in the States were Richard and Mary Crist. As rector of what the bishop considers to be the model parish in his diocese Richard has told me that he lets the parish run itself. That alone makes him a remarkable leader and in so far as his claim is true (he looked like a hard worker to me!) it is because for him the prayer life comes indisputably first and Richard holds himself quietly available to the call of the Holy Spirit.

Mary Crist has been endowed with the scriptural gift of prophecy which has brought her into contact with people in many parts of America and widely through the world. Words are presented to her aloud at dictation speed allowing her to write down any message which may be given. 'I hear him [Jesus] in a clear voice that is outside of myself. It is an external voice, not something I hear in my head or my heart . . . I realise others around me do not hear Jesus when he is speaking to me.' Mary also speaks of visual contact though 'it is more often I hear Jesus rather than see him.' Earlier she has written: 'I see Jesus as a real person, not as a hazy ghostlike figure. But I am aware that others around me do not see him. I see him with dark eyes and hair, most often wearing a simple sand-coloured robe of very rough material.' The messages may come at any time making it necessary for her to stop what she is doing in order to write them down. 'Most often I hear the Lord when I am quietly praying but he has been known to interrupt me at meetings, while driving or even while listening to a sermon . . . People ask me how I can be certain that the words I hear are really from Jesus. I know that this is true without a doubt. I hear and see him as clearly as I hear and see you. I have put myself under the authority and testing of the Church from the very beginning. I have a spiritual director, the bishop of my diocese, who provides guidance to protect the people, myself and the Church from error.'

Every year Mary, with the help of a large band of parish workers, sends out a Lenten journal with a reading and exercise for each day in Lent to seven hundred or more people at home or abroad.[2] This in itself would be work enough but enclosed with each journal is a 'Jesus letter' individual to each recipient and six or more Jesus directed individual Bible passages to be prayed over and studied. These have influenced many lives, including my own. 'I think of myself', writes Mary, 'as a "bearer of words" for the Lord. Over the fifteen years since the gift began ever so slowly I have given words and messages to over 2,000 people throughout the United States and around the world. I serve as a channel, bringing the words to those the Lord decides to send them to.'

In the language of the Church Mary would be known as a locutionist. The word is not used in the Bible though locutions abound. Some locutionists receive their messages in ecstasy – the visionaries of Medju-gorje are an example of this – but Mary is fully conscious of her surroundings when her words are given. The interplay between the personality of the agent of a locution and that of the receiver makes it necessary for a message to be received with caution lest the receiver has in some way unwittingly affected it. Mary is fully alive to this. The messages may vary in length from one short paragraph to thousands of words. I must have read about forty messages shown to me by various people. The words are always in accordance with Scripture and are given with understanding, tenderness and encouragement. Many, to my knowledge, have been deeply moved and helped by them. I do not doubt that they are inspired messages but at the same time I believe, as does Mary herself, that they should be read with discernment seeking the guidance of the Holy Spirit. Mary is completely dedicated to the service of the risen Lord in a relationship which began as a young child and has developed steadily ever since.

I have generally found the Bible passages relevant, and sometimes remarkably so, though not always understandable at first. In 1994 I received, as one of the six readings, the passage in the Acts of the Apostles (16:9–10) which runs: 'During the night Paul had a vision of a man of Macedonia, standing and begging him, "Come over to Macedonia and help us." After Paul received the vision we got ready at once to leave for Macedonia, concluding that God had called us to preach the gospel to them.' This made no sense to me until about two months later a Lutheran priest and his wife came to tell me that in the grounds of their home in Norway they felt called to build a retreat house chapel. They were, however, unfamiliar with the more catholic ways of prayer and everything depended on whether I could come and help them. I think I might well have refused the somewhat arduous journey and time-consuming assignment, but I was able to say at once that I already had my marching orders. What a richly blest visit that was! I went for two weeks with my friend and prayer companion Edna Jones and each day the four of us met several times for prayer followed by instruction or questions and gradually the project took form. Eric and Kirsten Rostboll were wonderful hosts and now have the most beautiful little chapel fifty yards from their front door to which retreatants come, the sleeping accommodation being already there.

I am not at liberty to quote from my Jesus letters as they are too personal to share except with a few close friends. Suffice it to say they are always gracious and encouraging, and usually demanding. Most demanding of all was the recent one asking me to write this book, something I would never have consented to do apart from this instruction which, after much wrestling in prayer, I was able to accept as the expression of God's will.

It is, however, of an earlier letter that I would like to speak here. People have often asked me if I spoke in tongues, sometimes with the implied opinion that I was not yet a true Christian if that gift had not come my way. I had replied that I did not have the gift, nor had I any desire to pray for it, but that I hoped I was open to receiving it if God so wished.

It had seemed to me it would be presumptuous to pray for any of the gifts of the Spirit listed by St Paul (1 Corinthians 12) in the absence of an indication to do so. I now believe I was wrong for, although Paul says at the end of the chapter quoted that love is the more excellent way, he also says we are to set our hearts upon the better gifts. And what we set our hearts upon is, after all, our prayer.

It was the Jesus letter of 1994 which brought home to me the error of my earlier thinking and convinced me that I had to pray for the gift of tongues and the gift of healing. Whereas before I had thought it would be presumptuous to pray for these gifts I was, in view of the letter, led to believe it would now be presumptuous not to do so. At that time I was editing a book, *Circles of Silence,* for *Julian Meetings* and was struck by two articles on the gift of tongues by Father Naters of the Cowley Fathers.[3] In due course I went to him to ask for the laying on of hands for the reception of the two gifts.

If readers are expecting me to say that I rose from that experience speaking in tongues as did Cornelius and his servants when visited by Simon Peter (Acts 10:44–8) they are in for a disappointment. It is true that there are many today – and they may be numbered in millions – who experience tongues in the same spontaneity of utterance as seems to have been usual in New Testament times. But there are others for whom tongues have to be worked at, starting perhaps with a single word to which other words may be gradually added. It is to this group that I belong. In what follows (comparing tongues with mantric prayer) it is from my own experience that I speak. It must be for others to determine how far my words are applicable to them. I speak in tongues (in private prayer only) in a very rudimentary way, the same words appearing in one order or another again and again; in fact it is so rudimentary that I almost wonder if I ought to be claiming that gift at all. But, and this is the important point, it has at times, and especially at times of stress, helped my prayer life. And I say that in case it should help the reader as well. An excellent beginning for anyone interested would be to study the two articles written by Fr Naters in the book referred to above.

Ever since reading *The Way of a Pilgrim* some sixty years ago, referred to in chapter 17, I have found great help in mantric prayer. It began with the Jesus Prayer but much has opened out since then. In mantric prayer a word or short sentence is chosen and allowed to act as a focal point for the mind. At times the mantra may be repeated continuously, at other times it may be allowed to come and go. In the end it will disappear altogether. In the early stages it may be repeated aloud and the action will be mostly in the mind. Later on, repetition in silence takes over (the lips and the tongue being still) and the mantra becomes lodged in the heart. Tongues has much in common with mantric prayer, but there are differences as well. I would list the similarities as seven:(1) Each way of prayer cuts out surface distractions which would otherwise arise. (2) The purpose of each is to engage the heart in prayer. Unless the heart be engaged there is no prayer at all. (3) Each is a means to the same end, which is (when the words have dropped away) the silence of the heart before God. (4) Each way of prayer is relaxing. A psychotherapist makes this as his only point on the value of tongues. He is right as far as he goes. But we need to be careful here since relaxation in itself is not prayer though it will be an aid to prayer. As for prayer itself there can be none unless the desire for God is present. (5) The full effectiveness of tongues or mantric prayer is to be found passively, that is to say rather than praying you allow yourself to be prayed. (6) Each can be used as an intercessory intention for a person or cause, just as an Office or Eucharist may be so used. (7) Each works towards the breaking through of the rational, fulfilling in this respect the function of a Zen koan, releasing inhibitions, putting the person more in touch with the subliminal consciousness, or the unconscious.

So much for the similarities. What then of the differences? Assuming, though it may not be a common practice, that tongues, like the mantra, may be 'spoken' in silence as well as aloud, I can find only two. (1) In mantric prayer the words are set for you. They are not only the same words each time but they come in the same order. In tongues the 'words' simply tumble out and even if they are the same, since they are in any case gibberish to you (but not to God who reads the heart), it does not matter in what order they come. For the proficient this allows for a greater liberty in the Spirit, a deeper rest to the memory and therefore to the mind, and thus a deeper relaxation. Anyone who is experienced in mantric prayer knows that for it to be effective the words have to be so well known that memory is scarcely operative. We could, as we might say, repeat the words in our sleep. And probably in the depths of the spirit we often do. Even so, I think in this respect, tongues (for the proficient) has the edge over mantric prayer. The mind is more deeply at rest. And (2) mantric prayer, as Christians normally use it, allows you to pray in a measure with the understanding as well as with the spirit, whereas in tongues (apart from a special revelation) you pray with the spirit only. St Paul allows either but in his first epistle to the Corinthians (chapter 14) seems to prefer prayer in which the understanding takes its part, though without insisting upon it. He tells the Corinthians that he was more proficient in tongues than any of them and it appears that he would pray sometimes with the understanding active and sometimes not. The passage may be compared with Romans 8:26-7 which reads, 'Likewise the Spirit helps us in our weakness; for we do not know how to pray as we ought, but the Spirit himself intercedes for us with sighs too deep for words. And he who searches the hearts of men knows what is the mind of the Spirit, because the Spirit intercedes for the saints according to the will of God' (RSV). It seems that Paul is here referring to, what we would call today, contemplative silence, but whatever form of prayer he is speaking of it is prayer without (on our part) the comprehension of what is being prayed. The Spirit understands but we don't, except in the sense that we may have offered our prayer beforehand for this or that intention. In these two verses Paul reveals the depths of his prayer life (and of what may be ours) more than anywhere else.

It is clear that speaking in tongues, unlike mantric prayer, is a *marked* scriptural phenomenon. Were it otherwise it would, I feel sure, be a highly suspect manifestation in most areas of the Church where it is acceptable today. Whilst Paul values tongues and insists that it is a gift of the Spirit, and thanks God that he has this gift, he is aware that used in public it can get out of control and be ego-inflating. Thus what ought to build up may easily, in corporate life, tend to destroy. Paul sees the value of tongues almost exclusively as a private gift.

For myself I have not given up mantric prayer since coming to that of tongues. It seems to me that each has its place and that if we are familiar with both we should use whatever may be most helpful at the time. For me that is normally mantric prayer. Neither is a final resting place, each being a preparation for the fuller silence which lies beyond. There will be days when that silence awaits us without the preliminaries of which we have spoken. But we cannot count on that and must be humble enough and flexible enough to use, when we need them, the aids which the Spirit offers.

How is one to understand the intercessory aspect of mantric prayer? When I was in India it was a common sight to see hundreds of men or women carrying on their heads a bowl of earth from one place to another in order to build a road or railway embankment. The amount each could carry on a single journey was infinitesimal. One person might perhaps complete the work in a thousand years. But put a thousand on the job and in a year the embankment would be there. I see a single mantric prayer as a bowl of earth on the head of one of those workers. In itself it seems nothing. And yet the railway line is built. So, too, every prayer offered with such devotion as may be given us helps in some infinitesimal way to extend the kingdom of God and to throw back the kingdom of evil. This one prayer may help a needy soul in the after life, a patient in the local hospital, a prisoner in a foreign land or the person I shall meet in the next ten minutes. I shall never know, at least not in this life, but I make my prayer as an act of faith, and it may be remembered that each time my faith is exercised it is increased. As each one goes faithfully on the boundaries of the kingdom are enlarged.

But, as we have seen, it is not one person who is employed but perhaps a thousand or more. And after a day's work the amount of earth moved is sufficient for all to see what has been done. How would it be if a thousand or more were occupied in mantric prayer? That is what you see happening in Medjugorje which I have described in an earlier chapter. It may well be that on any one day thousands of people are at work on their rosaries, and the prayers accumulate and achieve something for the extension of the kingdom which can be seen and felt and known. The prayers of Medjugorje build up (and I believe that in prayer as in marriage two is more than twice one) which is why it is a place where conversions take place, sanctifying grace is at work, love of one another is evident, miracles of physical as well as spiritual healing are often in evidence, and prayer goes out to accomplish its mission in all the world. Come back from Medjugorje and spiritually speaking you are in flat country. That is because our nation is as a tree partially stunted at the roots. It is indeed important to attend to the branches, to the needs of hospitals and schools and prisons. But it must always be the primary task of the Church to water the roots. The work on the branches will remain but they will blossom as never before.

Mantric prayer opens us, and others through us, to 'the impact of the truth which is in Jesus'. Allow me to quote from the closing paragraph of my rosary book, *A Doorway to Silence*.[4] With the necessary changes, the passage may be seen as in no way exclusive to the rosary.

> The rosary is a 'little way' asking of us no more than the simplicity of children, but to those practised in it it offers a rich reward.

This, however, may never be seen as an individual possession for it is of the very nature of love to radiate light and peace and joy and to spend itself quietly in helpful and practical ways. It is thus that the life of society is transformed, the leavening of the lump from within working what no government fiat could ever achieve. And so it must be that the witness of the Church will always be to the priority of prayer if its influence is to make impact on society as a whole.

Let me now turn to the question of healing which was the second gift I felt called to pray for on receipt of Mary Crist's letter. We should try to remember that the possession of any of the gifts of the Spirit exposes us to dangers and that it is more important to be grounded in the fruit of the Spirit than to possess the gifts. The fruit of the Spirit, as listed by St Paul in his epistle to the Galatians, is love, joy, peace; patience, kindness, goodness; faithfulness, gentleness, self-control. I have found it helpful to memorise these for their slow repetition can of itself be a spiritual therapy. They are easily memorised if it is noted that the first group are all of one syllable, the second of two and the third of three. Furthermore, that the second group and the third each follow the dominant vowels: *a i o* in the first case and *a e o* in the second. Whereas Paul speaks of gifts in the plural he speaks of fruit in the singular. For the fruit is indivisible. The 'fruits' listed are all aspects of the one love which governs them. Thus joy is love rejoicing and peace is love resting. Patience is love waiting, kindness is love acting and goodness is love being. Faithfulness is love trusting, gentleness is love nurturing and self-control is love discipliningning. I am doubtful whether anyone should ask for the gifts of the Spirit without a solid grounding in the fruit. In any case if, as now, we are talking of healing, the one who is rich in the fruit of the Spirit has to be a healer whether he or she knows it or not. Such people carry with them an atmosphere of healing which, simply by their presence, cannot but have a therapeutic effect on all who are open to receive it.

When one meets people who exercise the ministry of healing one is liable to hear the view that it is God's will that everyone should be healed of their infirmity or sickness, and that if they are not, there is some failure on the part of the minister or patient or those praying around them. In the long term that must be right, that we shall all ultimately be made whole and complete in body, mind and spirit. But the long term takes us beyond this life to the consummation of all things in Christ. In the short term, by which I mean the period this side of death, bodily sickness should often be seen as the condition needed for a while to enable healing to take place at a deeper than bodily level. God may sometimes call us aside from a busy life to do for us in sickness what he could never do in health. At such times a new world is often opened to us and we have time to reflect on matters of deeper moment than those which crowd into our minds in the stressful lives which belong to so many. In most cases the sickness is temporary, and we take up the thread of ordinary life again, now hopefully allowing ourselves more space for what ministers to our deepest needs. But in other cases the bodily sickness remains right up to the moment of death.

Christians who think differently from this have, it seems to me, to do some explaining away when it comes to considering St Paul's thorn in the flesh (2 Corinthians 12:7–10). I consider Paul's thorn in the flesh to be of crucial importance when we come to reflect on the ministry of healing. You will remember that Paul said there was given to him a thorn in the flesh, a messenger of Satan sent to buffet him, lest he should be exalted above measure. What form this ailment took we have no means of knowing and in that we may be blessed because we can then more easily identify it with our own. I find it interesting to note that Julian of Norwich believed that all who will be saved have this point of vulnerability, this Achilles' heel of Greek mythology as we might call it, which the enemy is quick to target. But we should not be downcast because God means this weakness to be for our good.

The nature of Paul's thorn is secondary. What is primary is the way in which he responded. It is important to note that his first response was not acceptance. It was protest. He prayed to the Lord three times, he says, that this affliction might be removed. We have a parallel here with Jesus in the garden of Gethsemane where we are told that three times he prayed that if it were possible his cup might be removed. Perhaps Paul had that very incident in mind. It was only after Paul had made his threefold protest that acceptance came. He received the reply: 'My grace is sufficient for you, for my strength is made perfect in weakness'. It is only then that Paul submitted and yet, as we know, he did more than submit, he rejoiced. He praised God for his infirmity: 'Most gladly will I glory in my weakness that the power of Christ may rest upon me'.

It is only with this theological background in view that I feel able to speak of the healing ministry for which, as I have said, I felt led to pray in obedience to one of Mary Crist's messages. But first I should say that

I resist calling it a healing ministry because that suggests to so many people that it is something to do exclusively with the body. I therefore call it a blessing/healing ministry as this makes the important point that the whole person is involved. Each one of us is a trinity in unity, a body-mind-spirit complex so that whatever is done to one part of our nature finds its repercussions in the other two. Thus the whole person is caught up in every act of healing where that word is understood in its complete sense. Before laying hands upon a newcomer who asks for this ministry I like to explain that there will always be a blessing and that God will give that blessing at whatever level he sees best. I then ask the person to sit upright in a comfortable chair and from behind lay my hands in the energy field above the recipient's head, the place where we would see the halo if we had the requisite psychic sensibility. I like to begin with a spoken prayer and sometimes to continue with such prayer, depending very much on the spiritual understanding of the one concerned. The whole takes about ten minutes of which perhaps, typically, half is in silence. The recipient is simply asked to be open and relaxed so that the energy of the Spirit may have as free a flow as possible. I am not aware of what takes place within the one to whom I am ministering though sometimes they like to volunteer this. What should be clear is that when nothing is felt it does not follow that the blessing/healing is less. Often it is the immature who have the felt and, sometimes, sharp reaction either because God sees they need this booster to their faith or because there are psychological blockages which impede the free flow of the Spirit. As a stream flows smoothly over a clear bed without leaping and bounding as it would if stones and rocks impeded its way, so will the Spirit tend to move peacefully in those whose lives are most truly hid with Christ in God. But that there are exceptions to this rule linked often to the psychic sensibility of the person concerned I do not doubt. To return to my own practice, I like to move my hands to rest on the recipient's head with a formal trinitarian blessing at the close of the session.

There are some who like to come a number of times and I can see nothing wrong in this; indeed it seems sensible and right if they are renewed and strengthened. If we may return again and again to receive the Eucharistic bread and wine it can hardly be wrong to act likewise in the lesser sacramental act of laying on of hands. A dependence upon the 'healer' could in some cases be a danger but in my limited experience it has not arisen. I believe we can be helped more than we ordinarily think by receiving this ministry from others suitably chosen (none who are not endeavouring to respond to God's call to holiness are suited to this work) and I frequently ask for it myself from those who are aspiring to make the same journey. I never feel drained or exhausted in exercising this ministry, nor do those who minister to me. I suppose it is that as we give so we receive. In fact we seem to receive more than we give, for refreshment is the word we would use to describe our experience. What is done takes place in a setting of quietness and trust. The ministry of healing is ill served by the noise and commotion we sometimes see accompanying it on our television screens. Recently there has been a well-publicised humorous/serious picture postcard making the point that the nearer we are to Jesus the less we need to shout. It stands not only for the healing ministry but for ministry at all levels.

26

The Psychical, the Spiritual and the Toronto Blessing

IN 1995 I WAS ASKED if I would be a Vice-President of the Churches' Fellowship for Psychical and Spiritual Studies (CFPSS) and to this I was happy to agree. I had for some years been a member of the Fellowship though had never contributed to its literature. The Fellowship was founded in 1953 by a group of clergy and laity in the conviction 'that psychical phenomena had great relevance to the Christian faith, both in life and death'. Full membership is open only to believing Christians who alone can vote or hold office. The present President (1997) is the Revd Dr Martin Israel whose spirituality and psychical awareness are well known to the many who read his books or attend his retreats. Among its patrons are the Archbishop of York (Dr David Hope), Dr Graham Leonard, formerly Bishop of London, and Lord Soper.

There are Christians who say they will have nothing to do with the psychic but this is a vain assertion since we are all immersed in it every day. Unfortunately they are apt to confuse the psychic with the dark regions of the occult which should be shunned as the devil himself. Every emotion, whether positive or negative, has a psychic charge. Communication in ordinary speech is in part a psychic phenomenon. The psychic is described as follows in a brochure for the CFPSS:

> It is basically a direct communication from the soul (or true self) of
> one person with another without rational mediation. No real
> relationship with people in fact can evade the psychic level, for it is
> here that we communicate with one another in truth. This applies to
> ordinary rational relationships, and sometimes, particularly in
> people who are closely attuned, the soul-contact can transcend the
> barriers of time and space; even, indeed the barrier of physical
> death. These experiences are not sought but occur spontaneously.

They are a part of the natural personality of human beings, and when properly understood need cause no embarrassment or fear. Some people are more sensitive than others, and if their sensitivity is dedicated to God they may be particularly valuable in the fields of healing and counselling, including counselling the bereaved.

People who are psychic to an abnormal degree are often known as sensitives. They are not necessarily better people (in a moral sense) than others. They may be saints but equally they may be rogues. I say this because it is important to realise from the outset that psychical capacity is in itself neither good nor bad. It is in theological parlance amoral or in more ordinary speech morally neutral. As a rough analogy you could see it as a telephone wire which can communicate rich blessings or pornographic trash whilst remaining neutral in itself. It is important that every Christian should be a spiritual person but it is not important that he or she should be a psychic person except in the sense that that capacity in a measure belongs to us all.

This leads us to consider the difference between the psychical and the spiritual. Our inquiry is hindered because the word spiritual is used in two different senses and we must first of all determine the sense in which we are to use it. Spiritual may be understood in contrast to the physical but that is not the normal New Testament sense and it is not the sense in which I shall mean it here. Thus, in this sense, you might speak of your neighbour's presence as a physical phenomenon whereas the presence of a ghost or spirit you would call spiritual. In this understanding of the word the archangel Gabriel is spiritual and the devil is spiritual (both being pure spirits). Whereas in the sense in which we shall use the word spiritual, following the New Testament, the archangel Gabriel remains spiritual whereas the devil is the most unspiritual being we can imagine.

How then does the New Testament understand the word spiritual? We have it in St Paul's writings. 'To be spiritually minded', he writes to the Romans (8:6), 'is life and peace.' There is no contrast here with the physical for Paul is clearly writing to those with physical bodies. The spiritual person is one who lives in the power of the Holy Spirit and who bears in their life the fruit of the Spirit: love, joy, peace; patience, kindness, goodness; faithfulness, gentleness, self-control. In comparing the psychical with the spiritual it is in this sense in which the word spiritual is here used.

The word psychic is defined in the dictionary as 'outside the possibilities defined by natural laws'. It has reference to paranormal phenomena such as telepathy, psychometry, clairvoyance, tongues, healing, prophecy. A sensitive may have special capacities within one or more of these fields. If he is a truly spiritual person he will exercise these powers for good. The prophets of Israel are a good example of this. If he is a rogue (an unspiritual person in our understanding of the word) he may use his powers to enslave and exploit and even destroy others. Practitioners in black magic are a flagrant example here. Thus it will be seen that a sensitive is a person with a tremendous potential for good or evil. A spiritually-minded sensitive such as for example the Curé d'Ars or Padre Pio may be the means of bringing countless blessings to countless people whereas an unspiritually-minded sensitive, a power greedy person intent on feeding his own ego, may be as the devil incarnate. All the more reason then for the Church not to ignore the psychic that its enormous potential may be captured for the kingdom of God. Hence the importance of the CFPSS and the reason for its caution in not allowing to full membership those who are not committed to the Christian way. It recognises that 'psychic studies are as likely to lead to harm as to good if pursued outside the realms of the spiritual life' which it defines as 'man's approach to God, through the practice of prayer, worship and service to his fellow-creatures'.

So long as the psychic is subsumed in the spiritual all is well. It is not then simply to be tolerated but is rather to be welcomed. Jesus was the supreme example of this. His psychic capacities were made evident in such incidents as seeing Nathanael meditating under the fig tree, discerning the past matrimonial life of the woman at the well, knowing from a distance that Lazarus had died. Most notable of all are the concluding words of chapter two of St John's Gospel. The Jerusalem Bible translates: '[Jesus] never needed evidence of anyone; he could tell what someone had within'.

Jesus expresses on two occasions his awareness of the dangers of the psychic. Here are words from the Sermon on the Mount.

> 'Not everyone who calls me, "Lord, Lord", will enter the kingdom of Heaven, but only those who do the will of my heavenly Father. When that day comes, many will say to me, "Lord, Lord, did we not prophesy in your name, cast out devils in your name, and in your name perform many miracles?" Then I will tell them to their

face, "I never knew you: out of my sight, you and your wicked ways." ' (Matthew 7:21–3)

Or again. St Luke tells us that Jesus sent out seventy-two disciples in pairs to prepare people in town and country for a visit from Jesus himself (10:1–20). Among the express commands was that they should heal the sick. They evidently returned highly elated at the sensational 'success' of their mission. For, as Luke writes:

> The seventy-two came back jubilant. 'In your name, Lord,' they
> said, 'even the devils submit to us.' He replied, 'I watched how
> Satan fell, like lighting, out of the sky. And now you see that I have
> given you power to tread underfoot snakes and scorpions and all
> the forces of the enemy, and nothing will ever harm you.
> Nevertheless, what you should rejoice over is not that the spirits
> submit to you, but that your names are enrolled in heaven.'

It usually happens that as a person grows spiritually psychic powers develop naturally without attention being paid to them, and this is safe and, further, beneficial because it is the spiritual by which the life is ruled. Even so, the degree of the psychic in a spiritually-minded person depends very largely on that person's psycho-physical make-up and not necessarily on the depth of their spirituality. Thus in the realm of the psychic a rogue could be a giant and a saint a dwarf. Whereas, in the realm of the spiritual, gianthood would belong to the saint and dwarfdom to the rogue.

It must always be desirable that the spiritual should catch up with the psychic since it is upon the spiritual that salvation depends. Whether it is desirable for the psychic to catch up with the spiritual is best left to the Holy Spirit in the ruling of one's life.

The following from Dr Martin Israel makes a valuable summary:

> The gifts of the Holy Spirit are essentially psychic in nature (and
> in no way to be belittled on that account), but the harvest of the
> Holy Spirit is genuinely spiritual, by which I mean leading to an
> encounter with God. Psychical gifts are excellent provided they
> are spiritually and not egoistically directed.

My life has not brought me much into contact with people of unusual psychic sensitivity but a close friend over the past ten years has been Geoffrey Treissman whom I have already referred to in this book. Geoffrey has marked healing gifts and I have, with many others, had cause to be grateful to him in times of injury or sickness. In common with many healers he is often able to locate the seat of a trouble as he moves his hands over the affected area. The healing energies of the Spirit are then directed to that point. 'Healer' is, incidentally, a word I hesitate to use lest it should disguise the fact that God is always the true healer. So long, however, as that is understood the word may be regarded as being as acceptable as that of 'doctor' who, too, is but the agent of God's healing work. More particularly I have called upon Geoff and Denise for their prayers in pastoral situations and their support has helped me through many addresses or retreats. Denise also has healing gifts.

Geoff has a further gift and a more unusual one. This has come to him unsought and enables him to see the individual aura, the energy field that surrounds each one of us. Geoffrey's auric diagrams, accompanied by their interpretation, have been a spur and encouragement to many (including myself) and often a basis for spiritual direction. Geoff is co-author of a well-established book, *Handbook of the Aura*,[1] and I would refer readers to this book if they wish to know more of his work. He has also, with my encouragement, produced an illustrated manuscript which hopefully will be published under the title *Auras of the Saints*. The book is designed to show the hidden glory which emanates from people of all faiths who have given themselves unreservedly to the service of God. It could make many aware of a spiritual dimension in human life waiting to be discovered, a dimension so largely suffocated in the pursuit of the transitory pleasures and awards which is all that secular society can offer. Some may find it hard to accept what I have written here but to gaze contemplatively on the revealed glory of the saints (Geoff would never do auras of lesser people unless asked for them by the person concerned) can hardly be anything but enriching to those who strive to follow in their way.

June Blythe is another psychic person whom I have come to know here in Norwich. She ministers healing in the name of God the Father and the angels and she prays with a beautiful simplicity. Her care for people is unbounding and she is ready to go to anyone, anywhere, at any time. I was introduced to June, seemingly by chance, only recently when she ministered to me before two (highly successful) cataract operations. I got into touch with June by means of the telephone but not all her patients are as sophisticated as that. One such was Dancing Proud. He had to send out his call for help from his stable in Newmarket by other means. June picked it up, at least she picked up that the first name was Dancing and she knew the signal came from Newmarket. So off she went stopping at a pub in the town and asking if there was a Dancing something horse in the place as she wanted to see him. She was told there was Dancing Proud but that he was very sick. However the publican knew his owner and arranged for June to go to the stables. There she found Dancing Proud lying out flat and managed to persuade those around him to let her into his stable where she sat on the ground beside him with her arm on his flank. After twenty minutes he got up onto his 'front knees' and whinnied to the astonishment of all. After a few days he had fully recovered. Most of June's patients are human and I think she has had no more horses but there are quite a few dogs and cats who have cause to be grateful to her.

My friend Mrs Anna Lee-Wood tells a heart-warming story in her book *Moments of Truth.*[2] The author is a committed Christian, the wife of an Anglican priest, who often receives messages from the beyond though she does not seek them. One night she was woken up by the sound of children's laughter. She asked if she could help. One of them replied:

> 'We are the children who died in the fire a short time ago. When we woke up we didn't know we had died, because we had all died in our sleep. Please will you tell our Mummy and Daddy not to be sad for us. Heaven is such a beautiful place and we have seen Jesus. Please tell them that he is far more wonderful than what they told us about him, and that he said that one day we will be all together again as a family.'

The author learnt later that the children's death had been caused by the fumes and so they had not been burnt by the fire. She was able to find the newspaper which had reported the tragedy and hence to discover the address of the parents who were greatly comforted. One reason I am anxious to tell this story is that, although we are right to be cautious about psychic phenomena, it indisputably illustrates that they may be a source of deep blessing. It would, in my view, be quite wrong for parents in such circumstances to try to contact their children, but for the author not to have listened when the contact was made from the other side would have surely been a betrayal of trust.

In 1995 publicity given to the Toronto blessing was at its peak and I was anxious to learn more for myself. For the sake of clarity I shall continue to refer to it as the Toronto blessing though I believe it would be more aptly termed (as it sometimes is) the Jerusalem blessing or yet more the blessing of Pentecost. Whatever I write about the Toronto blessing is bound to be controversial so let me introduce the subject with the aid of a story.

Some years ago I was one of a congregation in Great St Mary's Church in Cambridge sitting under a pulpit occupied by Archbishop Michael Ramsey. In a second pulpit a few yards to the right stood Dr Billy Graham. One of them would be asked a question which he would proceed to answer and the other would be given an opportunity to comment. Sometimes a debate would develop between the two. At one point Billy Graham said that he had always regarded the Archbishop as a saint and that on an early occasion in his ministry, when walking up the staircase in Lambeth Palace, the Archbishop had turned to him and said, 'Billy, I pray for you every day'. Deeply touched, Billy Graham asked the Archbishop how he worded his prayer. 'I pray, Billy, that the good that you do may be blessed and that the harm that you do may be overruled.' Naturally the reply brought the house down and I thought the Archbishop, who had seemingly forgotten the incident, might well burst a blood vessel as his body wriggled and shook with laughter.

So often have I reflected on that aptly worded prayer. It could be profitably used on countless causes and individually for all of us. I invite it now from the critical as I come to say a few words on the Toronto blessing.

With three friends I attended an evening service at Holy Trinity, Brompton, HTB as it is widely known. We first spent a period of quiet in the silent and prayer-charged atmosphere of the magnificent Oratory next door. The contrast as we entered HTB and heard the band tuning up with the full benefit of electronic magnification was enough to make us wonder if we should turn and run. However, I have to say that once the service began the band had toned down and by the time we reached the climax the music was soft and well suited to the devotions. I think the first thing which struck me was the friendliness of the place which was genuine and not aggressive or hearty. There was also a serenity and joy revealed on the faces of many young people. And the handclapping and other accompaniments appeared to be spontaneous and to come from the heart. As the ordered part of the service came to a close we stood for a short while in silence after which the leader quietly invoked the presence of the Holy Spirit. I think the words were simply, 'Holy Spirit, come among us', hardly necessary one might think at that stage of the service but then, if we insist upon being logical, we would never use them at all. Certainly the Holy Spirit answered the prayer dramatically and almost immediately people began to fall to the floor, slain in the Spirit, or resting in the Spirit as I prefer to say. It was not many that night, twenty at the most I would say. Some lay quietly, others shook, a few cried out and one was affected by laughter. A helper came to me and asked if I would like to be prayed for. I said that I would and he led me to a corner where he laid his hands on my head and prayed fluently and earnestly asking at one point that God would put me on the right track. I thought I sensed he was a little disappointed that I remained on my feet. I have to say his prayer did not come across to me as Spirit-filled though I had no doubt he was a good man doing his best to fulfil his obligations as a steward to a stranger within the gates. How often, I may ask, have my own prayers been the same! I thanked him, sincerely I trust, for I felt a bond had grown between us, though I was in no way elated.

What of those who fell down? Amidst all the comments, sympathetic, favourable or critical the wisest words seem to me to have come from the then Bishop of London (Dr David Hope): 'I'm not worried about them falling down, it's what happens when they get up which concerns me.' It is a case of by their fruit they shall be known. And the good fruit emerging from HTB and its sister churches in the Spirit can hardly be disputed, even if there are some who can point to failures along the way. These churches largely feed the Alpha course for theology and Bible study which is warmly commended by both Archbishops and the Bishop of London among many others. The course has reached 380,000 people (including Roman Catholics) in fifty-five countries in the past three years. Almost 5,000 churches are now running it and it is hoped that half a million people will be involved by the end of 1997. In addition HTB has a number of outlets for social service amongst various groups in need. Some may find, and rightly find, a different way in the Church but to limit the Holy Spirit to their way is to endeavour to encage him behind bars to which he will not submit.

It has been said that silence is God's first language and that everything else is but a poor translation. If that be so then ways of prayer of which we have spoken in earlier chapters – tongues, rosary, mantras – and other ways, as in the use of music, icons and the daily Office are secondary in nature. Amongst these may also be classified the accompanying of hymns or choruses with the movements familiar to Charismatics. One and all are secondary to contemplative silence but that does not mean they are unimportant. The question to be asked is whether they move the heart in that direction. So called 'happy-clappy' religion comes in for a good deal of derision but it is important to see it as but one way among many which can lead eventually to the establishment of the contemplative silence of which I have spoken. Several years ago I was asked to give two lectures on prayer to a gathering of Charismatics. A problem was that no one had told me they were Charismatics until I arrived in the lecture hall. Somewhat apprehensively I delivered what I had prepared on the lines on which I usually speak and it was very well received. In the prayer workshops afterwards we included an extended silence and the Charismatics took to it as easily as the prayer groups to which I am accustomed to speaking. The experience was a revelation to me and especially the singing in tongues which was Spirit-filled in a way I have not met elsewhere. I say this because it is easy to be superior about ways which do not happen to be our own without understanding that for those called to it the Charismatic way may be as good a lead in to deeper prayer as the ways with which we are familiar. What one asks is that each part of the Body of Christ should acknowledge the authenticity of the other.

It so happens that as I write my niece and godchild Gabrielle is in hospital recovering from a long and unusually complex operation. She is secretary to one of the Charismatic HTB group of churches. I saw her congregation on television just two Sundays ago, young, enthusiastic, singing their choruses to the customary bodily movements. I think some would have dismissed their way as superficial. Yet what happened when Gabrielle's nine-hour operation came along and she needed their support? They got together and arranged a forty-eight hour non-stop night and day watch of prayer each taking two appointed half-hours. This reveals a belief in the efficacy of prayer and a readiness to sacrifice time and comfort in its cause. It is demanding for most of us to keep watch in the early hours. I think many vicars of mainstream churches would be proud if their congregations volunteered to act accordingly. Thankfully I may add this pioneering operation has met with complete success.

What is happening at the level of the Spirit at HTB is in essence no different from what is taking place at Fr Jozo's church at Siroki-Brijeg about fifteen miles from Medjugorje. The sadness is that HTB might find it difficult to hear that. I received a distinctly dubious look when I told a steward that I had brought with me members of our rosary group. And maybe some at Medjugorje would disapprove of HTB though it would be against Mary's teaching and the ethos of the place to do so. It is a real sadness that we cannot reach out in affirmation of one another's work.

Fr Jozo draws hundreds of Medjugorje pilgrims to his church each week. After his talk most of his congregation go up to the sanctuary for his blessing. He walks along the line laying his hands with prayer for a few seconds on each pilgrim taking them two at a time. Immediately many fall backwards into the arms of hefty catchers who lay them gently on the floor. Most of them then have a good sleep in the Spirit until they arise perhaps twenty minutes later deeply refreshed. It can be as many as seventy per cent who fall though on the last occasion I was there it was, I would judge, less than twenty. I have heard doubters say they are pushed but you can't lightly push over someone who is not willing to go and in any case you could not in that way give them a Spirit-filled sleep. But I was not pushed though I have to add I did not fall. And I know Fr Jozo well enough to know he doesn't need to push anyone. I see what happens in that church as all part of the Medjugorje experience and that experience is provenly fruitful in thousands and I expect one may say millions of its pilgrims.

What is one to make of these outpourings of the Spirit in our modern world? There are some who believe it to be a preparation for the second coming and the gathering up of all things in Christ and this view is for them given added weight by the closeness of the new millennium. We cannot say, nor need we know. All that is asked of us is that we walk prepared. Others believe, and this is a belief in which I share, that apart from an extensive and radical turning to God we shall in the not too distant future experience cataclysmic events on a wide, if not global scale. The world, like my word processor, is designed to work in a certain way and if I do not follow the maker's instruction disaster is bound to follow. This does not presume wrath on the part of the maker of one or the other but either ignorance or obstinacy on the human scene in not following the rules laid down. As the popular song has it it is only love which makes the world go round, a sentiment with which we need not quarrel if we see love as that of the New Testament, the love which partakes of the nature of God's own love, outpouring, sacrificial, unconditional, seeking only the long-term good of the other. If the nation or the world becomes too short of that sort of love and substitutes for it a hedonistic love, hedonism being the doctrine that pleasure is the highest good, then in the very nature of things the joints will seize and disaster will follow.

It may well be that the luxuriant outpouring of the Holy Spirit in particular places in our day is a merciful preparation for the troublous times the world must pass through when many lives must be lost, and lost unprepared, apart from the chance now being offered. The preparation, too, would be for those who remain, often depleted in health and wealth and mourning the loss of those dear to them. And, too, for the faithful remnant who are left to build up the new civilisations. I am not claiming the mantle of a prophet and yet I don't think I speak in the world of fantasy. It may even be in my own lifetime that some of these things come to pass. Certainly some of the 'secrets' of Medjugorje indicate, as far as observers close to the visionaries can tell, that we are to expect testing times ahead. None of us can know. We can only grasp the opportunities which are offered and be assured in the words of the Lady Julian that he did not say you shall not be travailed or tempested but he did say that you shall not be overcome.

27

Julian of Norwich (1)

⚭⚭⚭

I HAVE WRITTEN BRIEFLY on the Julian Cell but on Julian herself I have said nothing. I knew almost nothing about her when I came to the cell in 1976 but since then her influence has grown steadily and my debt to her is incalculable. I must now try to make her known and explain her influence on my life. It happens that this year (1997) I was invited to give the annual Julian Lecture in St Julian's Church. I chose as my subject 'Julian, then and now: the mercy and forgiveness of God' because it is in that area that Julian has influenced me most. The lecture (which is slightly edited) has grown with me over the years and will be the best introduction to the interested reader of Julian herself and my indebtedness to her.

Julian is known to us today almost only through her book *The Revelations of Divine Love*, now widely acknowledged throughout the Christian world as one of the great classics of the spiritual life. Of independent contemporary witness there is simply the evidence of several wills, the record of a visit for spiritual counsel from the colourful Margery Kempe, and a mention from a scribe-editor in a brief introduction to the shorter version of her book. There he refers to Julian as a 'devout woman . . . who is a recluse at Norwich and still alive, A.D. 1413'. For the rest there is silence.

There are two versions of Julian's book of which the first was almost certainly written shortly after she received her sixteen showings of the love of God, fifteen in the early hours of 8 May 1373, and the sixteenth on the following night. After meditating upon her visions for many years she wrote an extended version which was completed in 1393. Almost certainly at some time between these dates she became an anchoress, living in a cell attached to St Julian's Church in Norwich. It is generally assumed that Julian took her name from the church which would then have been about four hundred years old.

Julian tells us that at the time of the showings she was thirty and a half years old and we thus know that she was born towards the end of 1342. She also tells us that in her young life she had prayed for three graces to be given her if it were God's will: the first that she might be given a revelation of Christ's Passion, the second that she might receive a bodily illness so severe that she would think that she would die, and the third that she might receive three wounds – the wound of contrition, the wound of compassion, and the wound of a longing of her will for God. The first two requests, she said, had passed from her mind but the third was with her continually. On that memorable day, falling that year on the third Sunday after Easter, her prayer was granted.

Julian had been lying desperately ill for about a week. In the early hours of 8 May, with her mother and friends at her bedside, the parish priest came to administer the last rites. Even as she was seemingly sinking into death, her eyes fastened upon a crucifix held before her by a serving boy, her life was remarkably restored. 'Suddenly all my pain was taken away and I was as fit and well as I have ever been.' The showings, centred upon the Holy Trinity and the Passion of Jesus, followed at once.

In reading Julian's book it is important to bear in mind for whom it was written. The scribe who adds a colophon at the end of the longer version expresses the fear lest it should fall into the hands of the impious and thus be misunderstood and misapplied. 'It is', he tells us, 'for God's faithful lovers', echoing Julian's own words that she is writing 'for men and women who, for God's love, hate sin and turn themselves to do God's will.' To such people, her 'even-Christians' as she calls them, she frequently refers.

In the colophon to which I have referred *The Revelations* is admirably summarised as 'a sublime and wonderful revelation of the unutterable love of God'. Simply to read the book prayerfully as a form of spiritual reading, without pausing to puzzle out the more difficult theological points – that will be a rewarding study later – is to expose oneself to be drenched in the all-embracing love of God, its length and breadth and depth and height, as St Paul speaks of it. But Julian is not simply a devotional writer whose treatise brings renewed hope and strength to troubled souls. She is, too, as is increasingly recognised today, an astute and perceptive theologian who has profound and important things to say, and who brings to bear new insights in the interpretation of God's love and purpose. Thomas Merton, who refers to her as a 'true theologian', regarded her as one of the two greatest English theologians of all time, and Richard Harries, now Bishop of Oxford, has, in a radio programme, speaking in a wider context, wondered if she may not one day be seen as the greatest woman this country has produced. With such tributes it behoves us to take Julian seriously and to listen carefully to what she has to say. Theology and devotion come together in Julian as they should always do in works of spirituality, and the value of her book as a devotional manual springs directly out of its theological integrity. In her recent study of Julian, Grace Jantzen aptly comments that 'Julian will settle neither for an undevotional theology nor for an untheological devotion'.

A wrath-free God

As Julian piles up image upon image to bring home to us the inexhaustible love of God certain features stand out. One is the constancy of God's love. No power in heaven or on earth – and that includes sin – can stop God loving us. God's love which is pure compassion, will search us out to the end in whatever state we may be. In this love there is, and can be, no wrath, a statement made by Julian no less than ten times, and four times she tells us it formed a part of each of her sixteen showings. When we fall into sin, it may seem to us (says Julian) that God is angry with us. But that is an appearance only. As Canon Michael McLean so well puts it, 'what we call anger (in God) is simply a name to express the sensation caused in a sinner by the fire of God's love.' The wrath, in fact, as Julian explains, is in us, and not in God, and when we are once again restored through grace (still following Julian) we shall 'see' that God was with us all the time, drawing us back to himself in tender love, even though we could not see it in that way at the time. The word 'wrath' for Julian, I should explain, has a wider meaning than plain anger but includes, in her own words, 'everything which is opposed to peace and love'.

Julian's teaching on the wrath-free nature of the love of God is made explicit in the fourteenth revelation which begins at chapter 41 and ends with chapter 63. It is not possible to quote much here, but those who are interested may care to consult chapters 45 to 49 of *The Revelations*. Julian was greatly exercised in her mind because her own revelation appeared to be at variance with the teaching of the Church, which taught her that sinners deserved blame and wrath. She refers to what was made known to her directly as the higher judgement whilst the lower judgement was what she received through the Church. And this lower judgement, she is at pains to say, she could by no means ignore. She writes in chapter 46:

And so in all this contemplation it seemed to me that it was necessary to see and to know that we are sinners and commit many evil deeds which we ought to forsake, and leave many deeds undone which we ought to do, so that we deserve pain, blame and wrath. And despite all this, I saw truly that our Lord was never angry, and never will be. Because he is God, he is good, he is truth, he is love, he is peace; and his power, his wisdom, his charity and his unity do not allow him to be angry. For I saw truly that it is against the property of his power to be angry, and against the property of his wisdom and against the property of his goodness. God is that goodness which cannot be angry for God is nothing but goodness. Our soul is united to him who is unchangeable goodness. And between God and our soul there is neither wrath nor forgiveness in his sight.

The passage as a whole is clear and needs no comment. But the last sentence may to some come as something of a shock. 'Between God and our soul there is neither wrath nor forgiveness in his sight.' It is a carefully worded and logical sentence. For if there is no wrath in God it must follow that there is no forgiveness *in his sight*. The reason God cannot forgive is because he has already done so. The reason I cannot come to this church is because I am already here. Yet it is not quite so simple as that because there was a time when I came to this church but there was no point in time when God forgave.

Julian is speaking here in a strictly logical and theological sense. There is no moment in time when God forgives because there can be no moment of time when he has been unforgiving. She doesn't always speak in this sense. At other times she uses the word forgiveness in the ordinary sense in which we use it. Thus in chapter 40 we have the sentence, 'And then we hope that God has forgiven our sin; and this is true.' And again in the same chapter we have, 'So sins are forgiven by grace and mercy'. And it is in this sense I shall continue to speak.

Personal application
What bearing does Julian's teaching at this point have on our own lives? Let me speak in personal terms and from there we can make application to ourselves. For most of my life I have believed that if I sinned against God and repented then God would forgive me my sin. And this is a blessed truth. But Julian's truth is yet more blessed. For Julian's truth is

that if I sin against God and don't repent then God still forgives me, though, (and this is vital), I can only appropriate that forgiveness, take it into myself and make it my own, after I have turned to him again. But the forgiveness is already there, whether I choose to take it or not. Julian is shown that God's love is pure compassion. This compassion, or we might say this all-forgiving love (for in him is no wrath) is streaming out to us all the time from the arms of God. It is there for the taking. And there is nothing I can do, however deeply I fall from grace, to turn that all-compassionate love into wrath. As Julian says, 'if God could be angry for any time, we should neither have life or place or being' (49).'[1]

An illustration I often use is this. If the sun were shining into your sitting room you could, if you wished, draw the curtains and live in the dark. But one thing you could never do, however thick the curtains and deep the darkness, you could never turn the sun's light into darkness. Draw the curtains back and there is the sun's light waiting once more to fill your room with light. And I could, if I wished, draw a curtain across my heart to separate myself from God's all-compassionate love and live in my own little darkness. But one thing I could never do, however thick the veil across my heart, I could not change God's compassionate love into wrath. Draw the curtains back, and there is that all-compassionate love waiting to stream into my life.

The truth may be put otherwise by saying that we may be responsive to God or we may fail to be responsive to God, but God is at all times and in all places responsive to us. God can never fail to be responsive to us. As Julian puts it in chapter 43: 'When we pray, the soul is made willing and responsive to God. There is no kind of prayer which can make God more responsive to the soul, for God is always constant in love.' Once we can make it our own, this doctrine of the wrath-free nature of God, we shall find it to be a liberating truth.

We must, however, be careful not to interpret this joyous gospel as though it implied that sin was of little account. Julian is no sentimentalist. 'Sin', she says, 'is the sharpest lash that any soul may be struck with' (39). And again, 'I was shown no harder hell than sin'. Julian firmly believes in hell, but she knows that it is our wrath and not God's which may take us there, the wrath in ourselves which we have not allowed God's compassionate love to quench. Furthermore, as Julian's writings make clear, the wrath-free character of God does not mean that we shall not suffer as our natures are cleansed in the purifying fire of his love.

What it means is this: that in our suffering God is on our side. And it is this which makes the difference between hope and despair.

This is not an acceptable theology to some. I doubt if it is often preached in our pulpits. Sermons speaking of God's wrath resting on his sinful people are not uncommon, and preachers who never make reference to God's wrath are also frequent, but sermons which state categorically that the wrath is in us, waiting to be quenched by God's all-compassionate love, are at least sufficiently rare for me never to have heard one myself. This is understandable because they might so easily be misunderstood. For a God for whom no wrath is possible could easily come across to many as an easy-going, apathetic figure, a lax, spoiling person for whom the fleeting happiness of his children is his chief concern. As a precaution against these dangerous misunderstandings of the nature of God's love it may well be, it seems to me, desirable that in our *human* vocabulary the word 'wrath' in relation to God should remain. It helps to safeguard certain qualities in God which might otherwise be forgotten. I would list three. It helps to safeguard God's holiness, the righteousness of his love and his abhorrence of evil. Secondly, it safeguards God's passionate concern for our own welfare. God is not indifferent, he cares and he cares mightily all the time. However far and fast we run he will never go away. And the third truth which the concept of wrath keeps alive is this – the awareness that if we persist in our own selfish ways without reference to the demands of God, as he would relate to each of our lives, then we are moving to our own destruction. But if we choose to keep the word 'wrath' in our own vocabulary we must be quite clear that there is no place for the word, as we understand it, in *God's* vocabulary. I think we might say of the wrath of God, if the phrase has to be used, and in the Bible, and especially the Old Testament, it often is used, something like this: Just as the so-called foolishness of God is wiser than the wisdom of men, so is the so-called wrath of God more compassionate than the compassion of men.

Relative and absolute truth

I think we must see the wrath of God, as expressed so often in the Old Testament, and less often in the New Testament, and incidentally never by Jesus, as expressing a relative truth. We are all familiar with relative truths and they serve us well until we are ready to move on to something more absolute. When I was a child I learnt through a well-known hymn that heaven was above the bright blue sky. It was sufficient to go on with but it wouldn't satisfy me now. The doctor gives us a diagnosis in terms relative to our understanding and that tells us how we are to proceed. To his medical colleague he is able to speak in more absolute terms. In the days of the Old Testament, the Jews were well served for centuries by a sacrificial system which included the day of atonement, but then with the coming of Jesus it came to be understood that the blood of bulls and goats could never take away sin. So, too, as I see it, belief in the wrath of God is a relative truth serving us well for a while in helping us safeguard truths I have earlier mentioned. And yet if anyone has the image of a wrathful God I would not press to take it from them until they feel ready to move on. We have to come to Julian when we are ready for her and we shall not be helped if we come before our time. It is a safe rule that if ever we have before us an image which is helpful, we are not to reject it until we can replace it with another image which is more helpful and takes us closer to the truth. Otherwise the danger is that we shall be left floundering in a spiritual vacuum. The point I am wishing to make is that we must hold ourselves open to be taken on in God's time to the more absolute truth which Julian offers. And I say 'in God's time' because to do the right thing at the wrong time is in fact to do the wrong thing. For many years, in fact for all of my sixty-six years before meeting Julian twenty-one years ago, I have lived in the earlier relative 'wrath of God/mercy of God' truth and it has been a great liberation to come to the other. And since what we believe of God determines our attitude to others this truth has an important social dimension as well.

There is plenty of wrath around. But it is, says Julian, in us and not in God. If Julian were writing today she would be using the terms of modern psychology and would be saying that we project our own wrath on to God and then see it as God's wrath coming towards us. God's work, for Julian, (it has been forcibly said) is 'to love the hell out of us', for everything in our nature which opposes peace and love – lust and greed, jealousy and covetousness, judgementalism, pride and anger – is a little bit of hell which remains in us. As we allow our natures to be exposed to God's all-compassionate love these contrary elements are dissolved. 'I must needs grant', says Julian, 'that the purpose of God's mercy and forgiveness is to lessen and quench our anger'.(48).

The influence of theology on behaviour

What I am saying of the character of God, as Julian expounds it, is, as I have indicated, immensely important for ourselves as individuals, or members of a family, or of the wider society around. For it is an inescapable truth that we ourselves become in character like unto, I will not say the one whom we worship, for that is not quite true, but we become like our mental image of the one we worship. Allow me to illustrate that with a story from my own childhood. When I was six years old I remember walking with my nurse when a Roman Catholic nun in full array walked out of a side street in front of us. To me she was a magnificent sight and to my young eyes she looked like a ship under full sail. I whispered to my nurse, 'Isn't she beautiful?' 'Hush, you musn't say that,' came the reply, 'she worships the Virgin Mary.' That was enough for me and I felt I must keep off that tack for ever. But I hope that in later years I may have grown wiser. We all know that instructed Catholics don't worship the Virgin Mary, but there may well be some who in their ignorance of the Church's teaching do exactly that. What I would want to say now is that if there is someone in the world who worships the Virgin Mary and sees in the Virgin Mary the fullness of compassion which Julian saw in God, then that ignorant person is closer to God as he truly is, than his orthodox Catholic brother who worships what he calls God, but whom he sees as a harsh, forbidding, wrathful person. That ignorant person will be a true Christian whereas the orthodox brother will present in his living a warped image of God. The importance of Julian is that she has put the all-compassionate nature of Mary, which the Catholic Church delights to proclaim, right into the middle of the Godhead itself.

When Thomas Merton spoke of Julian as being a true theologian he meant she was one whose vision of God was true. We all have our vision of God and in some measure all our visions are off target. Some of us may be but a few degrees to right or left of the bulls-eye, others may be wildly wide. Thomas Merton is saying that of all the people he knew, and he had an extensive knowledge of the saints, Julian's vision was the most true. It is this which is so important, this matter of being on target. For we grow, as I have said, into our image of the one we worship. If we see God as a tyrant, we too shall become tyrants, not for most of us on the world scene, but in the family, the church, the school, the hospital, wherever we are. Many of the world's dictators have been religious men. Their tyranny has been but a reflection of what they saw in God. It may be much better to be an atheist than to be a religious person with a seriously distorted image of the one we worship. I say 'may be' because atheists, too, can be tyrants as we know so well from the recent history of the Soviet Union. But a religious person who has a tyrannical image of God is bound to be a tyrant, his tyranny depending on the degree in which his faith is sincere. The more sincere he is the more thorough it will be. Saul of Tarsus, when persecuting the Church, was a deeply religious man acting consistently with his distorted image of the same God whom Jesus declared.

The thought can be followed through taking one by one the various false images which people hold. The one who worships a Father Christmas God will be kindly and spoiling and sentimental. Not that the original St Nicholas was like that, but then it is hard to see St Nicholas operating in Selfridges or Sainsbury's. The devotees of a policeman God will have their eyes set on law rather than grace. If for some, God is seen mainly as the Almighty Judge, then they themselves are likely to be censorious and judgemental. If our God is bigoted and narrow we shall be that way too, intolerant of other faiths and of other denominations than our own. The nationalistic God of Battles will make for a warlike tribe or nation. The early settlers in South Africa were religious people whose conception of a racialist God has left its mark on centuries of history. Our computer age could well usher in the image of a Company Director God leading the Church to become so overloaded with paperwork that the worshipping and pastoral side would be smothered. And so we might go on. For most of us it is not a matter of having one of these distorted images but a mixture of several.

The foregoing, it is hoped, makes it clear that worshippers who attach false images to God will absorb into their characters (more or less according to their measure of devotion) the distortions placed in the Godhead, leading to a consequent aberration of behaviour pattern. A recent writer has said of our love of God that it is the root of all evil, a startling saying, but in the light of what I have written it is easy to see the point he was making. Hence the importance of discovering the true image which an increasing number today believe Julian's Revelations set before us. Many must have found, as I have found myself, that the undistorted image of the wrath-free, all-compassionate God whose forgiveness is always coming to meet us (for God cannot deny his own nature) which Julian presents, must affect character in the direction of gentleness and forbearance, patience and understanding. The one who absorbs Julian can no longer believe in the 'Vengeance-is-mine-I-will-repay' type of God, excepting in the sense of a vengeance which returns good for evil thereby heaping coals of fire upon the offender's head. I think that many people in discovering Julian feel with me that they have come home. We know there is much to be tempered yet, but we believe ourselves to be in the right house.

Our love for one another must necessarily follow the same pattern as God's love for ourselves, a pattern in which, as we have seen, forgiveness *precedes* repentance and does not simply follow upon it, even though we know that the *appropriation* of forgiveness must await a renewed turning to God. Christian behaviour, as I have endeavoured to show, follows directly from Christian theology, and a sub-Christian theology as – it is maintained – is one which acknowledges wrath in God, must lead to a corresponding modification of our attitudes to one another. The direct link between the two – the nature of God's love for us and our love for one another – is unmistakably set before us in the words of Jesus: 'Love your enemies and pray for your persecutors, only so can you be children of your heavenly Father, who makes his sun to rise on the good and the bad alike, and sends his rain on the honest and dishonest' (Matthew 5:44–5). It is impossible to pray for one's enemies whilst one is *willingly* harbouring anger against them. Just as God's forgiveness is always coming towards us, so must our forgiveness be always going out to one another. There can be no saying to my brother or sister, 'You say you are sorry and then I'll forgive you'. My forgiveness must be reaching out to my brother before he is sorry. Though he reject it, it does not belong to me to withdraw it. It is in fact in the power of our outgoing love to one another that encouragement is offered towards reconciliation. Our brother is to be forgiven before he repents, even though he can only assimilate his forgiveness after he has turned again. I may add two quotations which admirably illustrate this point. The first from Archbishop Anthony Bloom reads: 'One should not expect to be forgiven because one has changed for the better, neither should one make such a change a condition for forgiving other people. It is only because one is forgiven, one is loved, that one can begin to change, not the other way round.' And Dorothy Sayers writes crisply: 'While God does not, and man dare not, demand repentance as a condition for *bestowing* pardon, repentance remains an essential condition for *receiving* it'. Julian is the apostle of reconciliation, her wisdom and sanity transcending all boundaries, and the strong and enduring love she holds out in the name of the crucified and risen Christ, is the only balm which may heal our souls.

If, then, our forgiveness is at all times to go out towards others does that mean we are to forget? The question is often asked in an international context: Is the Christian to forget the evils of the Nazi regime in Germany, the concentration camps, the Holocaust? The answer is clear. We are no more to forget the tyranny against which we fought, than we are to forget the yet greater evil, the crucifixion of the Son of God. There it stands, the cross of Jesus, on the pages of history, and must ever stand for all to see. The Church enshrines its memory in the heart of its liturgy and every time we say the creed we recall his death. But we are to forget in the sense that we are no longer to hold the remembrance of the scene *against* those who laid him bare, and this sort of forgetting is what we mean by forgiveness. Or to put it otherwise, God does not require us to forget, forgetting is in fact an impossibility where any event affects us deeply (can any forget a wartime bereavement?) but God does require us to forgive and by his grace we are enabled to do so. If we do not, hoping thereby to punish another, time will only reveal that we have punished ourselves. It is not for us to sit in moral judgement upon any person, and in any case by what measuring line do we measure the extent of another's sin against that of our own? It may be that the hearts of some are hardened and that they cannot receive the forgiveness which God or man is offering to them. Nevertheless the spirit of forgiveness must continue to flow, and lest it be betrayed into condescension, it must flow in the remembrance of the forgiveness which we have received of God and which we all need of one another.

The harm of continued self-blame

These thoughts take me on to our next Julian theme. God does not blame us for our sins. This is not just an isolated thought in Julian's writings. She returns to it no less than ten times. God is not in the business of blaming. But it is a thought which worried her because her revelation was here contrary to all that the Church had led her to believe. 'I saw our Lord', she writes, 'putting no more blame on us than if we were as clean and holy as the angels in heaven' (50). Julian, we remember, is writing for her 'even-Christians', for people such as ourselves who are often despondent over our failures, and yet who long to grow in the knowledge and love of God. For such people, Julian sees clearly, self-blame, especially where it is prolonged, will be a serious stumbling-block to our growth in Christ. Julian's picture is that after a fall her even-Christians should make a brief act of contrition ('Do not blame yourself too much', she writes in chapter 77) and then go on their way without looking back in self-recrimination. Too often we blame ourselves, not realising that such irritation with ourselves is in reality pride sheltering under the guise of humility. The primary meaning of the Greek word for forgiveness (*aphesis*) is release, in this context release from guilt and fear. Julian was greatly concerned to tell her readers that it is not God who would bind us, but rather that we, through want of faith in his promises, so often fail to take possession of the release God is offering us.

What lies at the heart of the matter is this. We mistake our self-blame for humility. In chapter 73 Julian is speaking to a situation in which we cannot let go of our past sins. In Julian's own words:

> When we begin to hate sin and to amend ourselves according to
> the laws of Holy Church, there still persists a fear which hinders
> us, by looking at ourselves and our sins committed in the past, and
> some of us because of everyday sins ... And the perception of
> this makes us so woe begone and depressed that we cannot see any
> consolation.

And here comes the punchline: 'sometimes we mistake this fear for humility'. But it is not humility, says Julian, but 'a reprehensible blindness and weakness'. But she adds that whilst we are able to despise other sins, we are unable to despise this one for the simple reason that we are unable to recognise it as sin, kidding ourselves all the time that we are being humble. Here we have a not uncommon example of pride masquerading as humility. We think we are honouring God in continuing with self-blame but in truth we are dishonouring him, blaspheming him would not be too strong a word, because we are denying the generosity of God's love. We are blind (Julian argues) as to the nature of love and because of this blindness we make a mistaken response to God. True humility, Julian would have us know, comes not from the denial of God's love but from its acknowledgement, 'for love makes his power and wisdom very humble to us'. We have measured God's love by our own, but so far is it beyond our own that 'no creature can comprehend how greatly, how sweetly and how tenderly our maker loves us' (6). Our horizons are limited by our poverty in love. We have to break through the barrier by faith so that we may reach God's perspective, and when we have done this we shall see self-blame for what it is, an indulgence on our part enabling us to live within our sterile limitations at the expense of dishonouring God.

Here is a true story. The details may not be exact but the point remains. Wendy went to spend a few days with her friend Anne. On Anne's mantelpiece was a beautiful piece of Dresden china given her by her father shortly before he died. Wendy admired it, took it into her hands and let it slip to the floor where it now lay in many pieces. Her apologies were profuse. How could she be so clumsy, and with something so beautiful and so valuable? Moreover, since it had sentimental as well as market value it was irreplaceable. How could she ever forgive herself for being so careless? Anne took it well, telling Wendy that accidents happen to everyone, that she must put the matter behind her, that she freely forgave her and that she really must forgive herself. But Wendy could not let the matter rest. Time and again through the morning she would refer to her calamity, blaming herself anew and apologising again and again. Finally Anne spoke out plainly: 'Wendy, you have come to spend three days with me. You've already ruined the first morning for both of us and if you go on in the same way you will ruin the whole visit. For God's sake put the matter behind you and don't refer to the incident again. If you could see things in a right proportion you would know that the breaking of the china is quite a small thing compared with all the negativity, the wallowing in self-blame and guilt, and the destruction you have brought to my house.' It was exactly the plain speaking Wendy needed, for in some perverse way she thought she was doing something praiseworthy in her continued expressions of blame, and from then on relationships began to improve and at least two days were not wasted. If I were to say that God speaks to us when we persist in self-blame in much the same way as Anne spoke to Wendy, I would not be misinterpreting Julian's teaching at this point. Perhaps we have here a simple parable on which many might profitably reflect.

There is a great deal in Julian's writings which supports what has been said, often directly when she returns to the subject of blame and even more often when she speaks of the joy in which we should live because God is working out his salvation in us. Self-blame, whereby we return again and again in a spirit of remorse to the failures of the past is, of course, the enemy of that joy. That is why Julian sees it as the hammer blow of the devil. 'Our enemy', she writes, 'tries to depress us with false fears which he proposes. His intention is to make us so weary and dejected, that we let the sight of our everlasting friend slip from our minds' (76). But the enemy is the great deceiver, the father of lies as Jesus describes him. The truth belongs to God. And God's truth, as it was to her 'astonishment' shown to Julian, was that God looked upon his servant 'with pity and not with blame' (82). Indeed she goes further and says that all that has been a shame to those who shall be saved shall be turned into honour and joy (39). And further still, that when our healing is complete our wounds shall be seen by God 'not as wounds but as honours' (39). Julian's teaching in this whole area in which we have been speaking is, in her great parable of the Lord and the servant, linked to the atoning work of Jesus. She writes: 'So has our good Lord Jesus taken upon himself all our blame; and therefore our Father may not, does not wish to assign more blame to us than to his own beloved son Jesus Christ' (51). There is an echo of that life-bearing sentence in George Herbert's well-loved poem, 'Love bade me welcome', 'And know you not, says Love, who bore the blame?' The whole poem, we may note in passing, is pure Julian.

Justice swallowed up in mercy

What I have written, or rather what Julian has written, must seem shocking to some. If all this be true what becomes of God's justice? The possibility of God being angry has already been denied. Is God's justice to be swept away as well? The answer is yes: in the logic of Julian's thought God's justice has to go. God is unjust, that is to say if we measure justice by our ordinary accepted standards. To soften the shock it might be put like this: 'Just as the foolishness of God is wiser than the wisdom of men, so is the injustice of God more just than the justice of men.' Or more simply: 'God's injustice is the highest form of justice.' That accords well with something Pope John Paul II has written: 'True mercy is the most profound form of justice.' In Julian we find 'justice is swallowed up in mercy'. I take the phrase from Canon A.M. Allchin though he is using it, not of Julian, but of a saint who in many ways is very close to her, Isaac of Syria. Isaac spells out this theme in a way in which Julian does not and it will be worth following him through for a few minutes. Isaac, by way of introduction, was Bishop of Nineveh in the seventh century. He is held to be one of the greatest writers in the Christian East and in the Orthodox Church he is undergoing a renaissance today.

Isaac writes as follows:

> Do not speak of God as just, for his justice is not in evidence in his actions towards you. How can you call God just when you read the gospel lesson concerning the hiring of the workmen in the

vineyard? How can someone call God just when he comes across
the story of the prodigal son who frittered away all his belongings
in riotous living – yet merely in response to his contrition his father
ran and fell on his neck and gave him authority over all his
possessions? . . . It is God's own son who testifies about him in
this way. Where then is this 'justice' in God, seeing that, although
we were sinners, Christ died for us. If he is so compassionate in
this, we have faith that he will not change.

Justice and mercy, as we commonly use those words, are concepts we
need in a fallen world to help hold the fabric of society together. No law
court could run on the principle of the parable of the prodigal son, and
no business could flourish on the example of the labourers in the vineyard. And yet those parables remain valid in portraying the nature of
God's dealing with us. 'As the heavens are higher than the earth, so are
my ways higher than your ways, saith the Lord' (Isaiah 55:9).

The point we have to learn is this: God's justice is revealed not in the
way in which we ordinarily think according to our customary usage of
that word, but in the way in which we respond to his mercy. Look back
to the parable of the prodigal son. Take a look at the elder brother. I
picture him as a diligent, dutiful, hard-working young man, a fair overseer
on the farm, a moral and upright person. And how was he judged? He
was judged by the manner in which he responded (or more accurately
in this case, failed to respond) to his father's mercy. He could not accept
the compassionate forgiving love of God shown to his brother and so he
was excluded from the celebration. Look at the labourers in the vineyard.
They too were judged by their incapacity to respond to the compassion
of the owner of the vineyard.

What I am saying has been vividly portrayed in one of the most
insightful books of the Old Testament, the book of Jonah. Jonah was told
by God to go to preach to the city of Nineveh, a city notorious for its
wickedness, but instead Jonah ran in the other direction and tried to
take a ship to Spain. This is not the place to follow Jonah in the adven-
tures ascribed to him. It is enough to say that they led him to repentance
and that when God asked him a second time to go to Nineveh he at
once obeyed. Why did he refuse in the first place? It was not because he
was afraid for his own skin. But in another sense he was afraid, he was
afraid Nineveh would hear his message and repent. He knew how great
was the depths of God's mercy and he couldn't bear to see it exercised

on a city so wicked as Nineveh. You will remember, that in response to Jonah's preaching, Nineveh did repent and the allegory tells how the king and the people and even the animals wore sackcloth and fasted. And God, just as Jonah had expected, forgave them. And now, Jonah, thoroughly angry, explains his behaviour. I quote from the Good News Bible:

> 'Lord, didn't I say before I left home that that is just what you would do? That's why I did my best to run away to Spain! I knew that you are a loving and merciful God, always patient, always kind, and always ready to change your mind and not punish.' (4:2)

And God gently rebuked Jonah for his anger. That isn't the end of the story but it is all that we need for our purpose. The question I want to ask is how was Jonah judged? He was judged by the way in which he failed to respond to God's mercy on the people of Nineveh.

Or take the case of the two dying thieves on Calvary. Luke tells us that one of them hurled insults at Jesus: 'Aren't you the Messiah? Save yourself and us.' But the other said, 'We deserve our fate, but he has done nothing wrong. Lord, remember me when you come into your kingdom.' And Jesus assured him that that day he would be with him in Paradise. This man had no opportunity to live out a changed life or to make reparation. He was judged purely on his response to God's mercy. His companion could receive no promise because he was unable to respond to the mercy which was equally available to them both.

Sharing in the heavenly banquet

Julian would, of course, have followed us in all that has just been said. The underlying theme of her book is a witness to that. Let us put the Bible aside and try to see this in contemporary terms. I ask you to imagine a member of your church, a person of upright character and well respected in the congregation (as Jonah would have been in the synagogue) dying and presenting themself for admission at the doorway of heaven. But before the door opens our church member becomes aware of another figure awaiting admission, a figure from the distant past, perhaps, recognised as one who had been of 'unsavoury' character, or, perhaps, a figure known indirectly through the mass media, maybe someone held up before the public eye as an icon of evil. And instead of rejoicing with the angels of God that this person has found repentance and forgiveness, our parish member draws back and the portals open and the penitent passes through. Like the elder brother of the parable our parish member is unwilling to share the heavenly banquet with company such as this. He is judged by the manner in which he responds, or in this case fails to respond, to God's mercy to the one who has been welcomed within. An unforgiving soul can never be in heaven, not because of any arbitrary decision on God's part (God continues to love an unforgiving soul) but simply because heaven would cease to be heaven if an unforgiving soul were somehow to slip in. That church member could, of course, be any of us. Even so we would know that there would be those who would be praying here below that the good work God had begun in us might be perfected in the day of Jesus Christ. That perfection would consist in the cleansing away of the elements of self-righteousness which remained. Only then can 'those who will be saved' be one and all 'right merry in heaven' for they will be rejoicing not only in their own salvation but in the salvation of all who share their bliss.

I am not saying it is easy to forgive. It may be that forgiveness needs more grace than anything else we are ever asked to do. Forgiveness presents a great challenge to us all especially where the injury has been done against ourselves or those whom we dearly love. Perfection in forgiveness goes hand in hand with perfection in humility. We should not therefore be surprised if we cannot forgive as generously as we would wish. Forgiveness has to be worked at like everything else in the Christian life. So long as we are willing to forgive and our hearts are opened in prayer for the other person, God will work upon that until full forgiveness is possible. The more we are able to enter into the reality of all that God has forgiven us the more possible it will be for us to forgive others.

And here we come back to Julian for I do not know that anyone has spoken more tenderly in relationship to the sins of others.

> The soul which would remain at peace when another's sins come
> to mind, must fly as from the pains of hell asking God's protection
> and help. Looking at another's sin clouds the eyes of the soul,
> hiding for the time being the fair beauty of God – unless we look
> upon this sinner with contrition with him, compassion on him, and
> a holy longing to God for him. Otherwise it must harm and
> disquiet and hinder the soul that looks on these sins. (76)

Sometimes in India I would walk round the garth of the Cowley Fathers and Wantage Sisters, the cemetery of those who had lived their lives in the joys and sorrows of India. And on each grave was a simple wooden cross with just two words written on it: 'Jesus, mercy.' You cannot get deeper than that. And that is where Julian was and where we all have to be.

Julian writes:

> He who is highest and closest to God may see himself – and needs to do so – as a sinner like me; and I who am the least and lowest who shall be saved may be comforted with him who is the highest. (78)

And now, by way of closing, I would like to read a remarkable prayer. It is a poem prayer, written by Lord Hailsham as the epilogue to his autobiographical book, *A Sparrow's Flight*. As the prologue to his book Lord Hailsham has quoted a well-known passage from the Venerable Bede's *Ecclesiastical History*. At an assembly near York in the year 627, before Eadwine, the pagan king of Northumbria, an unknown member has spoken. 'Such,' he said, 'O king, seems to me the present life on earth, as if . . . on a winter's night a sparrow should swiftly fly into the hall and, coming in one door, instantly fly out through another . . . Somewhat like this appears the life of man. But of what follows or what went before we are utterly ignorant.' Taking up this theme, Lord Hailsham calls his poem 'The Sparrow's Prayer':

> Father, before this sparrow's earthly flight
> Ends in the darkness of a winter's night;
> Father, without whose word no sparrow falls,
> Hear this, Thy weary sparrow, when he calls.
> Mercy, not justice, is his contrite prayer,
> Cancel his guilt and drive away despair;
> Speak but the word, and make his spirit whole,
> Cleanse the dark places of his heart and soul.
> Speak but the word, and set his spirit free;
> Mercy, not justice, still his constant plea.
> So shall Thy sparrow, crumpled wings restored,
> Soar like a lark, and glorify his Lord.

There ends the lecture. A question arising from it which is often asked me is this: 'You say that there is no wrath in God, and Jesus says we should be perfect even as our Father is perfect. Does that mean we should not get angry?' Julian gives no direct answer to that question. Indirectly she answers us by saying that the mercy of God and his forgiveness abate and dispel our wrath (48).

If we look to the New Testament we must say it is suspicious of human anger though it does not forbid it. Jesus says in the Sermon on the Mount that anyone who is angry with his brother without a cause is in moral danger. Various degrees of anger are then mentioned (Matthew 5:22). The words 'without a cause' are in some manuscripts only, and it is generally thought that they were added by a copyist, no doubt to help clarify Jesus' meaning. In fact they probably obscure it. Perhaps the New English Bible is the best interpreter of the meaning of Jesus. 'Anyone who nurses anger against his brother must be brought to judgement. If he abuses his brother he must answer for it before the court; if he sneers at him he will have to answer for it in the fires of hell.' A sharp, almost reflex, outburst of anger in the presence of an evil deed is hardly blame-worthy, it is the nursing of the anger which will be destructive. Paul reinforces this when he writes: 'If you are angry, do not let anger lead you into sin; do not let sunset find you still nursing it; leave no loop-hole for the devil' (Ephesians 4:26–7). Again, anger is not forbidden. The Bible does not say 'No' but it does say 'Look out!' And it says that once our anger is out we are not to hold on to it.

I think myself that in this matter of anger we have to be true to ourselves according to the state of our development in Christ. I was once watching the news on television when a prison van was shown drawn up outside the law courts. Inside the van was a man who had perpetrated some sensational crime which had captured the imagination of the nation. In the room with me were two young men in their late teens. One of them rose from his seat and angrily banged the television screen calling out 'no, no, not that'. I felt there was nobility in that. What of his companion? This young man remained seated in an attitude of apathy and indifference. The reaction of the angry young man was far superior to his. But now let us suppose a mature member of our church congre-gation had been in the room watching with us. It would have been insufferable if she had banged the screen! She would, one hopes, have taken that prisoner's sin and suffering into herself, and together with it the suffering of the victim and of the victim's parents and family. She would have borne it all in her heart and offered it at the foot of the cross. To an outside observer her reaction might have seemed identical with that of the apathetic young man. But in reality it would have been poles apart. And that angry young man who stood in the middle? I admired him because he did his own thing for his particular stage of the Christian journey. He was incensed at the crime and sorry for the victims but that is as far as his understanding went at that time. If he had attempted to imitate the patience of our church member (patience being not a passive virtue but the quality of life which makes suffering creative) he would have been putting on a false front and that would have helped no one. He did what God asked of him in his own particular state of life. That was ten years ago. He has now moved on.

28

Julian of Norwich (2)

THE FOREGOING CHAPTER DEALS with only one aspect of Julian's teaching, though one which runs as a golden thread through her book. It is the aspect which has had the most to teach me personally, helping me to move to a vision of God which allows for a liberty of spirit beyond my grasp in earlier years. The chapter in many ways reflects a pilgrim's progress in my life, and that I have been able to make it belongs above all to Julian with her vision of an all-compassionate God who looks upon his struggling servants with pity and not with blame. Yet my faulty image, I make bold to say, was not mine alone but belonged in wide measure to the Church. Sunday by Sunday, and at periods weekday by weekday, I had said for many decades, together with millions of my fellow-Christians, 'Provoking most justly thy wrath and indignation against us' and accepted the words unquestionably as true. Liturgy works largely by dropping seeds into the unconscious and for the most part we are impregnated unawares. The words quoted from the prayer of confession in *The Book of Common Prayer* no longer form a part of the liturgy as commonly used in the Church today, but so often as I have been taken back to them, I have been left wondering how I could have accepted them over many years. Add to that the daily reminder of God's wrath in the first canticle of matins and the then oft-used prayer of the litany, 'Be not angry with us for ever' (both omitted in the ASB), and the words which almost opened compline, 'let thine anger cease from us', and it is easy to receive the impression (notwithstanding balancing factors elsewhere) of a God swifter to blame than to bless, far removed from Julian's picture of one 'who loves us and enjoys us' and 'who is swift to clasp us to himself, for we are his joy and his delight'. I know there are many who still hark back longingly to the old forms of prayer but, fortunately, it is the grandeur and the cadence of the language and its power to provoke the numinous (all so true) rather than the theology it portrays which mostly holds them and, in so far as they are to be found in church at all, little harm may be done. The more seriously we take our theology, the more will be its power to affect our lives for good or ill. Recently I had to speak in St Julian's to thirty young men and women mostly preparing for ordination, and in an unprepared talk I found myself stressing that their lecturers were not to be judged as true theologians by their grasp of the academic niceties of the schools in which they were so much more versed than the Lady Julian, but by their capacity to portray God as he truly is. That I believed to be Julian's strength and to be the justification for Thomas Merton's assessment that she was one of the greatest of English theologians.

And yet what would I have done without this Church which so lovingly sustained me, fed me with the bread of life, raised me when I fell, and in my fellow travellers encompassed me with so much patience and forbearance? Without her I would have been lost and confused, floundering without rules and guidelines, as are so many in our troubled secular society today. The Church has been my mother and to complain that she has been less than a perfect mother would be ungenerous in the extreme. I consider myself to have been exceptionally fortunate in those fellow church people I have met, who have directed me and encouraged me, whose lives are in some cases briefly recaptured in these pages. Of these Julian stands first for, although unseen by the outer eye, she has through the magic of her writing been made more visible to the eye within than many whom I have loved and known in the ordinary ways of life. One day, if ever I am allowed to approach the exalted plane in which she must now rest, I hope to be able to thank her for the encouragement and hope with which she has endowed me in my later years. And I do not doubt that I would have been brought to her sooner if I had been ready to absorb the treasures she holds out to those who can respond to her gentle spirit.

An interest for many in Julian today is her teaching on the motherhood of God (mostly 59 to 61). She is by no means the first in the field though it is in her writings that the subject finds its most exhaustive treatment. As far back as the Old Testament we have Isaiah's words, 'As a mother comforts her son, so will I comfort you' (66:13). More familiar are the words of Jesus likening himself to a hen who would gather her chicks under her wings. St Anselm takes this up with, 'But you, too, good Jesus, are you not also a mother? Is not he a mother who like a hen gathers his chicks between his wings?' Even such a 'masculine' saint as Augustine writes that God exercises 'fatherly authority and maternal love'. In post-Julian times we find John of the Cross speaking of God as one who gives the soul 'the breast of his tender love'. And later still Pope Clement of Alexandria speaks of 'the Father's loving breasts' and 'the milk of the Father'.[1]

It is desirable that we should get away from the exclusively masculine image of God. I have stressed earlier how our images of the God we worship must affect us at the level of our daily living and there can be no doubt that the exclusively masculine image of God has contributed greatly to the absurd and offensive supposition that men are superior to women which has so marred the history of the Christian Church. It would be silly to suggest that men and women – or, indeed, any two people – are equal in God's sight (God doesn't suffer from cataract!), but that all are equal in his love goes without saying and everything worthwhile for both sexes flows from this truth.[2] It would be equally foolish to move to a full feminist theology for it is balance and not the exaltation of one sex over another which is required. When Julian speaks of God she keeps this gender balance writing, for example, that 'He is our Mother'. Or again, 'As truly as God is our Father, so truly is God our Mother'. But nowhere does Julian call God 'She'. Those who object to the feminine pronoun being used of God today can therefore look to Julian for their support. I have to say I think Julian is illogical here, but in going as far as she did she doubtless went to the limit of thought acceptable to her day.

There are many who will accept the word 'mother' in relation to God but who stop short at the word 'she'. I am convinced that this is a misunderstanding based on a failure to understand that the pronouns 'he' and 'she' have a different meaning when used in relationship to God to what they have in relationship to ourselves. The pronouns 'he' and 'she' when used of one another refer entirely to the physical structure of the body. A man may have a markedly feminine personality yet because the body's physical structure is this and not that the pronoun 'he' must always apply. Likewise a woman may have markedly masculine traits, yet the physical structure of the body determines that the pronoun 'she' be always used. Thus the pronouns 'he' and 'she' when used of one another have no reference whatever to aspects of character or personality, but depend entirely on the configuration of the material body. But God is infinite spiritual Being and to speak of God in terms of this or that bodily configuration makes nonsense. It follows therefore that 'he' or 'she' when applied to God has reference solely to character and personality. But, as we have seen, this is the one area where 'he' or 'she' as applied to ourselves has no application at all.

What then do we mean when we call God both Father and Mother and use the corresponding pronouns he and she? By calling God both he and she we mean that the character traits we have come to associate especially with manhood and the more tender traits we traditionally link with womanhood are, in the Godhead – raised to perfection – integrated into one harmonious whole. The perception of God's character is enlarged and enriched by the masculine and feminine finding their integration in him, and because we become, as I have already said, not like the one we worship but like our mental image of the one we worship, our own characters move towards integration and are enlarged accordingly.

What are the objections to calling God Mother as well as Father? The one which comes most readily to mind is that Jesus referred to God exclusively as Father. This is weighty but can by no means be considered conclusive. Jesus said to his disciples that he had many things to say to them which they were not then able to bear (John 16:12) adding that the Spirit of truth would later lead them into the fullness of truth. It may well be that a truth awaiting the Church as it puts on its maturity in Christ is this one I have been discussing. For myself I find it hard to see how anyone on rational grounds, as distinct from grounds of historical conditioning, or psychological grounds, could object to what has been propounded, of which the basis (all except the feminine pronoun) is to be found in Julian.

Although Julian speaks freely of God as our Mother she sees the office of motherhood as belonging in a special way to Jesus. 'All the lovely works and all the most loving offices of beloved motherhood are appropriated to the second person.' She writes of 'our true mother Jesus who is all love and bears us into joy and endless living'. As a mother feeds her child with her milk so 'our beloved mother Jesus feeds us with himself' and 'in tender courtesy he gives us the blessed sacrament, the treasured food of life'. Jesus, our mother, is likened to a 'kind nurse who has no other care but the welfare of her child'. 'It is', says Julian, 'his responsibility to save us, it is his glory to do so, and it is his will that we should know it.' With Julian the initiative is always with God whose inexhaustible love is poured out to meet us at all times.

I turn briefly to the subject of prayer. In my book *With Pity not With*

Blame I have written on Julian's teaching here under the headings of yearning, beseeching and beholding. Julian nowhere sets out a method of prayer as does her contemporary writer, the unknown author of *The Cloud of Unknowing*, but needless to say her book breathes the spirit of prayer throughout. Most of the direct teaching, which is profound if deceptively simple, is confined to three chapters in the centre of her *Revelations*. For many, as for myself, Julian has been the great encourager. Perhaps nothing she has written on prayer is more important than her insistence on perseverance, even when the wind is sharply in our faces, and we may be sure that the experience at times of the seeming futility of prayer was something Julian herself had to face and overcome. A part of chapter 41 reads:

> So he says this, 'Pray inwardly, even though you find no joy in it. For it does good, though you feel nothing, see nothing, yes, even though you think you cannot pray. For when you are dry and empty, sick and weak, your prayers please me, though there be little enough to please you. All believing prayer is precious to me . . . God accepts the good-will and work of his servants, no matter how we feel. It pleases God that by the help of his grace we should work away at our praying and our living, directing all our powers to him until in the fulness of joy we have him whom we seek – Jesus.'

For Julian, prayer is our offering to God. It doesn't have to 'work', not at least in the sense in which we are likely to think of it working. It has to be offered with all the simplicity a child may offer its mother a daisy chain (my image) and it will never be wasted even though we are not likely in this life to know for most of the time how it will be used. And, like mercy, prayer is twice blest. It blesses the one who prays as well as the person prayed for. For prayer 'ones [unites] the soul to God'. And there can be no higher blessing than that, as Julian makes clear in her own prayer: 'God of your goodness, give me yourself, for you are enough for me. There is nothing less I can ask that is worthy of you, and if I ask for anything less I shall always be lacking, for only in you I have all' (5). The words are reminiscent of St Augustine: 'He who asks of God/ anything less than God/ regards the gifts of God/ more than the giver./ Has God then no reward?/ Only himself.'

Nor are we to be deflected from our prayer life because we feel our love for God is too small. Our knowledge of our love for God is a very little matter: our knowledge of God's love for us is what counts. And I suppose one might say that Julian's whole book is written with the intention of making that known. All Julian asks of us in our prayers is that they shall be made with such love and devotion as God gives us. What he gives is his business. We don't in any way have to work ourselves up as though to show God we are more loving and devoted than we feel. We just have to pray. We are back again to quantity. Quantity belongs to us, quality to God so long as our desire is to offer ourselves as well as we can.

Julian is through and through incarnational and she is thoroughly biblical in her evaluation of human nature. For her, God is concerned with every aspect of our humanity – and, too, of the natural world – and there is no part which is outside the fullness of redemption. In a passage which for sheer beauty and delicacy matches any writing in her book, she speaks of God's regard for all of our human nature right down to its lowest level.

> A man walks upright, and the food in his body is shut in as if in a well-made purse. When the time of his necessity comes the purse is opened and then shut again in most seemly fashion. And it is God who does this, as it is shown when he says that he comes down to us in our humblest needs. For he does not despise what he has made, nor does he disdain to serve us in the simplest natural functions of our body, for love of the soul which he created in his likeness. For as the body is clad in the cloth, and the flesh in the skin, and the bones in the flesh, and the heart in the trunk, so are we, soul and body, clad and enclosed in the goodness of God. (To be found in ch. 6 of Paris ms. only.)

Julian views our human nature in a very different way from that in which we commonly see it. If a man enriches himself by dishonest practice or a woman falls into prostitution we are apt to comment that after all 'it is only human nature'. If Julian were to see a man rapt in contemplative prayer or a woman sharing her last crust in a refugee camp she could, in consistency with her thought, make that very same remark. God made our nature basically good and it is when we deliberately practise deceit or lust that we are being, not true, but untrue to our human nature. Jesus took upon himself our human nature in all its fullness and in him human nature is revealed as God intended it to be. Our human nature is destined in God's hope for us to be raised to the height of glory. In his stimulating contribution to *Julian: Woman of our Day*, Father John-Julian, founder of the Episcopalian Order of Julian of Norwich in the USA, makes the important point that for Julian we are perfectible because of our human nature and not in spite of it. It is because we have the stamp of the Master upon us, the stamp of him who created human nature, and whose Son took on the fullness of our human nature, that we can be brought to the fullness of perfection. Our human nature is, in fact, the guarantee of our perfectibility. Although this is entirely in line with the doctrine of the Church ('Grace perfects nature') in practice it would seem that the truth has often been forgotten, our human nature being seen as in some way a barrier to our perfection. Theology and conduct are, as we have seen, inextricably linked and it is when our theology goes wrong at this point that Christian asceticism is mistakenly conceived. If I am perfectible only *in spite of* my human nature, then the more I can crush this so regarded obstacle, the better it will be. Such thoughts may be the path to all sorts of fruitless excesses, for my poor repressed human nature may come bouncing back on me and wreak its revenge in all sorts of startling and unexpected ways. But if it is *because* of my human nature I can be brought to perfection then spirit and body are partners in one great enterprise. We shall still need discipline (a suspect word in many quarters today but one with which the Christian life – at least until it has reached the perfection of love – can never do without) – for human nature is a frail commodity and may easily run amok and land me in a frightful mess. But once we get our theology right, a right understanding and practice of asceticism will follow.[3]

I have frequently referred to Julian's 'teaching' and it has seemed right to do so. Yet Julian makes the claim for herself that she is no teacher. What she would have us understand is that what she expounds is 'on the Shewing of Him who is the sovereign teacher.' Julian as always sinks into the background that God may be exalted. And so it is that she writes, 'You shall soon forget me (and do so that I shall not hinder you) and behold Jesus who is teacher of all.'[4]

As with the earlier saints of whom I have written I append some memorable sayings from Julian. They are taken from *Enfolded in Love*[5] or *In Love Enclosed*.[6]

He loves us and enjoys us, and so he wills that we love him and enjoy him, and firmly trust him; and all shall be well.

It is God's will that we should rejoice with him in our salvation, and that we should be cheered and strengthened by it.

He delights in us for ever, as we shall in him, by his grace.

He is quick to clasp us to himself, for we are his joy and his delight, and he is our salvation and our life.

Our lover desires that our soul should cling to him with all its might, and that we should ever hold fast to his goodness. For this above all pleases God and strengthens the soul.

When a soul holds on to God in trust, whether in seeking him or contemplating him, this is the highest worship it can bring.

Our soul rests in God its true peace; our soul stands in God its true strength, and is deep-rooted in God for endless love.

The simple enjoyment of our Lord is in itself a most blessed form of thanksgiving.

The love that God most high has for our soul is so great that it surpasses understanding.

The testing experience of falling will lead to a deep and wonderful knowledge of the constancy of God's love, which neither can nor will be broken because of sin. To understand this is of great profit.

He says, 'Do not blame yourself too much, thinking that your trouble and distress is all your fault. For it is not my will you should be unduly sad and despondent.'

Our enemy tries to depress us by false fears which he proposes. His intention is to make us so weary and dejected, that we let the blessed sight of our everlasting friend slip from our minds.

He is endless and has made us for his own self only, and has restored us by his blessed Passion. And he does all this through his goodness.

If we fall we are to get up quickly; for the worst pain a soul can have is to let sin take it away from God.

He did not say, 'You shall not be tempest-tossed, you shall not be work-weary, you shall not be discomforted.' But he said, 'You shall not be overcome.' God wants us to heed these words so that we shall always be strong in trust, both in sorrow and in joy.

Flee to our Lord and we shall be comforted. Touch him and we shall be made clean. Cling to him and we shall be safe and sound from every kind of danger. For our courteous Lord wills that we should be as at home with him as heart may think or soul may desire.

God is our sure rock, and he shall be our whole joy, and make us as changeless as he is when we reach the heavens.

Julian was one of four fourteenth-century English mystics. The other three were Richard Rolle, Walter Hilton and the unknown author of *The Cloud of Unknowing*. A saying from each, in the above order of authors, is appended.

> When wilt thou come, Jesu my joy, and rescue me from woe,
> And give thyself to me, and be, with me for ever so?
> All my desires would be fulfilled if that were given to me.
> All my desires are one desire, and that for naught but thee.

Believe that you are chosen by the mercy of God to be saved as one of His elect. Never depart from this hope, whatever you see or hear, or whatever temptations come upon you. And even though you think yourself a sinner only worthy of hell, because you do no good and do not serve God as you ought, hold fast to this faith and hope, ask mercy, and all shall be well.

By love he may be gotten and holden; by thought never.

Epilogue

‎⸺❦⸻

IT HAS BEEN SAID THAT LIFE must be lived forwards but understood backwards. So it must be for me. My life has been like a large jigsaw puzzle where it has often been impossible to see how this piece or that contributed to the picture, but as the whole has come together the purpose has been made clear.

Interestingly to me I have never sought any of the posts other than the first appointment from Cambridge, but have accepted work as it was offered and believe I can see the hand of Providence in taking me to each school, parish, Bede House and finally the Julian Cell. I fancy most older people can do the same.

In my case, as the jigsaw was nearing completion, I received what was perhaps the greatest surprise in my life. The administrator of the trustees of the Templeton Trust phoned me one day in November 1994 to say I had been awarded the UK individual Templeton prize. This is awarded biannually to any member of the United Kingdom of any faith or none to mark a contribution in the field of spirituality, in my case 'for fostering Christian devotion through an apostle of hope, Dame Julian of Norwich'. I saw myself to be the recipient on behalf of many here in Norwich who have helped to make Julian better known.

As I now look back over many years it is with deep gratitude to God for the love which has shaped me and would not let me go, but also in penitential sorrow for my sins and failings. And yet, without seeking to make excuse, it is for our comfort that even these may be caught up in the providence of God to work in us that humility without which no virtue can flower. For this we may be truly thankful even though, as we look forward, we continue to lay our frailties before God that his healing work may be completed.

It cannot be long before death separates me from many loving friends who visit me in my small flat close to the Julian Shrine in Norwich and talk with me and pray with me which is my greatest joy. For this I owe gratitude, above all, to Julian for there is something special about those who have discovered her and they come from all over the world to share their treasure. How then can I better end than with Julian's own words describing her vision at the end of time when all people of peace and goodwill shall be gathered up in Christ?

> When judgement is given and we are all brought up above, then we shall see clearly in God the secrets now hidden from us. In that day not one of us will want to say, Lord, if it had been done this way, it would have been well done.' But we shall all say with one voice, 'Lord, blest may you be. For it is so and it is well. And now we see clearly that all things are done as it was ordained before anything was made.'

Notes

Chapter 1: Early Days

1. Lisle Combe, St Lawrence, Isle of Wight, is a fascinating, comfortable house offering bed and breakfast.
2. D.W.A. Pelham (1812–51).

Chapter 4: King Edward VI School, Southampton

1. Taken from *Old Edwardians Journal, Issue 1*. Written by Jack Taylor, at the school from 1924–31.

Chapter 5: Cambridge Days

1. Now known as The Delhi Brotherhood.
2. For particulars of the American ministry of Bryan Green I am indebted to *Bryan Green: Parson-Evangelist*, published by The Bryan Green Society Ltd, 68 Southern Road, Thame, OX9 2DZ.

Chapter 7: Westminster School (2)

1. Today, however, the ordained members of the community are generally known as 'Father'.
2. I owe this story and the previous one to *Brother Douglas: Apostle of the Outcast*, by Father Francis ssf. The book gives an admirable account of Brother Douglas' work and mission, and his contribution to the Church and nation.
3. I read this summary, I forget where, perhaps forty years ago. I have quoted from memory as best I can. I have a vague recollection that it comes from the writings of Archbishop William Temple.

Chapter 9: The Hallett War School

1. I am grateful to Grace Jantzen for this illustration. See Julian of Norwich by Grace Jantzen (SPCK, 1987), p. 182.

Chapter 14: Poona: Parish and Convent

1. Since relating this story I have been introduced to 'The Song of the Magnificat', a long narrative poem written by Edith Nesbitt (1858–1924). It was recited on Radio 4: unfortunately I heard only the last fifty lines. The point of the story is the same but the singer with the beautiful voice was a monk

visiting a monastery where the singing was abysmal. The visiting monk was invited to sing the Magnificat alone but 'his heart is chained to earth' and not a note penetrated heaven. The poem ends with the angel saying to the monks, so conscious of their poor voices: 'The sweetest of earth's music came from you/ The music of a noble life and true.' My story is clearly a garbled version of this poem.

2. The Venerable Ronald Cole, *The Times*, 2 August 1996.

Chapter 17: Curé d'Ars and Caussade

1. I have taken the quotations on the Curé d'Ars from *A Dictionary of Christian Spirituality* (SCM Press), edited by Gordon S. Wakefield. Article on the Curé d'Ars by Francis H. House.

Chapter 18: The Anchorhold and Bede House

1. Geoffrey Harding, *On lying down in Church* (Churchman Publishing Ltd).

Chapter 19: Ibiza and the Rosary

1. Another rosary, and one which is making rapid strides around the world today, is that of the *Divine Mercy* incorporating words given to Blessed (Sister) Faustina of Poland. The decade prayer which replaces the Hail Mary runs: 'For the sake of his sorrowful Passion, have Mercy on us and on the whole world.' Two advantages are that it is theologically acceptable to all denominations and that because it is widely spread the user will more easily find a companion in its use. For a descriptive leaflet send 76 pence to the Padre Pio Information Centre, Tankerton, Kent, CT5 2DF. Readers of this chapter who have problems with the Hail Mary could well substitute the above prayer, saying the Our Father on the medallion only and letting the rest remain the same, and moving to the full use later if they wished. It takes but six minutes!

Chapter 21: Medjugorje (2)

1. Mary Craig, *Spark from Heaven: The Mystery of the Madonna of Medjugorje* (Hodder and Stoughton, 1988), p. 71.
2. Wayne Weible, *Medjugorje: The Mission* (Orleans, Mass.: Paraclete Press), p. 251.
3. Mary Craig, op. cit., p. 117.
4. Dr Ljudevit Rupcic, *The Truth about Medjugorje* (Ljubuski-Humae), p. 18.
5. Mary Craig, op. cit., p. 149.
6. Mary Craig, op. cit., p. 149.
7. Mary Craig, op. cit., p. 154.
8. Mary Craig, op. cit., p. 151.
9. Rupcic, op. cit., p. 65.

Chapter 22: Lourdes

1. Merlin Carothers, *Prison to Praise* (Hodder and Stoughton, 1972).
2. See the final chapter of *Walking and Leaping* (Kingsway Publications, 1974).
3. The sympathy of Pope John Paul II for Medjugorje is well known and many quotations might be given. To Fr Jozo, referred to in this chapter, he said on 17 June 1992: 'I give you my blessing. Take courage. I am with you. Tell

Medjugorje I am with you. Protect Medjugorje.' Any official pronouncement must await the findings of the Commission appointed to enquire into the authenticity of the visions. An enigmatic Medjugorje-related saying of the Pope runs: 'Sometimes the people follow the bishops, sometimes the bishops follow the people.'

Chapter 23: The Julian Cell, Retreats and Books

1. Now Jean Herschel. Jean married the Revd Richard Herschel of the Episcopal Church, USA, on 30 September 1997.

Chapter 25: America, Norway, Tongues and Healing

1. *A Lesson of Love* (DLT, 1988).
2. Thus it was when this chapter was written. But from 1998 the journal will cover the full year. Readers who wish to receive it should write to Mrs Mary Crist at 301 West Hintz Road, Prospect Heights, Illinois 60070, USA.
3. Robert Llewelyn (ed.), *Circles of Silence: Explorations in Prayer with Julian Meetings* (DLT, 1994). Articles by James Naters ssJE, pp. 115–19.
4. Robert Llewelyn, *A Doorway to Silence: The contemplative use of the rosary* (DLT, 1986).

Chapter 26: The Psychical, the Spiritual and the Toronto Blessing

1. Laneta Gregory and Geoffrey Treissman, *Handbook of the Aura* (Ashgrove Press).
2. *Moments of Truth* is available from Mrs Anna Lee-Wood, White Wings, West Bexington, Dorchester, Dorset, DT2 9DE at £5.50, post free. Cheques to Mrs Anna Lee-Wood.

Chapter 27: Julian of Norwich (1)

1. The figure in brackets refers throughout to the chapter number in *Revelations of Divine Love*.

Chapter 28: Julian of Norwich (2)

1. In this paragraph I am indebted to J. Leclerq's preface to *Julian of Norwich: Showings* by Edmund Colledge osA and James Walsh sJ (New York: Paulist Press, 1978).
2. The distinction between God's sight and God's love I owe to Archbishop Geoffrey Fisher. St Paul recognises our inequality in the sight of God in 1 Corinthians 12. Our equality in the love of God is illustrated by Jesus in Matthew 5:43–7.
3. I have in this section drawn freely on my book *With Pity not With Blame* (DLT, 1982).
4. In this paragraph I have drawn from chapter 6 of the Shorter Text.
5. Robert Llewelyn (ed.), *Enfolded in Love: Daily Readings with Julian of Norwich* (DLT, 1994).
6. Robert Llewelyn (ed.), *In Love Enclosed: More Daily Readings with Julian of Norwich* (DLT, 1994).

1. *Selective Index of Names*

2. *Selective Index of Places*

3. *Reflections on Prayer and Spirituality*